African Regional Organizations

African Regional Organizations

edited by
DOMENICO MAZZEO

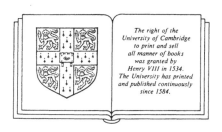

The right of the
University of Cambridge
to print and sell
all manner of books
was granted by
Henry VIII in 1534.
The University has printed
and published continuously
since 1584.

CAMBRIDGE UNIVERSITY PRESS

Cambridge
London   New York   New Rochelle
Melbourne   Sydney

CAMBRIDGE
UNIVERSITY PRESS

University Printing House, Cambridge CB2 8BS, United Kingdom

Published in the United States of America by Cambridge University Press, New York

Cambridge University Press is part of the University of Cambridge.

It furthers the University's mission by disseminating knowledge in the pursuit of education, learning and research at the highest international levels of excellence.

www.cambridge.org
Information on this title: www.cambridge.org/9780521317665

© Cambridge University Press 1984

First published 1984
Re-issued 2014

A catalogue record for this publication is available from the British Library

Library of Congress Catalogue card number: 83–25257

ISBN 978-0-521-26246-0 Hardback
ISBN 978-0-521-31766-5 Paperback

Cambridge University Press has no responsibility for the persistence or accuracy of URLs for external or third-party internet websites referred to in this publication, and does not guarantee that any content on such websites is, or will remain, accurate or appropriate.

Contents

List of tables, figures and map

The Contributors

S. K. B. ASANTE graduated in History from the University of Ghana and received the M.Sc. in Economics and Ph.D. in International Relations from the London School of Economics. A Senior Lecturer at the University of Ghana, he has also taught in Nigeria and the United States, contributed papers at numerous international conferences, and published widely on international economic relations, development studies and pan-Africanism. He is the author of *Pan-African Protest: West Africa and the Italo-Ethiopian Crisis* (Longman, 1977) and has almost completed for publication a full-scale study on *ECOWAS: a Case Study in Economic Integration Among Developing Countries*.

RICHARD FREDLAND is Chairman of the Political Science Department of Indiana University at Indianapolis where he has been on the faculty since 1970. He teaches international relations and is particularly interested in international organizations in Africa. In 1977 he was on sabbatical leave in Nairobi. He is the author of *Africa Faces the World*, a study of international relations in Africa; an article on the Organizations of African Unity, *African Affairs*, 1973; and *Integration and Disintegration in East Africa*, co-edited with Christian Potholm (University Press of America, 1980).

LEON GORDENKER, professor of politics at the Center of International Studies, Princeton University, is a scholar of wide experience in academic teaching and research and the functioning of international organizations. His major publications include *The UN Secretary-General and the Maintenance of Peace* (Columbia University Press, 1967); *The UN in International Politics* (Princeton University Press, 1971); and *International Aid and National Decisions: Development Programmes in Malawi, Tanzania and Zambia* (Princeton University Press, 1976).

ISEBILL V. GRUHN is professor of politics at the University of California, Santa Cruz. She received her B.A. from Dickinson College; M.A. from the School of Advanced International Studies of Johns Hopkins University; and her Ph.D. from the University of California, Berkeley. She is the author of *Regionalism Reconsidered: the Economic Commission for Africa*, as well as numerous monographs and articles concerned with inter-African affairs and International Policy towards Africa. Professor Gruhn has travelled widely throughout the African continent over the past two decades.

K. MATHEWS received the B.A. in Political Science from Kerala University, the M.A. in International Relations from Delhi University and the Ph.D. in International Relations from Jawaharlal Nehru University. He is teaching International Organizations at the University of Nigeria, Nsukka. He previously taught at the University of Dar es Salaam and Delhi University. Professor Mathews is the author of a dozen articles and as many conference papers and co-editor of *The Foreign Policy of Tanzania: a reader* (Tanzanian Publishing House, 1981).

DOMENICO MAZZEO is teaching international organizations and international relations at the University of Nairobi. He is the author of *Foreign Assistance and the East African Common Services* (Weltforum Verlag, Munich, 1976). He has also published on the UN and decolonization, problems of cooperation in East Africa, and the State and the Transnational Corporation. He is currently engaged in a major research project on *Cooperation in Science and Technology in Africa*.

PETER MEYNS received his Ph.D. in Economics from the Free University of Berlin. He has taught at the Universities of Dar es Salaam, Berlin and Zambia, where he also served as Head of the Department of African Development Studies. He has published widely on liberation movements and the domestic and foreign policy of southern African countries. He is the author of *The revolutionary war of liberation in Angola, Guinea Bissau and Mozambique; National independence and rural development in the Third World: the case of Tanzania;* and *Mozambique in the year 2 of independence.*

LYNN K. MYTELKA is a professor of political economy at Carleton University. The author of books on regional integration, multinational corporations and technology transfer in both Africa and Latin America; she has also served as a consultant to UNCTAD, the UN Economic Commission for Africa, the Andean Group and the International Development Research Centre (IDRC).

FRANCIS V. WODIE is a lawyer, holder of a Ph.D. in Law, M.A. Degrees in Public Law and Philosophy, and postgraduate Diplomas in Political Science. He is Dean of the Faculty of Law of the University of Abidjan and professor of Law at the Faculties of Law of the Universities of Abidjan and Algiers.

1 Introduction: the regional trend

DOMENICO MAZZEO

General factors

The majority of African countries became independent in an era of regionalist euphoria. In the 1950s and early 1960s, the regional trend was reinvigorated worldwide by several interacting factors, notably the existence of the United Nations (UN), a raging East-West conflict, the progress of decolonization and new technological developments. On the African continent, the idea of post-independence cooperation was further promoted by the common anti-colonial struggle, particularly as embodied in the pan-Africanist creed and movement.

Although it represented the institutionalization of the globalist approach to the regulation of international relations, the UN contributed in several ways to the growth of regionalism. In anticipation of the East-West conflict, doubts on the merits of the global collective security system had already been expressed during the debate leading to the creation of the UN. Consequently, regional security arrangements were permitted under the UN Charter. A regionalist view was even encouraged by the principle of equitable geographical representation in UN elective bodies. In particular, the establishment of the UN Regional Economic Commissions and Regional Offices of major UN Agencies gave new impetus to regional cooperation in the technical and economic fields, on a continental and subcontinental scale. As decolonization progressed, by its very existence and the principle of universal membership, the UN system offered unprecedented opportunities for diplomatic and other forms of interaction among newly independent countries. The formation of continentally-based groups within the organization facilitated the harmonization of views and eventually of policies on common problems, particularly on those issues related to national liberation, racial equality and some aspects of economic

1

relations with the industrialized countries. Such opportunities were of great significance to Africa, where feelings on the above issues were more intense and where a relatively low degree of intracontinental rivalries – at least as compared to the prevailing situation in Europe or Asia – allowed the emergence of some kind of continental attitude. But it was probably the collapse of the global collective security system under the stress of the East-West conflict, that seemed to prove unequivocally the soundness of the regional approach and brought to prominence the regionalist clauses of the UN Charter.

Born from the rivalries of two newly emerged superpowers, the Soviet Union and the United States of America, championing two opposed socio-economic systems, the East-West conflict urged the consolidation of contrasting strategic and economic blocs. The North Atlantic Treaty Organization (NATO) and the Warsaw Pact, the European Economic Community and the Council for Mutual Economic Aid (Comecon), to some extent the result of the East-West conflict and the demarcation of the most important zones of influence of the superpowers, still remain the symbols of a relatively successful regional order, if not a new regional justice. The East-West conflict also promoted, by contrast, the rise of the non-aligned movement. Partly aimed at containing and possibly reducing this conflict, the movement provided new guidelines and a framework for increasing cooperation among developing countries, at a continental and intercontinental level, cooperation made feasible with the advance of decolonization.

Regional cooperation and decolonization are intimately related processes. The severance of traditional colonial relationships not only made possible new forms of cooperation among former colonial possessions, but also created conditions that favoured cooperation among ex-colonial powers. Faced with the devastation of the Second World War, the prospects and reality of losing their empires, and the rise of two non-Western European superpowers, Western European countries, including major colonial powers, felt the urgency of joining forces to preserve their security and welfare. Regional ties, on a continental and subcontinental level, also appeared to newly independent countries as an instrument for safeguarding their recently acquired political freedom and possibly attaining a higher degree of economic independence.

Finally, technological development created some of the most compelling conditions for the establishment of strong security and economic communities of states, particularly among industrialized countries. This gave the impression that the era of the nation-state had already elapsed, at least in the industrialized world.

In brief, the growth of regionalism has been stimulated by technological advances and the spread of decolonization in an atmosphere of East-West conflict. In other words, the major forces behind the regional trend are technology, nationalism and ideology. Technology may have played a more important role in bringing industrialized countries closer together, nationalism the developing countries. The greater extent to which regional cooperation is considered by developing countries as an instrument for the satisfaction of basic national aspirations also explains the higher degree of ambiguity of the regional process in the Third World. Ideology, while contributing to the partition of Europe, was an element of cohesiveness within each of the two halves of the continent. Cutting across subregions, ideology has so far played a much more negative role in regional cooperation among developing countries, particularly in Asia and Africa.

Attempts at regional cooperation have proliferated for over two decades in Latin America and Africa, and more recently even in Asia. But such cooperation has flourished mainly among the highly industrialized countries of Europe. This has convinced some students of international relations that regional cooperation is a privilege of the industrialized countries. In any case, the theory of regional cooperation has clearly been coloured by the aspirations and experience of industrialized countries, notably of Europe.

Schools of thought

The theory of regional cooperation or integration[1] was elaborated mainly as a response to the major concerns of Europe after the Second World War: containment of nationalism and the promotion of economies of scale. These concerns have been the central themes and shared objectives of the two main schools of thought on regional cooperation, the federalist and the functionalist,[2] though the respective integrationist strategies of the two schools differ, because their basic assumptions are different.

For the federalist school, these objectives could be better attained by launching a frontal attack on national sovereignty. This implies the adoption of a common constitution and the creation of joint institutions or a central government. Through its legal, administrative, budgetary and, if necessary, coercive power, the central government would give birth to an integrated economy and community attitudes. Subscribing to the tenet that politics rules economics, the federalist school sees in the political elites, notably in the role of strong and committed personalities, the key to federation.

The functionalist school, instead, accepts the idea of the predominance of economics over politics, a kind of economic determinism so dear to classical liberalism and Marxism. Economic integration should precede political integration. But economic integration can only be a slow and gradual process. Gradualism implies a movement from the easiest to the more complex aspects of regional cooperation. Since different sectors of the economy and eventually different interest groups may be brought together at different times, gradualism also assumes the existence of a certain degree of social and economic pluralism. From the marriage of gradualism and determinism, in an atmosphere of pluralism, are born the major contributions of the functionalist school to theorizing on regional cooperation: the concept of incrementalism or the spill-over effect from lower to higher forms/levels of regional cooperation, and the concept of shifting loyalties of the concerned interest groups from national to supranational institutions. In brief, for the functionalist school, nationalism and ideology are forces too strong to succumb to a frontal political attack. They will only be eroded by a slow process of technical and economic cooperation, hence the importance attached to the role of experts and economic interest groups in the integration process. For the functionalists, political integration is the child of growing economic inter-dependence, usually the mark of a relatively high level of economic diversification or development.

The most popular of the two schools, in theory and practice, has been the functionalist school. The whole debate on regional cooperation has generally taken for granted the validity of the market approach and incrementalism. This is evident in the conception of regional cooperation as a process and the discussion of its major stages or forms. Economic cooperation was supposed to start with the creation of a free trade area or the liberalization of the movement of goods regionally produced. The next stage would have been the establishment of a customs union or the adoption of a common external tariff, thus allowing also the free movement of imported goods. From a successful customs union one would have moved into a common market, which calls for the free movement of all factors of production: goods, capital and labour. The whole process of cooperation may have ended in an economic and, eventually, a political union or federation, where all aspects of economic and foreign policy would be jointly managed.

On the basis of mutual criticism and experience, the two schools of thought partly re-examined their respective positions. Most federalists came to accept the idea of regional cooperation as a process of negotiation and experimentation, and increasingly appreciated the importance of socio-economic forces in this process. The functionalists questioned their faith in economic determinism and acknowledged the autonomous role of political decisions. The validity of incrementalism was, at the best, restricted to the economic field, while the emphasis on the depoliticization of the integration process was abandoned.

In practice, regional cooperation has often combined federalist and functionalist elements. This is particularly evident in the first major attempt at regional cooperation in Western Europe: the creation of the European Coal and Steel Community in 1952. Through intergovernmental agreement, a supranational authority was established from the outset to regulate a major sector of economic activities. The Treaty of Rome of 1957 adopted a gradualist approach to economic cooperation, but clearly proclaimed its political, quasi-federal, final objective.

Major theoreticians, notably of the functionalist school,[3] warned against applying the general concept of regional cooperation, in particular the European model, outside the environment of industrialized countries. Nevertheless, enthusiasm for regional cooperation ran high among Third World leaders and among scholars concerned with developing countries, especially during the 1960s. In Asia, a situation of almost continuous war and pervasive rivalries, cutting across the various subregions of the continent, did not permit much formalization of regional cooperation, with the exception of the Association of South East Asian Nations (ASEAN) and the Gulf Cooperation Council, created in 1967 and 1981, respectively. In Latin America, where thought about regional cooperation was highly articulated and action systematically undertaken at the continental and subcontinental level, regional cooperation ran almost exclusively on functionalist lines. In Africa and the Middle East, both the federalist and functionalist schemes were tried. Attempts at federations in Africa south of the Sahara are not unknown. But the record for the number of still-born federations undoubtedly belongs to the Arab-speaking countries of North Africa and the Middle East. In Africa south of the Sahara, the general feeling was more favourable to a functional approach to regional cooperation. In the whole of Africa, however, the idea of regional cooperation on a continental or subcontinental scale easily took root in the fertile soil of pan-Africanism.

Pan-Africanism and intra-African cooperation

Pan-Africanism was essentially the consciousness of the right of the African peoples to cultural, political and economic independence, that is to equality with the other nations of the world. Linked with the anti-colonial struggle, it served as an instrument for the awakening of African nationalism or, more exactly, the nationalism of the peoples within each colonial territory. Partly due to a lack of time, the policies of the colonial powers and indigenous interest groups, pan-Africanism did not have a chance, prior to the achievement of independence of the majority of the African peoples, to become sufficiently structured, nor to develop into a doctrine for post-independence cooperation in Africa. It remained a creed more than a movement, a feeling more than an organization. Apart from *ad hoc* pan-African conferences and their supporting secretariats, little was done to create widespread pan-African political forces and infrastructures, in the form of pan-African liberation movements, political parties, trade unions or even youth leagues, on which to build post-independence pan-African cooperation, if not unity. This remained either the dream of a few isolated individuals or the cover for national expansionist policies.[4] Once independence was achieved, the meaning and objectives of pan-Africanism were generally domesticated. National integration and national development took precedence over the concern for intra-African cooperation.

Following the independence of many African countries, the already uncertain pan-Africanist movement was further weakened by contrasting views on how best to implement intra-African cooperation. Broadly speaking, there was a federalist and functionalist interpretation of pan-Africanism. The federalist approach was not, and probably could not have been, seriously considered by the majority of African leaders. The functionalist approach seemed a more acceptable form of cooperation among independent African countries. But, in the almost complete absence of relevant infrastructures and the extremely low level of industrialization, it was also realized that prospects for a pan-African common market were, in the short run, meagre indeed. Some forms of coordination of economic policy at the pan-African level could undoubtedly be pursued, notably with respect to infrastructural development and external economic relations. However, it was generally felt, particularly in French-speaking West Africa and English-speaking East Africa, that the more promising comprehensive forms of economic cooperation could eventually be achieved only at the sub-continental level. After all, this was more in tune with colonial experiences in Africa and regional experiments elsewhere. These subcontinental common markets could, hopefully, become the building blocks of a pan-African common market.

In conformity with the mood of the time, development was identified with industrialization and the validity of the market approach to regional cooperation was uncritically accepted. Because they favoured economies of scale, common markets were seen as ideal instruments of industrialization in Africa. In fact, together with a general scarcity of skills and capital, and the colonially inherited structure of foreign trade, the small market size of most African countries was considered a major obstacle to the transformation of the continent's rich natural resources into diversified production. The need for regional cooperation was probably more intensely felt in Africa than elsewhere in the Third World. But if needs were severe, capabilities were low. One could hardly fail to realize that the actual conditions for the establishment of common markets in Africa were practically non-existent. This realization did not, however, discourage practical experiments and their theoretical justifications. Emphasis was put on the dynamic effects or the more long-term benefits of common markets, as explained by regional integration theories, including Viner's Customs Union Theory. It was argued that, though common markets among developing countries may not find complementary economies, they are expected to create regional economic complementarity; though they may start being trade-diverting, they can become trade-creating. One might have even been tempted to believe that developing regional economic diversification could be easier than bringing together already diversified, hence competitive, national economies!

The danger with this kind of reasoning is to overlook the present, upon which the future to a good extent depends, and eventually fail to match needs with capabilities. Faced with the crucial problems of nation-building, incipient administrations, weak infrastructures and little diversification of national economies, African governments found it near to impossible to tackle successfully most regional cooperation issues. The distribution of benefits among partners of regional groups and the allocation of industries on a regional basis proved particularly intractable. The search for immediate results, so compelling in a situation of underdevelopment, leaves little time for implementing more structural readjustments, upon which long-term benefits rest.

Poor results and the search for alternatives

In Africa, as in other parts of the Third World, regional experiments have produced few satisfactory results. Under the weight of this negative experience and in the light of new development theories, the regionalist faith of scholars and policy-makers was shaken. The wide acceptance of the structuralist views of the Economic Commission for Latin America, including its more radical interpretation, the dependency theory, stimulated a growing interest in two apparently opposed development orientations: one stressing the need to restructure the international economic order or to create a New International Economic Order, the other emphasizing national self-reliance. The two development orientations stem from the same root: the realization, or at least the assumption, that the underdevelopment of Third World countries is due to the integration of these countries into the international capitalist system, under conditions of uneven power. So, either the type of dependent links of the periphery with the centre have to be reformed or they have to be severed.

The development approach based on the New International Economic Order stands for global negotiations and proclaims the need for a new type of North-South relations, including improved terms of trade, aid and monetary transactions, more favourable to developing countries. It proposes to reform, not to abandon, the international capitalist system. Some partial achievements of this approach are the adoption of the General Scheme of Preferences, aimed at stimulating exports of manufactured goods from developing countries into the market of industrialized countries, and the creation of the Special Drawing Rights. Other still unfulfilled and perhaps more ambitious expectations of this approach include the stabilization of export earnings of developing countries and, eventually, the indexing of the prices of Third World commodity exports upon the prices of their imports of capital goods from industrialized countries, as well as the adoption of a new Law of the Sea and a Code of Conduct on Trans-national Corporations. In brief, this approach favours cooperation between developing and developed countries, and is inclined to recommend an export-oriented development strategy, even if this implies collaborating with trans-national corporations.

The national self-reliance approach insists on a more nationally generated, self-contained development effort. It rather encourages a disengagement from the international, notably capitalist, system. To that effect, it opts, in the short-run, for a basic needs development strategy[5] and, in the long-run, for greater diversification of national economies, so to satisfy through domestic production as many national needs as possible. This may require the adoption of a socialist development model.

There has been a tendency among scholars in recent years to consider the establishment of a New International Economic Order, national self-reliance and regional cooperation as divergent development paths. This view is generally not shared by the authors of this book, who rather see the three approaches as basically complementary, a point brought to light also by the original position of the Economic Commission for Latin America on these issues. In any case, even if the interests of scholars in regional cooperation drastically declined in the 1970s, the concern of policy-makers for some form of collective self-reliance among developing countries was less severely affected, as confirmed by evidence provided in this book. In the light of experience and the new development orientations, the objectives and forms of regional cooperation are more carefully scrutinized and new trends are emerging.

With respect to Africa,[6] three major developments deserve to be mentioned. First, African countries are moving from a type of regional cooperation anchored to colonial experience to regional cooperation based on common problems, cutting across colonial divisions. Second, after two decades of independence, African countries are increasingly realizing that their basic development problems remain similar, despite the adoption of different political and socio-economic systems. Conflicting ideologies seem, therefore, to be allowed to play a less disruptive role within regional groups. Third, the emphasis on the comprehensive market approach to regional cooperation is gradually, if not replaced, at least more often combined with a preference for cooperation in specific programmes and projects. The effect of the above trends could be to put intra-African cooperation on a more solid and promising basis.

Scope and organization of the book

On the basis of a relatively representative sample of African organizations, this book aims mainly at providing a comparative study of past problems, present trends and future prospects of intra-African cooperation, at a continental and subcontinental level. To our knowledge, this is the first major work on African regional[7] organizations, combining in one book the study of continental and subcontinental African institutions of a security, political, financial and common market type.[8] One of the merits of this approach is to provide the reader with a better grasp of the possible complementarities between continental and subcontinental cooperation as instruments for building or strengthening the national capacity for development on the one hand and for helping restructure the international system on the other. All chapters of the book are original contributions. They benefit from a time perspective of two decades of efforts at intra-African cooperation. As practical attempts at cooperation in Africa continue unabated, a look at the experience and difficulties of the past 20 years may suggest well-founded guidelines for future action in this respect.

This study does in fact hope to contribute to a deeper understanding of the reasons why regional cooperation in Africa has so far not produced the expected results, and whether and how such cooperation could still serve as an engine of development. To that effect, we will re-examine the major tenets of the established theory and practice of regional cooperation and suggest new avenues for thought and action in this field. In particular, we would like to find out whether the production-oriented approach (trade liberalization and allocation of industries) to intra-African cooperation should be pursued or whether such cooperation should rather be geared to the service sector with the aim of increasing individual member countries' capacity for more self-sustained national development.

The book addresses itself to scholars, policy-makers and, hopefully, wider sections of the public with an interest in international organizations or the more general field of international relations. It is primarily intended to fill a gap in the regional component of university courses on the subject. Systematic studies of global organizations are not lacking. To the editor's knowledge, no relative comprehensive books on regional organizations in Africa or Latin America exist, in the sense outlined above. At the same time, our analysis could provide guidelines for action by policy-makers, whether within governmental circles or international organizations themselves. Policy implications are transparent in the general re-examination of aims and forms of regional cooperation. They are even more obvious in the discussion of more specific issues, such as the production versus services approach to cooperation and the inter-industry versus intra-industry specialization, or the question of complementarity between global, continental and subcontinental organizations.

The content of the book can be divided into two parts: the first on African continental cooperation (Chapters 2 to 5), the second on African subcontinental organizations (Chapters 6 to 10). Considering the special significance of the UN to African countries, the first part opens with an analysis of the link between the UN system and intra-African cooperation in the political and economic spheres (Chapters 2 and 3). This is followed by a study of the more peculiar African continental institutions: the Organization of African Unity (OAU) in Chapter 4, and the African Development Bank and the African Development Fund in Chapter 5. Chapter 6 on the African and Malagasy/Mauritian Common Organization (OCAM), the widest and loosest attempt at rallying most of the Francophone African countries, provides a bridge between pan-African organizations and more geographically confined regional groups. Chapters 7 and 8 give examples of partial or total failure of two of the more classical experiments at regional cooperation in Africa: the Central African Customs and Economic Union (UDEAC) and the East African Community (EAC). Chapters 9 and 10 discuss new attempts at regional economic cooperation on the continent, namely the ambitious Economic Community of West African States (ECOWAS) and the more subtle

Southern African Development Coordination Conference (SADCC). In the light of the experience of UDEAC and the EAC, the chances of success of the two relatively different approaches to regional cooperation of ECOWAS and SADCC can be better evaluated. The Conclusion (Chapter 11) summarizes problems, trends and prospects of intra-African cooperation in the light of a redefinition of the whole concept of regionalism.

NOTES

1 Originally, theorists preferred the term integration, which hinted at the possibility of creating regional supranational authorities and, in the long-run, replacing the present system of nation-states by a new system of regional states. In theory and practice, the stability of the nation-state system and the permanence of the negotiating process within regional groups have been increasingly recognized, hence our preference for the looser, but more realistic term cooperation.
2 Several authors consider the Communication Theory as a third major approach to the study of regional cooperation. We see it essentially as a branch of the functionalist approach, concerned mainly with the measurement of the regional process in terms of attitudes, transactions and institutional relevance. Therefore we do not feel here the need for a special reference to the Communication Theory.
3 See, in particular, E. B. Haas, *The Uniting of Europe* (Stanford University Press), 1968 edn, pp. xxxvi and 316; and 'International Integration: the European and the Universal Process', *International Organization* xv (1961), pp. 104–5, 117.
4 Kwame Nkrumah remained an almost solitary champion of the idea of the United States of Africa. In the early 1960s, Morocco's membership in the so called more radical group of African states was partly motivated by its desire to annex Mauritania.
5 Satisfaction of basic needs is broadly assimilated with the availability of a balanced diet, decent housing, health and educational services for the great majority of the population. Linked to the 'small is beautiful' philosophy, the basic needs strategy has particularly strong reservations about a development approach based on the use of capital-intensive technology. Instead, it calls for reliance on local resources, including technology, to meet local needs. It implies a sustained effort to create, as a first priority, relatively efficient and diversified agricultural and infrastructural systems throughout the country.
6 UNDP, *African Experiences in Technical Cooperation among Developing Countries*, Conference of Governmental Experts on Technical Cooperation among African Countries, Nairobi, Kenya, 12–20 May 1980, notably pp. 7–9.
7 The meaning of the term 'regional' is generally clarified by the authors in their respective chapters. As far as the title of the book is concerned, 'regional' refers both to continental and subcontinental organizations or cooperation.
8 A couple of comparative studies on African subcontinental economic cooperation

were published in the mid-1960s. In the 1970s, the more scanty research in this field was either oriented toward case studies or had an intercontinental outlook with fragmented evidence from various continents. Specific references are given in the Bibliography at the end of this book.

2 The UN and political cooperation in Africa

LEON GORDENKER

Introduction

Nearly a quarter of a century has gone by since the United Nations (UN) adopted its ringing declaration against colonialism[1] and thus signalled the beginning of a flood of newly independent states into the ranks of its members. Fifty members of the Organization of African Unity (OAU) are members of the UN, constituting nearly a third of the participants in the global organization. Only one people of a colonial territory in Africa, those of Namibia, still seek formal independence. The process of decolonization is thus nearly complete, although human rights issues, notably in South Africa, remain to be decided or managed. Enough time has passed and enough political change has taken place so that some clear trends in the international organization of Africa can be traced from the past and analyzed in a contemporary political framework.

African participation in the UN system has been prominent and ceaseless during the last quarter century. The UN system encourages regional cooperation both with symbols and with practical steps. It does not, of course, guarantee such regional political cooperation or offer explicit inducements to further it. Rather it offers opportunities by which participants in regional cooperation can increase their influence in global policy-making (or attempts at it), achieve certain material benefits and give their political preferences publicity and, often, legitimacy.

This chapter examines the process by which participation in the UN system affects political cooperation in Africa. It deals with institutional arrangements and doctrinal interpretations. It examines inducements to political cooperation and suggests what benefits may be derived. Finally, it outlines limits to African political cooperation in the UN system that derive from reactions by other governments, from the nature of the system and from African factors. The term 'political' covers attempts to decide upon and execute common policies to deal with issues that affect whole societies and involve choices that imply differential costs and benefits. The perspective of the chapter will be that of global rather than regional politics; it is based on the assumptions that the state system will continue to function in forms not sharply different from the past and that governments usually make autonomous decisions for which they take responsibility.

The UN and regionalism

The UN system generally encourages regional political cooperation. Formal provisions appear in the UN Charter for regional organizations to settle disputes among members, which are enjoined in any case to try such devices before appealing to the Security Council.[2] These provisions represent a response to demands for hemispheric autonomy on the part of the governments of the American continent.[3] They also imply encouragement for cooperation to promote the general welfare, as much of the history of inter-American cooperation involved not defence and security but rather economic and social programmes.

Regional arrangements for the promotion of peace and security via the UN system relate both to the pacific settlement of international disputes and to the enforcement of the broad prohibition against the use of force in international relations. The first of these lines of action was intended by the drafters of the UN Charter to have paramount importance at the regional level, if for no other reason than the expectation that enforcement action would rarely be necessary. Enforcement action would result either from premeditated violation of the UN Charter, leading to self-defence responses which could involve regional organizations, or from a failure of pacific settlement. Therefore, non-violent procedures logically have special importance to maintenance of the peace. The UN Charter places on members of regional organizations the obligation to make every effort to settle local disputes in regional agencies before bringing them to the attention of the Security Council. The Council itself is instructed to encourage such regional settlement.[4] But it still has the right to intervene on its own initiative in a local dispute which it believes may threaten peace and security.[5] Thus, the arrangements in the UN system for dealing with peace and security can be understood as simultaneously embodying centralizing and decentralizing tendencies. The Security Council is given primacy in managing the maintenance of peace but is supposed to restrict its attention to the most dangerous or general disputes, encouraging regional organizations to do their work without involving the whole world.

Centralization predominates in the formal arrangements for the use of enforcement action under the UN system. Here the scope of regional action is much restricted. The Security Council must take a decision first to use a regional organization for coercive action.[6] The only exceptions relate to the now nugatory category of action against the former enemy states of the Second World War and to collective self-defence.[7] The Charter envisages the possibility of organization for collective self-defence which by implication is different from broad-scope regional organization with duties of pacific settlement of disputes.[8] It is the legal cover for such bodies as the North Atlantic Treaty Organization or the Warsaw Treaty Organization which have military purposes defined by alliances. It is not certain, however, that any such elaborate institutionalization was intended by the founders of the UN. Nevertheless, even in this military area of organization, where a largely diplomatic, consensual system has the lowest capacity for persuasion, the members are legally obliged to report their defensive actions at once to the Security Council. These reports were intended to ensure the centralization of decision in regard to aggression.

In addition, other processual features of the UN system encourage regional approaches. Election of non-permanent members of the Security Council involves attention to geographical distribution;[9] regional groups have been formed from the beginning to put forward candidates and the new African members followed suit. When the Security Council was enlarged to 15 members in 1965, it was understood that five seats would be reserved for Africa.[10] This accretion to UN practice in fact grew out of the belief among African governments that the smaller original size of the Council failed to represent the interests of the continent. Election of judges to the International Court of Justice also relies on regional groupings, these organized in accordance with the statutes of the Permanent Court of Arbitration.[11] In the General Assembly and other large conciliar organs of the UN system, vice-presidents and committee chairmen also are selected to reflect the geographical diversity of the members; this, too, encourages regional distributions.[12] Appointments to the upper ranks of the international secretariats of the UN system also show special attention to the need for geographical distribution, enjoined by the Charter for the entire UN Secretariat. The senior appointments almost always involve consultations with leading governments of regions and have a representational quality of dubious conformity to the principles of the international civil services.[13]

Formal constitutional arrangements for regional cooperation in economic and social fields and in the treatment of colonialism contrast sharply with those for the maintenance of international peace. The UN

Charter does not explicitly mention regional cooperation for the general welfare or for the treatment of colonial issues. Neither the General Assembly nor the Economic and Social or Trusteeship Councils are under any injunction to employ or to establish regional bodies. The main instruments for promoting the general welfare in economic and social areas were to be specialized agencies, which by example from the past, would have the global membership characteristic of the International Labour Organization or the Universal Postal Union. The broad organizational powers given to the General Assembly and the coordinative tasks settled upon the economic and Social Council did not exclude regional organizations but neither did they specifically encourage them. As for the colonial issues, their handling was divided between the Trusteeship Council, which had close supervisory functions with regard to a few, closely-defined territories, and the General Assembly which had broad powers of recommendation but little specific authority to deal with those colonial areas not under the Trusteeship system. In neither case, was regional organization a formal factor.

Within this framework, initiatives soon appeared by governments for the creation of organs of the UN devoted to regional cooperation. This led to the establishment of regional economic commissions, first for Europe and the Far East and later for Latin America and, in 1958, for Africa. The creation of the Economic Commission for Latin America, in particular, accorded with longer-term organizational trends in the region, while those in Europe had definite roots in wartime cooperation and postwar emergency. The establishment of the UN Economic Commission for Africa had a clear relationship to the strong ideas of African solidarity and unity that emerged with the mounting onslaught on colonialism.[14]

The creation of regional commissions for economic cooperation within the UN framework clearly reflected ideological notions about the promise of regional cooperation. On the one hand, proponents sought the advantages of geographical proximity and cultural kinship. On the other, they were anxious to defend themselves against strong extra-regional, usually colonial, influences. Furthermore, regional organization would lead to influence by strong regional governments with less effect from outside powers. In this sense, regional organization aimed at parochial control, based on what supporters held was a better understanding of local needs and problems. In addition, this line of argument joined with another that insisted on the efficiency of decentralization above that of global approaches.[15] Together, the pressure for regional control of regional affairs and the doctrine of decentralization, which incidentally matched the horizontal organization of the nation-state system, affected the structure of specialized agencies. This effect reached broadest proportions in the World Health Organization which has a formally regional decisional pattern. Other specialized agencies formed regional offices and encouraged regional and subregional gatherings for various purposes relevant to their overall mandates.

Instrumental use of the UN by African governments

African governments have used the formal institutional structures of the UN system in several instrumental ways and in relation to a long list of issues. This section of the chapter deals with the instrumental employment of the UN system by African governments, while the subsequent section will take up some of the leading issues. The instrumental aspects of the UN system relate to the decisional process and the operation of institutions, rather than primarily to particular issues.[16]

Above all, African governments have used the UN as a means of giving global priority to issues important to them. They have done this by using the large African membership of the UN to place and retain items on the agenda and by reacting quickly as a group to challenges. The OAU has served as a primary instrument of global agenda setting.[17]

That the OAU would have such a function was made clear by the constitution of the regional organization. That document sets out as a main purpose of the OAU the harmonization of international cooperative policies among African governments and refers to the UN as a solid foundation for such cooperation.[18] The point was sharpened by OAU decisions to establish mutual relations with the UN and to create permanent representation for the regional body at UN headquarters.[19]

African governments have frequently sought and obtained the formal and active support of the OAU in pressing their cases at the UN. Such African issues as apartheid have been on the UN agenda continuously. The permanent representatives of the OAU speak frequently on behalf of governments in the region. Whenever the OAU can create a common position on an issue before the General Assembly, the African group becomes an essential element in any consensus. Furthermore, in the Security Council, African representatives often have been able to present a common regional position and representatives of the OAU are always present as observers during meetings. Thus, the UN serves as an instrument by which the African governments can assure a hearing for their views and can broaden consideration of what they develop as regional issues.[20]

The UN policy-making process can also legitimate African positions by demonstrating that they have support from a wide segment of the states of the world. Whenever an African position, or a recommendation developed by cooperating African countries, is adopted by the General Assembly or other organs, its supporters can claim that their views have legitimacy. When recommendations and declarations are repeated by UN organs year after year, regional points of view become more familiar to other governments. They may also become more persuasive or else the subject of deals for support. Thus, African governments have frequently supported the Arab governments and received their support in turn on issues of importance to each region. Furthermore, it becomes easier to assert that an African position has the force of law, after it is repeatedly given strong backing by a large majority of governments. It can then be asserted that a rule of law has demonstrably been accepted. This is, of course, a controversial procedure, but because accepted rules emerge from arguments, the legitimacy of an African position may be enhanced in the eyes of other governments.

Legitimating a position may be important in creating coercive pressure against those who oppose it. African positions on colonialism and racism have been subject to this process. As the legitimacy of the African view is increasingly accepted, the UN machinery can be employed to put pressure on those who maintain illegitimate practices. This pressure can range from strong efforts to persuade up to organized deprivation by economic means and conceivably military action against a recalcitrant. The Security Council, in particular, can be employed to organize mandatory programmes, as it has with regard to arms shipments to South Africa[21] and economic relations with Ian Smith's regime in the erstwhile Rhodesia.[22]

Agenda setting, legitimating and the creation of binding rules all relate to broad fields of policy apart from problems of maintaining the peace. Economic cooperation to spur economic development has been a permanent part of the UN agenda since the decline of colonialism. The African governments have taken a leading role in seeking cooperation for economic development through the UN system.[23] This search has two distinctive aspects that apply generally to UN promotion of the general welfare.

The first of these aspects may be characterized as planning. It is the attempt to set out clear goals for cooperation, to determine priorities and to encourage governments to conform. This approach has involved the use of technical skills that are represented in such bodies as the UN Commission for Development Planning. It sets out the schemes adopted by the UN General Assembly as the global development strategies for the Development Decades. The third Development Decade is now under way. Such planning has had joint and individual political support from African governments.

The planning approach, emphasizing deliberate cooperation, has also involved institutional changes and efforts to dominate the political junction points. The African governments took a prominent share in the reorganization of the UN system to promote what the General Assembly called a New International Economic Order.[24] They strongly supported the appointment of a senior official, just below the rank of Secretary-General, in the UN Secretariat as the superior coordinator of economic and social affairs: a ranking Ghanaian diplomat, Kenneth Dadzie, was the first named to the post. Furthermore, African governments have successfully insisted on more representation in various deliberative organs, ranging from the Economic and Social Council to the more specialized directing bodies of operating agencies.

The second aspect of the promotion of the general welfare involves the furnishing of material assistance. Here the African governments sought to increase the aid proffered through the UN system and joined with other developing countries to attempt to enlarge existing programmes and to create new ones. This effort was an integral part of the widening of the scope of operations by the International Bank for Reconstruction and Development and by the International Monetary Fund.[25]

Such long-term facilities contrast sharply with the emergency needs of African countries, which are exemplified by the vast flows of refugees on the continent. Here, too, African governments sought successfully to call attention to a human disaster and to employ the UN machinery to increase the flow of material assistance. The conference in Geneva during the first part of 1981 was a tribute to their success.[26]

The fact that the UN system offers instrumental opportunities which African governments have used to their benefit does not, however, signify general satisfaction. Such approaches encounter resistance, both from within and outside of Africa. Not every attempt to use the UN machinery instrumentally, fully or even partly succeeds. Especially when the aim of African governments has to do with redistribution of resources from the rich to the poorer or with the use of strong pressure by means not in the possession of African governments, the outcomes may create discontent. That such dissatisfaction frequently surfaces in speeches in the UN General Assembly can be treated as quite normal in a political institution, for only the deceived could believe that the purpose of international cooperation could easily be accomplished to the satisfaction of all participants.

The UN and some major African issues

African inputs into the global system and the necessarily broad framework of global cooperation have had mutual effects. But effects alone do not make contentious issues vanish. In fact, the UN system frequently highlights important African issues and conflicts. This section of the chapter will deal with some of them.

At the beginning of the 1980s, the dominant African political issue in the UN system reflected the unsettled situation of southern Africa.[27] Cooperating closely in regional and subregional groupings, African governments had been an integral element in the progress of Zimbabwe towards independence. The African governments had pressed the United Kingdom to eliminate the white-dominated Smith regime even before its unilateral declaration of independence in 1965. They had later led the way in the Security Council to the imposition of mandatory economic sanctions that certainly had a punishing but not a decisive effect, for South Africa and a few other states allowed the boycott to be penetrated.

Nevertheless, the end of the Smith regime once again demonstrated what the effort to use coercion had earlier made equally clear: even a united Africa could neither force the resistant Smith regime nor the governments that could exert maximum pressure to act against their will. The independence of Zimbabwe required both political pressure and fighting on the African side and cooperation from extra-African governments.

Southern Africa remains disturbed after the successful progress of Zimbabwe to independence. Two main factors create this turbulence. The first, the independence of Namibia, is an issue characterized by the intimate concern of the UN system for the last 35 years. It is ineluctably bound up with the denial of human rights in South Africa under the apartheid system, a second southern African issue of paramount concern to the rest of Africa. Had African sentiment alone dominated, both of these issues would long ago have been laid to rest. Were they to vanish, however, southern Africa would still be subject to disturbance until Angola found a better political footing and diminished its dependence on the presence of Cuban troops whose welcome no doubt wears thinner with each passing year but whose services remain valuable.

The complex bundle of southern African issues has been subject to dynamic, varied treatment in the UN system.[28] The African governments have employed the UN instrumentally and with a high degree of unity to keep pressure on the powerful extra-African governments. These have gradually responded with more zeal and have cooperated with the neighbours of Zimbabwe and South Africa, the 'front-line' states. Considerable progress was made on Namibia in the late 1970s, even though the remarkable obstinacy of South Africa, the effective administrator of the territory, remains for all to see. Meantime, through the UN system, legal rules and political decisions, including the establishment of specialized machinery for Namibia, have provided the basis for a smooth transition to independence whenever the negotiations centred on the Security Council succeed. Furthermore, the African governments have continually employed the General Assembly to demand heavier coercion against South Africa, but this remains a symbolic gesture so long as the United States, France, West Germany, the United Kingdom and other powerful extra-African states interpret their roles as primarily diplomatic.

The violation of human rights in South Africa disturbs not only African opinion but also groups spread throughout the world. It calls forth moral denunciations from Communist and democratic, pluralistic governments alike. The UN system has been brought by its members, led by the African group, to join in condemning the conduct of the white South African government and some hesitating steps toward coercion, such as a mandatory boycott of arms sales to South Africa, have been undertaken. In several guises, the South African guerilla groups abroad have received modest assistance from the UN system. South African refugees also receive educational and other benefits. But outside of Africa, no consensus or commitment has emerged to use extra-continental force to overturn apartheid. Thus, the extreme programmes of the African governments have been turned aside, whatever the majority of the General Assembly, and the several more specialized committees it has formed to deal with the subject, may recommend. It demonstrates to all those who remain unaware that the UN system is essentially a set of organizations for voluntary participation.[29]

The sharp antagonism of African opinion and the behaviour of South Africa pose broader issues for Africa in the UN system than mere tactics. Indeed, at a tactical level, African cooperation has been highly successful. It has kept southern African issues continuously on the agenda of the General Assembly and the Security Council. It has driven the South African representatives out of the General Assembly and has compelled the withdrawal of South Africa from the International Labour Organization, the UN Educational Scientific and Cultural Organization (UNESCO) and other specialized agencies. It has built a long series of symbolic resolutions and doctrinal declarations upon which the argument that apartheid is a threat to peace can be based. It has seen the positions of the OAU on the matter adopted in the General Assembly. And

Africa has achieved a high degree of tactical cooperation with the Arab governments and other Third World countries on the matter.

Yet Africa does not function effortlessly as a continental force in the UN system despite much rhetoric about unity in the OAU. No group of governments more keenly defends national independence than those of Africa. As a result, disputes among African governments either do not come to the UN for treatment, as in the case of the conflict between Somalia and Ethiopia, or else elicit a sputtering, equivocal unresponsiveness as in the Tanzanian invasion of Uganda, that mirrors the cracks in the alleged African consensus. The machinery of the OAU can be engaged to play off against the UN so that disputes are treated effectively in neither one nor the other. Even on so clear a violation of UN doctrine as the case of human rights in South Africa, where the African governments have insisted that the General Assembly appeal for an economic boycott, some of the nearby governments continue to trade and others maintain formal or practical diplomatic relations with Pretoria.

Furthermore, the treatment of serious African political disturbances with excruciating human results does not necessarily get pushed onto the global agenda. Nothing was heard of the deaths of some 80,000 BaHutu during political turbulence in Burundi during the mid-1970s. The unrestrained murderousness of the regime in Uganda did not prevent its leader, General Idi Amin, from representing Africa before the UN General Assembly which ultimately recommends policies for global protection of human rights. Similar comments relate to the unlamented Macias regime in Equatorial Guinea. While treatment of refugees by African governments has been remarkably helpful and gentle in comparison with Southeast Asia or with Europe immediately before the Second World War, the rest of the world has not been encouraged to enquire into the causes of the flights of millions.

Thus, participation in the UN system opens up to attack the plausibility of the notion that African governments can settle their own affairs among themselves. Even when the principle is not directly challenged, many governments and some sections of public opinion outside of Africa are keenly aware of the disparity between supporting high-minded declarations on the denial of human rights in South Africa and outside of Africa and the behaviour of some African states towards their neighbours and their own people. It can be argued that nationalism and autonomy of governments in Africa should be no more privileged than in any other region.

Furthermore, the very machinery of the UN system develops a certain intrusive quality as its operations proceed and benefits obtained from it on a national basis encourage individualistic rather than joint behaviour by governments. The leading role developed by the front-line states in dealing with southern Africa and in negotiating with the contact group of the Security Council tends to reduce the persuasiveness of the broader African position. Furthermore, cross-cutting links between individual governments and extra-African organizations and states have a similar effect. For instance, some of the North African governments have close links with other Arab states and take part, along with some of the sub-Saharan governments, in the Islamic Conference. Almost all of the African governments join in the non-aligned movement, a few are members of the Organization of Petroleum Exporting Countries. Many have important treaty links with the European Community which, despite its title, makes decisions which necessarily have political implications.

In addition, loans and technical assistance from the several organizations which are part of or associated with the UN system, such as the UN Development Programme or the World Bank, are obtained on a national or sub-regional basis. Governments have every incentive to act autonomously in this area, for their abilities as competitors for scarce resources are rewarded. Such competitiveness cannot avoid influencing the positions member governments take on broader political and economic issues, such as those posed by the Declaration on the New International Economic Order, which had strong backing from African governments.

Conclusion

The political role of Africa in the UN system has unquestionably been an influential one. In its simplest form, it relies on sheer numbers. But such simplicity fails to relay either the complexity of international politics or the rich variety of opportunities for national governments. The fact is that African governments have used the consultative possibilities of the OAU and other organizations to originate and elaborate joint positions which can influence the UN system. They have repeatedly demonstrated their capacity to exert such influence in the General Assembly and its manifold political subsidiaries. They have participated effectively in setting out priorities in the global political economy. African representatives are omnipresent and necessary to decisions throughout the UN system.

Yet Africa has no more unity of ideas, approaches, aims and methods in the UN system than it has on the ground of the continent. Much of the doctrine on such subjects as southern Africa represents a lowest common denominator of national policies or has hardly much more meaning than a pious wish. Sometimes the language employed is so broad and abstract as to mean whatever governments wish it to mean. Sometimes it is mere doctrine without the capacity to induce its targets to act. Africa has to live with its own diversity both at home and in the UN system.

Unity of opinion and adroit tactics by the African governments do not necessarily produce the desired outcomes in the UN system. These often depend on the willingness of extra-African governments to act. Especially in southern Africa has this been the case, for if the only manner in which to deal with South Africa requires coercion, its costs usually cannot or will not be met by African governments. The consequence is that joint African positions on particular political issues reintroduce the extra-African influences to a continent whose governments have continuously tried to eliminate them.

The use of the UN system to achieve political goals acceptable to Africa has the effect of generalizing the issues so that many more governments become involved. Whether dealing with the issues requires economic strength, broad support among diverse publics and sustained commitment, the UN involvement may be highly beneficial. Such benefits are involved in the development of a doctrine on human rights, especially racism, and on the emergency treatment of refugees, which can be seen as a result of political decisions. But such benefits can also involve tactical concessions in order to make it possible to achieve broader support. As a negotiating theatre, the UN can offer some advantages. It has settled procedures for formal decisions, can furnish experienced international civil servants as advisers and encourages many sorts of less formal contacts among the representatives of almost every government in the world.

African participation in political activities in the UN system, finally, involves certain paradoxes. African governments trumpet their desire for independence, but a common African position in political discussion in the UN requires a reduction of autonomy. The common African position accepted in the OAU looks forward to a continent which deals with its own disputes and common enterprises and is influential in the UN. But participation in the UN necessarily challenges extreme autonomy.

NOTES

1 UN General Assembly Resolution 1514 (1960).
2 UN Charter, Article 33 (1).
3 Leland M. Goodrich, Edvard Hambro, Anne P. Simons, *Charter of the United Nations*, Columbia University Press, New York, 3rd rev. edn, 1969, p. 263.
4 UN Charter, Article 52 (3).
5 UN Charter, Article 34.

6 UN Charter, Article 53.
7 UN Charter, Article 107.
8 UN Charter, Article 51.
9 UN Charter, Article 23 (1).
0 Leland M. Goodrich, 'The UN Security Council' in James Barros (ed.), *The United Nations: Past, Present and Future*, The Free Press, New York, 1972, p. 32.
1 Statute of the International Court of Justice, Article 4.
2 Stephen G. Xydis, 'The General Assembly', in Barros, *The United Nations*, pp. 66–7.
3 Leon Gordenker, *The UN Secretary-General and the Maintenance of Peace*, Columbia University Press, New York, 1967, p. 91.
4 James S. Magee, 'ECA and the Paradox of African Cooperation', *International Conciliation*, 580, (1970).
5 Walter R. Sharp, *Field Administration in the United Nations System*, Praeger, New York, 1961, pp. 507–12.
6 On the UN decisional process, see Johan Kaufmann, *United Nations Decision Making*, Sijthoff & Nordhoff, Alphen aan den Rijn, 1980, Chapter 7 and *passim*.
7 Berhanyku Andemicael, *The OAU and the UN*, Africana Publishing Co., New York, 1976, pp. 29–30.
8 OAU Charter, Preamble and Article 2.
9 OAU Summit Conference Resolution C, 25 May 1963; UN General Assembly Resolution 2011 (XX); and UN-OAU Agreement of 1965, reprinted in Andemicael, *OAU and the UN*, pp. 301–4.
0 See Andemicael, *OAU and the UN*, Part I, on OAU activities in UN security cases. No more recent, comprehensive account seems available. Also see his article in Andemicael, *Regionalism and the United Nations*, Oceana Publications, Dobbs Ferry, N.Y., 1979, pp. 225–98.
1 UN Security Council Resolution 418 (1977).
2 UN Security Council Resolutions 232 (1966) and 253 (1968).
3 See Andemicael, *OAU and the UN*, Part II, for detailed but rather legalistic discussion. Also see Parley W. Newman, Jr., 'United Nations Regional Economic Commissions and Their Relations with Regional Organizations in Developing Areas', in Andemicael, *Regionalism*, pp. 374–8.
4 The recommended framework for the New International Economic Order is contained in UN General Assembly Resolutions 3201 (S-VI) and 3202 (S-VI), adopted on 1 May 1974. The restructuring of the UN system was mandated by the General Assembly in UN General Assembly Resolution 3362 (S-VII), adopted on 16 September 1975. The Sixth and Seventh Special Sessions of the General Assembly, which adopted these resolutions, saw heavy African participation.
25 African efforts also have successfully singled out continental problems for specific treatment by the UN and its subsidiaries, e.g., Sudano-Sahelian desertification. See UN General Assembly Resolution 35/72.
26 See United Nations, International Conference on Assistance to Refugees in Africa, Documents A/Conf. 106/1 and Add. 1 and A/Conf. 106/3 and ICARA *Report* (a periodical published by the UN High Commissioner for Refugees) for current information. The UN General Assembly in 1980 con-

tinued its earlier practice of adopting a series of resolutions on African refugee situations.

27 The situation in South Africa continues to dominate the treatment of the southern African sub-region. See Richard E. Bissell, *Apartheid and International Organization*, Westview Press, Boulder, Col., 1977, *passim* for an account of the developments centred around South African racial policy. Kenneth Grundy, *Confrontation and Accommodation in Southern Africa*, University of California Press, Berkeley, 1973 makes clear the structural factors that give South Africa special importance in the region.

28 In addition to Bissell, *Apartheid*, see the annual *Issues Before the United Nations General Assembly*, published by the United Nations Association of the United States, New York.

29 Resolutions of the General Assembly now routinely accuse unnamed NATO members, Israel and multinational corporations of involvement in the maintenance of apartheid. This line echoes complaints adopted in the UN General Assembly's Special Committee on Apartheid. The governments charged simply brush aside such language as a guide to action, even if they equally routinely protest both the accuracy and the fairness of the charges. For a recent sample of this self-defeating sort of diplomacy, see UN General Assembly Resolution 35/32. The 15 governments which voted against the resolution included those whose cooperation is most needed for effective pressure. The great powers included in the majority have scrupulously avoided making any commitment as to action through the UN system.

3 The Economic Commission for Africa

ISEBILL V. GRUHN

Introduction

The Economic Commission for Africa (ECA), which in 1983 will celebrate its 25th birthday, is one of the Regional Commissions of the United Nations' economic and social structure, and as such is not, strictly speaking, an African organization. However, the ECA has over the years played a pivotal role in African regional cooperation, directly through its own policies and programmes and more indirectly by serving as parent, midwife and concerned cousin to many African regional organizations and mechanisms. The ECA comprises 49 independent African states. Throughout most of its history it has been under the stewardship of two prominent West Africans: Dr. Robert Gardiner of Ghana, who was Executive Secretary from 1962 to 1975, and his successor, Dr. Adebayo Adedeji of Nigeria.

The UN Economic and Social Council established the Economic Commission for Africa on 29 April 1958. Addis Ababa, Ethiopia, was selected as the site for its headquarters. Like the UN's other regional commissions, ECA operates under the general supervision of the Economic and Social Council and of the General Assembly. The terms of reference of the ECA require:

a) that the Commission initiate and participate in measures for facilitating concerted action to relieve the economic and technological problems of Africa;

b) that it make or sponsor investigations into economic and technological problems of development;

c) that it undertake or sponsor the collection, evaluation and dissemination of economic, technological and statistical information;

d) that it perform such advisory services as countries of the region may desire, provided that these do not overlap with those provided by other bodies of the UN or its specialized agencies;

e) that it assist the UN Economic and Social Council, at its request, in discharging its functions within the region in connection with any economic problems including those in the field of technical assistance;

f) that it assist in the development of coordinated policies for promoting economic and technological development in the region;

g) and that it deal, where appropriate, with the social aspects of economic development and with the relationship between economic and social factors.[1]

The terms of reference for the ECA, like those of other UN regional commissions, implicitly include a dual mandate: act as part of the UN's international structure, but also serve the special needs of the specific region. The mandate of the regional commissions has been sufficiently vague to allow each one to define its own personality, and to reflect the special needs of each region as well as to redefine needs within a region over time. I have written elsewhere[2] that the ECA has developed its institutional structure and programmatic personality without resolving the conflict arising from the competing and overlapping demands of the dual mandate. As a consequence, the ECA more than other UN regional commissions, has continually both mirrored and generated international and African trends of thought and action regarding regional cooperation and integration. Beyond its own intrinsic import as an institution, ECA constitutes a good focal point around which to pose a range of questions about the feasibility and viability of past, present, and future efforts regarding African regional organization and about the fostering and hindering forces that the international economic and social structure imposes upon such efforts.

The context which gave birth to the ECA

In Africa, the political and cultural imperative of African unity dominated the independence and post-independence ideologies of Africa's key leadership. Whether it was Kwame Nkrumah's advocacy of continental unity through pan-Africanism, or the more cultural and literary themes of Negritude as advanced by Leopold Senghor, the theme was one of uniting the peoples and cultures of Africa. The uniting of Africa, both politically and culturally, appeared essential for political, psychological, and cultural liberation from colonial oppression. The uniting of Africa also appeared to many African leaders as necessary for coping with a post-Second World War cold war context, and for overcoming the economic development obstacles on the African continent. However, by 1960 about half the continent had attained political independence, and the establishment of so many small, seemingly unviable states, along with their tendency to quickly form ideological blocs, made it clear that the uniting of the African continent carried with it far more obstacles than doctrines such as pan-Africanism could overcome. The Organization of African Unity (OAU), founded in 1963 under the aegis of then-conservative Ethiopia, was a far cry from Nkrumah's vision of 'union government for Africa.' At best the OAU was perceived as an embryonic compromise – a means of creating a minimal foundation upon which African unity might someday be built.

A number of miscalculations on the part of ideologues led to calls for unity when the political, economic, and social realities increasingly indicated schisms amongst newly politically independent states. In retrospect, it should not surprise us that independence movements and their leadership concerned themselves largely with shaping national identities rather than collective continental problem solving. National leadership was clearly not interested in divesting itself of its newly won authority at the national level in the name of some continental authority.

Perhaps even more concretely, attempting to integrate the administrative and economic affairs of states with differing colonial heritages raised serious obstacles. The colonial period had formed political and economic entities with few structural links between them. Most African countries had economies which were competitive with rather than complementary to those of their neighbours. Even adjacent states commonly utilized different bureaucratic practices, different accounting systems, different monetary zones. Few, if any, transportation and communication links existed; instead links with metropoles were, after independence, transformed into bilateral relationships most appropriately described as neo-colonial. Thus, even building limited interstate relationships of a meaningful kind carried with it inherited and continuing obstacles which were both serious and widespread.

In the early post-independence years, the usual life cycle of an inter-African organization started with a series of interstate conferences which culminated in a charter signing ceremony attended by the heads of state and the selection of a headquarters site. Next, an organizational bureaucracy was created which promptly ran into financial difficulties. Bureaucratic disarray and loss of interest by the membership soon followed. The rhetoric of cooperation, coordination, indeed integration and unity, gave way, and the organization became a so-called 'paper organization.' African leaders were understandably in a hurry; they wanted quick solutions to their countries' many problems. There was little patience with incremental organization building and engaging in the slow and tedious process of slowly creating the infrastructure of interstate relations. Political actors caught up in the euphoria of post-independence Africa fully confronted neither the structural obstacles to national economic development, nor the structural obstacles to building mutually beneficial cooperative links with continental neighbours. As new, untried regional institutions were chartered they were of course confronted with the overwhelming problems of the development needs of the African continent. African leadership soon became disillusioned with the promises of continental unity and various types of regionalism. Growing cynicism and disillusionment amongst African leaders and their followers throughout the 1960s constituted the political milieu confronting the ECA. This was the very clientele which the ECA had to prod into interstate cooperation for the purpose of social and economic development.

The ECA's activities were also influenced during this early period by the theoretical and academic discussions, mostly Western, regarding regionalism. For young economists and political scientists interested in African affairs, studies of post-Second World War European reconstruction lent the hope that regional integration could be applicable to the African context. But this theorizing by Western scholars was generated more by contemporary fashion than by intimate acquaintance with African circumstances.

At this point it is useful to differentiate between the terms 'regional cooperation' and 'regional integration.' Regional cooperation is a vague term applied to any interstate activity with less than universal participation designed to meet some common need. The term regional integration has acquired several quite technical definitions, but for our purposes it will be defined as the process or the achieved reality of national units sharing part or all of their decision-making authority with an emerging international institution.[3] As applied to Africa, 'region' almost always refers not to the continent as a whole, but to some sub-group of African states.

Throughout the 1960s the number of regional integration studies on Africa increased and, quite expectedly, almost all aspects of the African situation were found to be at variance with the European one which had originally given rise to theorizing about regional integration. Nevertheless, the belief persisted that African variations could either be accounted for by the theory through some additional variables, or could, with some adjustments, be made to explain and predict the likelihood of failure of regional integration schemes in Africa. As Africans themselves lost their euphoria about the prospects of continental and regional institutions, a more realistic examination of African circumstances began to appear.[4]

But it is not the range and the twists and turns of these debates amongst Western scholars and critiques of them by Marxists that interests us here;[5] we merely wish to indicate the second context in which the ECA operated. The evolution of the ECA as an institution, its programmes and activities, were not merely affected by the circumstances and conditions of the region, but by the ideas and theories prevalent regarding the role that regional cooperation and/or integration can have in the development process. These theories, while largely non-African in origin, nevertheless constituted a key element in the ECA's conceptualization and execution of its task.

In addition, the ECA operated within the context of a third milieu, namely the bureaucratic maze of the UN family of agencies. The ECA was, after all, not a free standing institution, but rather a link in a chain of often overlapping, competing UN agencies. As a consequence, the ECA's institutional structure and programmatic battle plans were, from the very onset, not merely a reflection of African realities, ideologies, and Western theories about regionalism, but also a reflection of the uncertainties and complexities of defining the ECA's role within a larger set of organizational ideologies and bureaucratic mazes.

Finally, the ECA, like any organization concerned with economic and social development in the Third World, had to take cognizance of the international milieu. Cold war politics, aid strategies of donors, and other international environmental factors had the power to foster or hinder the activities, and directly or indirectly help to define the role of a regional commission. The ECA's infancy and adolescence in the 1960s should be judged against the background of these forces.

While the ECA reflects the milieu in which it was established, it also had the opportunity to help change its environment. Before discussing the ECA more directly, it will be helpful to move past the 1960s into the 1970s and 1980s to indicate how the empirical and conceptual context, and hence the ECA's milieu, have changed.

Recent trends

Political actors, as well as those writing in scholarly journals, have seen evidence in recent years of the decreasing relevance of regional integration in Africa. This is based in large part on consistent failures of various regional integration efforts in Africa (e.g., the demise of the East African Community), and the failures of so many organizations to develop institutional and programmatic viability. The failures of regional integration efforts during the 1960s and early 1970s, along with the frustrations of development strategies in general, have won attention for two additional but seemingly contradictory sets of ideologies. The first, popular with actors and theorists alike, is that economic and social development in Africa must come about through so-called 'self-reliance.' Self-reliance here meaning not merely reduced dependency upon neo-colonial ties, but also autonomous state institution building and development along with 'collective self-reliance' (multinational and regional development). The second set of theories and strategies, again popular with theorists and ideologues, as well as actors, concerns the so-called New International Economic Order (NIEO). Here the argument is that neither national nor regional efforts can overcome the international structural impediments which will forever replicate the inequality between the Have and Have-Not states. According to this thesis, regional efforts constitute, at best, sticking plasters, not cures, for African disadvantage and underdevelopment. First, it should be pointed out that national self-reliance and seeking to develop a NIEO are not incompatible notions, since it can be argued, and many do, that a NIEO is a precondition for greater national self-reliance or that greater self-reliance is a psychological as well as structural precondition for creating a NIEO. In short, it is not necessarily inconsistent to argue that the current dependency relationship of African states on a global economic order needs to be changed by simultaneously creating changes in the international structure and generating greater national and regional competency in the economic and social realm.

There is, however, little question that NIEO and self-reliance have in recent years replaced regional integration and African unity as catch phrases in both political and economic discourse. It also appears evident that neither a NIEO nor self-reliance can be willed into existence, however desirable and agreeable either or both would be for the economic and social well-being of African countries and peoples. Also, it now appears reasonably clear that self-reliance and a NIEO require of African countries, individually and collectively, rather similar skills and resources as regional cooperation and integration schemes called for. Development and change call for institutional capacity, manpower capacity, well-functioning domestic and foreign policy-making processes; and proper distribution and redistribution of national resources. Even if one were to imagine the availability of vast new resources generated, for example, by a NIEO, the lack of absorption capacity of such resources, especially in small and least developed countries which make up more than half the states in Africa, would still be a serious problem. In short, a NIEO, self-reliance, and, for that matter, interstate cooperation, still require Africa to address the fundamental questions of capacity building. And, capacity building in

Africa, while not necessarily solvable through regional integration, may require at least some form of regional cooperation.

Ironically, now that regionalism has fallen out of favour amongst development theorists and ideologues calling for NIEO and self-reliance, the actual practice of regional institution building in Africa is at an all-time high. The explanation is simple.

Some of the obstacles which stood in the way of regional schemes in the early 1960s have been removed (though admittedly some new ones have been erected) such as a stronger sense of national identity. For example, the linkages between African states and the metropoles are no longer perceived to be as secure, reliable, and favourable as they used to be for most African states. The lack of intercourse amongst African states has been replaced by slowly increasing interstate movement of goods and peoples. Interstate communications have been improved. Thus, currency clearing houses and institutional arrangements to facilitate monetary and financial transactions now make more sense and are in the self-interest of states. As goods and people move across borders, institutional mechanisms to facilitate this become not merely theoretically but practically essential. And as goods and people and other transactions increase, more interstate infrastructure and institution-building is desired. Interstate highway building, the development of a continental information network, a West African Currency Clearing House, the establishment of the Economic Community of West African States (ECOWAS) with its range of agreements amongst its 16 member states – the very institutions and' policies called for in the 1960s and relegated to paper organizations – have now become viable, functioning regional mechanisms. The preconditions which were absent in the 1960s and which established the gap between regional integration theorizing and African self-interested practice, have now begun to change. This change is part of a larger syndrome of development experience over the past 20 years and can be easily distorted by only highlighting the above. However, it is accurate to say that regional cooperation and regional institution-building have increased in velocity at the very time when attention has been diverted from them.

It will be seen that the ECA has both generated and reflected some of these evolutionary changes. At any given time the ECA has played some role at both the theoretical and practical levels. I think it can be unequivocally stated that, in 1981, while theorists and frequently rhetoricians are occupied with matters other than regionalism as a vehicle for development, regionalism as a process and goal is alive and increasingly well on the African continent. The ECA continues to play an interesting role in this drama of international, regional, and national forces, which, though often conflicting, continue to grope for political, economic, and social solutions to problems confronting an underdeveloped continent.

The ECA'S organization, leadership and mission

The Gardiner era

Robert Gardiner's influence dominated the first part of the ECA's life as an organization. His style and posture was that of a national and international civil servant. It was his intention, even if not always realized, that the ECA should steer a neutral course and not get into the fray of inter-African and national African politics. In true UN style, studies and documents written by the ECA were not supposed to offend governments. It was to be the ECA's task to show African leaders and governments what was feasible, and to provide the informational background upon which decisions could be made. The ECA's image both continentally and internationally was meant to be that of a bureaucratic servant to client governments. Although Gardiner emphasized the ECA's UN connection, he recognized that the ECA's viability in Africa required that it should not be seen as yet another internationally staffed UN agency made up of individuals with little knowledge and even less sensitivity to Africa. Gardiner sought to Africanize the staff of the ECA as promptly as possible. By 1968, 60 per cent of the professional staff was African; by 1976 the figure was closer to 80 per cent, and it is even higher today. However, given the paucity of trained Africans, especially during the first decade of the post-independence period, and the limited enthusiasm of most French-speaking African governments for the ECA, the Africanization had two effects. First, most of the staff was trained in law or the social sciences; and second, most of the staff was drawn from English-speaking Africa with proportionally large contingencies from Ghana and Nigeria. Thus, during Gardiner's tenure and beyond, the ECA's staff was made up of generalists better prepared to handle administrative work than the technical aspects of development planning. In this respect the ECA's staff resembles the secretariat of UN headquarters rather than that of a technical division of one of the UN's specialized agencies.

Throughout Gardiner's tenure at the ECA, his leadership and style did not produce either a well-defined organizational ideology or a sense of intellectual excitement that would inspire the dedication of the ECA staff or give its work output an identity and visibility among its clients. Indeed, when Gardiner retired in 1975, few leaders and governments in Africa believed the ECA to be a potent instrument.[6] The ECA's low profile obscured some of the real contributions it had made. Member governments and other UN agencies were frequently so unfamiliar with the ECA's work that they were unable to draw on and utilize the many studies, reports, and technical assistance facilities provided.

Only in the international realm did Gardiner's moderation enhance the ECA's image. To Western ears, the ECA's moderation and modest levels of competency within the UN structure came as a welcome relief compared to the more strident rhetoric of the OAU, its institutional incapacity to deal with development issues, and the moribund nature of sub-regional organization. Then, too, the ECA under Gardiner echoed the views fashionable among Western development experts. The early fascination with regional integration as a vehicle for generating and sustaining development was evident when the ECA set up sub-regional offices intended to serve as foci for regional integration. Similarly, the Western penchant for doing background studies, especially popular with the American Agency for International Development, was mirrored by the ECA's heavy investment during its first decade in collecting data and undertaking feasibility studies. The international development community's emphasis on industrialization was also echoed by the ECA.

In fact, the ECA managed, throughout the 1960s, to give off an image of a totally non-threatening and somewhat ineffectual organization in each of the realms in which it operated. Internationally, in view of its dual mandate as an arm of the UN machinery, the ECA's role partly overlapped and competed with that of other agencies, but its general striving to upgrade the African continent's development capacity was not unwelcome. In its second role, as a builder of African interstate institutions, the ECA's work was consistent with international and African thought on the matter. Here the ECA can indeed claim paternity, or at least a midwife role, for a large range of interstate African institutions including the African Development Bank, the West African Currency Clearing House, and ECOWAS. Third, the ECA's efforts to expand its own institutional role by erecting sub-regional offices and offering its own administrative structure as foci for regional integration and cooperation also proved consistent with African and international assumptions of the time, though it must be quickly added here that the reality was a long way from the ideal. The ECA's sub-regional bureaux never became fully operational and certainly never became nuclei for sub-regional integration.

Under Gardiner's stewardship then, the ECA, rather than resolving its dual mandate, sought to serve in various capacities as an arm of the UN system, simultaneously offering itself as the centrepiece for African integration, and fostering non-ECA tied inter-African institution building. It was a tall order for any institution to serve several functions as diverse and potentially conflictual as these. But since the ECA was not a highly visible and threateningly activist mechanism under Gardiner, impotence, rather than conflict, constituted the most common consequence of the rather awesome agenda.

It is useful to digress for a moment to point out that the ECA's organizational structure, mission and style under Gardiner's leadership were a matter both of design and default. This can best be seen by briefly comparing the ECA with another UN Regional Commission, namely the Economic Commission for Latin America (ECLA). The ECLA developed a very different and distinctive development ideology under the much more dynamic leadership of its executive secretary, Raul Prebisch. The ECLA, of course, served a different constituency as well – one with considerable political schism but greater cultural and linguistic uniformity, a longer post-colonial history, and relatively better economic health. Nevertheless, the ECLA made some very different choices from its very inception. Unlike the ECA, the ECLA sought to avoid an elaborate organizational structure, either at headquarters or as part of an outreach programme. Instead Prebisch concentrated the ECLA's energies in a relatively small (about 100 professionals) secretariat into which he sought to gather the best minds in Latin American economic and social development thinking. By 1960 the ECLA had become a high powered think-tank for what is still acknowledged by advocates and critics alike as an important analysis of underdevelopment. Rather than merely reflecting and echoing the current wisdom in the development community, the ECLA forged a distinctive development ideology. In essence, this ideology held that the economic disadvantage of Third World countries stemmed from the fact that they are situated in the periphery in an international economic system that has resulted from, and is perpetuated by, giving Third World countries unfavourable terms of trade. To attack these disadvantages, industrialized 'core' states would have to be persuaded to reverse this pattern and create in its stead a mechanism that would guarantee preferential status for the less-developed countries in the periphery. Latin American regional cooperation and integration was perceived as an essential step in the reorganization of centre-periphery relations.

The ECLA made it its mission to influence international thinking about, and understanding of, the nature of underdevelopment with the aim of changing the international economic structure. In this sense the ECLA conceived of itself as a lobbyist for Latin American interests and, more broadly, Third World interests in general. The ECLA was staffed as a think-tank to develop strategies for inducing the UN and other bilateral and multilateral actors to accept its views on the need to restructure the international system. Along with this mission the ECLA did attempt to produce studies upon which its clientele could focus their own development strategies, a perceived necessary concomitant to global structural change.

Much can be said about the ECLA's strategies, its achievements, and failures, but this is not our purpose here.[7] What is relevant to our discussion is that the ECLA, unlike the ECA, was perceived both in its own region and internationally, as a truly Latin American organization, and not as an administrative arm of the UN. And the ECLA had a well-developed and visible ideology which contained a development assessment and strategy for which the organization became a missionary, both in Latin America and internationally. This, it can easily be seen, marks the ECA and the ECLA as quite distinctive Regional Commissions, despite the fact that the charge for each from the UN's Economic and Social Council was identical. In a comparative and critical perspective, the ECA failed, during Gardiner's reign, to develop a distinctive and governing perspective *vis-à-vis* regional and international development strategies. It should therefore come as no surprise that when the Gardiner era ended and the Adedeji era began in 1975, the issue was not merely one of a change in leadership. It quickly became a matter of real concern whether Adedeji would somehow sharpen the focus and mission of the ECA and generate a more activist role both in Africa and internationally.

The Adedeji era

Adebayo Adedeji took over the helm at the ECA after the retirement of Robert Gardiner in 1975. Adedeji was educated abroad with an MA in public administration from Harvard and a PhD in economics from the University of London. However, Adedeji had returned home to Nigeria where, among other things, he served as a Federal Commissioner and as Minister of Economic Development and Reconstruction. Given his background and personality, it was assumed that he would perceive his role as Executive Secretary of the ECA more as a lobbyist and salesman for African needs and strategies and less as an international civil servant. Indeed, the record to date indicates that under his stewardship the ECA is more visible and activist, especially on the African continent itself.

In fairness to Robert Gardiner, it should be pointed out that he served during an era in African development when laying the groundwork institutionally, statistically, and programmatically was certainly appropriate. When Adedeji came to power, it had become increasingly clear that post-independence development strategies simply were not making adequate inroads. In fact, Adedeji often points out in speeches that, after 20 years of independence, African economies are deteriorating.[8]

Consequently, Adedeji has taken an activist role in pressing African governments to realize the urgency of the situation. He seems to be saying the following: the African continent is in a state of crisis; things are getting worse. With a population said to be likely to double from some 400 million to 800 million by the turn of the century, Africa is not keeping up with the needed food, energy, and other essential economic and social needs. The growing crises during the past 20 years have been due as much to a lack of know-how and enterprise as to a lack of money. Adedeji seems concerned that there are too many inter-African institutions which compete and duplicate; he thus appears to be placing an emphasis on making institutions work rather than merely generating more paper organizations. Adedeji emphasizes what he calls 'self-sustaining internal growth', the mobilization of African states, inter-African institutions, and African resources, and gives less weight to the NIEO. The ECA's early emphasis on inter-African cooperation has not been dropped; in fact much importance is placed on a call for building reliable physical links between markets of the continent so that more cooperation and integration can indeed take place. But, Adedeji stresses self-reliance and self-sustainment, though not necessarily self-sufficiency.[9]

It seems to me that in his public utterances Adedeji stresses two things. First, that African states, individually and collectively, need to energize themselves and more directly confront the 'crises of the Continent', to do something for themselves. Second, the ECA as an organization and Adedeji as its leader are seeking to play the role of catalyst rather than that of an executing agency, but at the same time continuing in some of its missions to provide interstate cooperative and integrative institutional and infra-structural assistance. So, for example, the work begun in 1971 on a Trans-African Highway which is to link Mombasa to Lagos continues. Work continues on a Pan-African Telecommunications network (PANAFTEL). Adedeji also seems anxious to sustain the existing network of inter-African institutions to make them work better, and to get African governments to view them as important mechanisms deserving of financial and other support. These institutions include: the African Centre for Applied Research and Training in Social Development; the African Development Bank; the African Centre for Engineering Design and Manufacturing; the Regional Centre for Training in Aerial Surveys; the Regional Centre for Population Studies; and others. Taken as a whole, the ECA's aim under Adedeji appears to be to activate the energies of the leaders of the continent and the existing institutional structures into confronting the African situation. The specific guidelines to be used evolved in the following way.

At the 16th session of the Assembly of Heads of State and Government of the OAU in Monrovia, Liberia in July 1979, the 'Monrovia Strategy for Economic Development of Africa' and the associated 'Monrovia Declaration of Commitment on Guidelines and Measures for National and Collective Self-Reliance in Social and Economic Development for the Establishment of a New International Economic Order' were adopted. The Assembly also decided to hold an extraordinary session on economic problems of Africa, in Nigeria, before the next ordinary session. In the operative paragraph of the resolution containing this decision, the Assembly directed the Administrative Secretary-General of the OAU, in cooperation with the Executive Secretary of the United Nations ECA and the ministers of member states responsible for economic development, to prepare the ground for the proposed extraordinary session. The resulting document, plus amendments made to the Plan and approved by the African States was published by the OAU under the title 'Lagos Plan of Action for the Implementation of the Monrovia Strategy for Economic Development of Africa.' It has become known as the Lagos Plan.[10] Without going into the details of the plan itself, it is worth noting that the identification of issues, problems, goals and strategies bears a considerable resemblance to Annual Reports of the ECA. It helps frame the ECA's operational context, providing visibility and a framework, both politically and institutionally, for African self-reliance and collective action. This is consistent with the ECA's more catalytic role under Adedeji, and its renewed efforts to combine forces with the OAU.

Two further questions are appropriate to ask regarding the ECA's evolution: how has the ECA as an organization changed, if at all; and to what extent has it made any inroads in resolving its dual mandate under Adedeji? To take the second question first, I believe it is too early to respond, apart from pointing out what appear to be modest changes of direction. Under Adedeji the ECA appears to have taken a clue from the ECLA experience and is concentrating a little more on generating a continental strategy for development, rather than seeking to play the role of executing agency for the UN system. How far Adedeji and the ECA will go in developing a genuine ideology and capacity to influence its clientele and direct their development strategies accordingly remains to be seen.

With respect to the first question, the situation is also still somewhat murky. In his first years in office, Adedeji appears to have devoted more attention to generating visibility for himself and the ECA on the African continent than attending to the badly needed organizational capacity building at the ECA headquarters itself. Admittedly, the ECA's organizational structure chart has been somewhat streamlined. A Policy and

Program Co-ordinating Office has been placed directly under the Executive and Deputy Executive Secretary, as has a Technical Assistance and Co-ordination and Operations Office. In addition, some of the substantive divisions have been reorganized. Still, the bureaucratic malaise within the organization and its functional ineffectiveness show no visible signs of improvement. Action Plans called for by ECA's Annual Reports and the Lagos Plan will see little effective follow-through unless the administrative and technical competency of ECA headquarters is upgraded. It appears to be the case that Adedeji would like to move the ECA in the direction of a first-rate think-tank with the sort of reputation that the ECLA enjoyed under Prebisch. But such a reputation calls for men and women of very high calibre on the staff, further organizational streamlining, and the further resolution of the issue of whether the ECA is meant to be a catalyst or an executing agency. For now, the ECA headquarters has yet to receive the necessary time and attention from Adedeji, who spends much of his time on the road mobilizing governments and institutions.

By the 1980s, the African staffing of the organization and Adedeji's role as a lobbyist within Africa and for Africa internationally, have detracted from the ECA's 'arm of the UN' image. But, by the same token, the fact that a substantial part of the ECA's budget is derived from the UN system has given the ECA a level of solvency not enjoyed either by the OAU or other inter-African institutions funded through African membership contributions. While the task of African development outlined in the ECA's annual programme reviews and proposals may always exceed its resources, this must be seen in a relative light, especially with respect to the OAU which has also consistently, and frequently competitively, claimed a role for itself in the economic and social development field. Adedeji appears to be sensitive, as was his predecessor, to the need to work out a productive relationship with the OAU – note that the Lagos Plan is a combined ECA-OAU enterprise. The relationships between the OAU and the ECA has been an uncomfortable one. The OAU's aim to involve itself in African social and economic development has been consistently undermined by its institutional and budgetary limitations. Similarly the ECA, especially during Gardiner's leadership, was always uncomfortable and somewhat on the defensive about the fact that, as a UN agency, it was not a genuinely African organization. There thus evolved a somewhat tentative and troubled marriage of convenience. The OAU would lend its political support to the ECA's activities as a co-sponsor of meetings, proposals and the like. Thus the actual work of the ECA was given a political certification by the OAU. The OAU as co-sponsor could then claim that it participates in economic and social activities and institution-building on the African continent. The benefits and potential liabilities of this arrangement have cut both ways. Now under the stewardship of Adedeji, some greater politicization of the ECA, its activities and role has taken place. By the same token the OAU has renewed, rhetorically at least, its commitment and desire to get into economic and social development. The differential in staff and financial circumstances separating the two organizations remains as before. Whether Adedeji's more politically activist role will eventually produce increased and open conflict between the two organizations, or whether a diplomatic alliance will continue, remains an open question. Should the ECA develop over time political leverage for its economic and social policies along with a continental and international role as lobbyist for Africa, a serious dilemma will arise for the OAU. Will its own claims and aspirations for developing its own economic and social development capacity be perceived as credible by even its most ardent supporters? This whole terrain remains very fuzzy at the time of writing. What is relevant for our discussion is that changes that occur with respect to the ECA's capacity as an organization and its role in the future economic and social developments on the African continent, also affect the relationship of the ECA to other continental and regional institutions seeking to or claiming to address similar issues. Since Adedeji appears to be altering the ECA's role and function, it is worth watching to see if these changes will produce any impact with respect to the OAU and its potential future role in African regional development.

Regional self-reliance in the future: the ECA role

Few inside or outside the African continent would, in the 1980s, quarrel with the notion that greater regional self-reliance is both desirable and necessary for Africa. Even in the global realm, most small or economically weak African states profit from exerting collective leverage on behalf of the continent at international forums. And the ECA, despite all its past failures and current shortcomings, still constitutes one of the most viable and potentially potent forces for fostering regional cooperation on the African continent.

Starting in the late 1970s, the ECA abandoned existing sub-regional offices, converting them into Multinational Programming and Operational Centres (MULPOCs). The distribution of MULPOCs and the ECA's organizational structure are shown in Map 3.1 and Fig. 3.1.

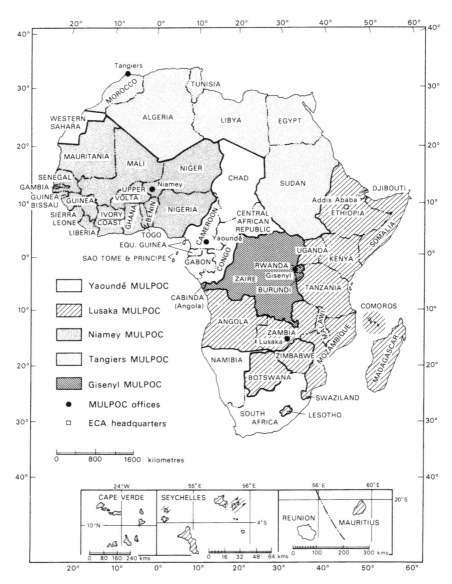

Map 3.1   The distribution of MULPOCs in Africa

MULPOCs are intended to be operational arms of ECA to facilitate sub-regional planning, and also to provide capacity and technical expertise within the sub-regions. Whether, in the long run, MULPOCs will facilitate sub-regional interstate organizations such as ECOWAS or compete with them is far from clear. What is clear is that the ECA headquarters still constitutes the core of the ECA's operations. Thus, the quality of the headquarters staff and its work will continue to determine the ECA's utility to its clients. The ECA headquarters comprises a number of Divisions which in turn are divided into even more functionally specific units. The Divisions are: Socio-Economic Research and Planning; joint ECA/FAO Agriculture; joint ECA/UNIDO Industry; International Trade and Finance; Social Development; Natural Resources; Transport, Communications and Tourism; Public Administration, Management and Manpower; Statistics; and Population. While some of these Divisions are reasonably permanent and well staffed, others are almost entirely dependent on bilaterally funded or otherwise seconded temporary staff. In many of the technical areas the expertise simply does not exist with which to carry out the programme generated by the ECA itself. In short, the capacity of the ECA to carry out its own annual work plan is seriously undermined and restricted by the inadequate staffing at headquarters. Many of the studies and reports are either of low quality or not realistically aimed, given the ECA's or the client's resources for implementation. It could also be argued that, given the resources available, the ECA is spreading itself too thin, taking on too many subjects and problems. Although relatively better endowed and better functioning than many interstate African organizations, the ECA still falls very much short in its actual capacity to implement its own work programmes and agendas. If in the years to come, it moves more in the direction of serving as a think-tank for development strategies, that move should determine the direction of upgrading staff and organizational output. If, on the other hand, the ECA wishes to continue to play the role of a UN executing agency, then, of course, a different sort of upgrading is called for. As long as it straddles the fence regarding these different functions, it will be difficult for the ECA to reform itself and upgrade the quality of its work and its effectiveness in fostering African development.

On the more positive side is the ECA's role as a catalyst among its clientele. Perhaps the ECA's greatest contribution in Africa to date, and one which continues into the present, is its role as facilitator for inter-African institution building. ECA has played a very important role in the establishment of the African Development Bank, ECOWAS, and Regional

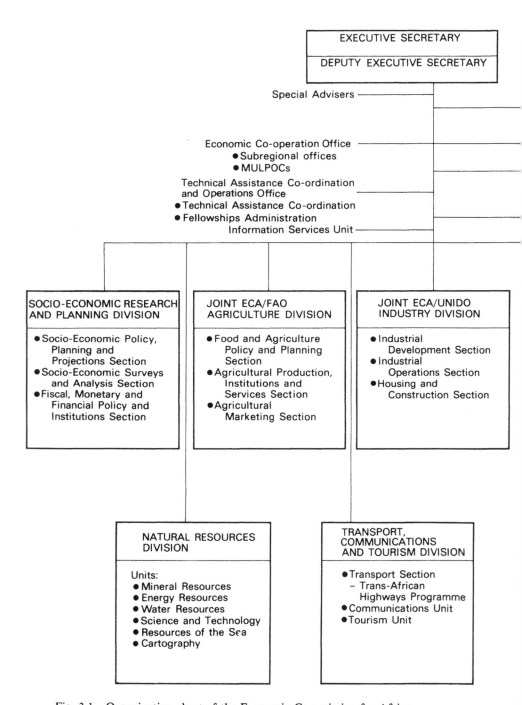

Fig. 3.1 Organization chart of the Economic Commission for Africa

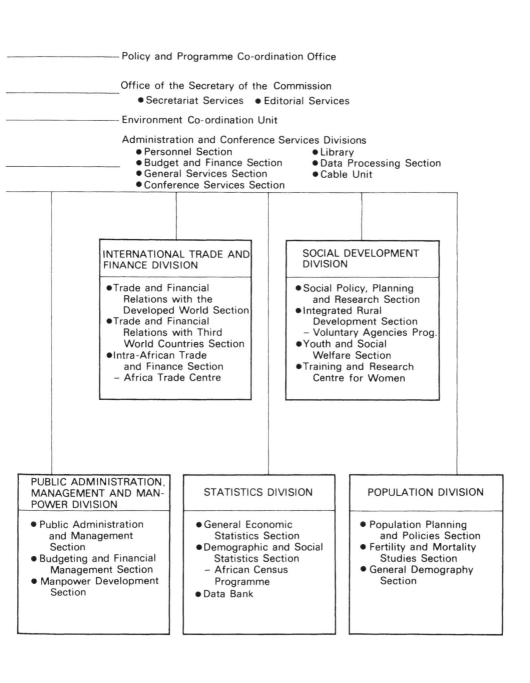

Policy and Programme Co-ordination Office

Office of the Secretary of the Commission
● Secretariat Services   ● Editorial Services

Environment Co-ordination Unit

Administration and Conference Services Divisions
● Personnel Section   ● Library
● Budget and Finance Section   ● Data Processing Section
● General Services Section   ● Cable Unit
● Conference Services Section

INTERNATIONAL TRADE AND FINANCE DIVISION

● Trade and Financial Relations with the Developed World Section
● Trade and Financial Relations with Third World Countries Section
● Intra-African Trade and Finance Section
– Africa Trade Centre

SOCIAL DEVELOPMENT DIVISION

● Social Policy, Planning and Research Section
● Integrated Rural Development Section
– Voluntary Agencies Prog.
● Youth and Social Welfare Section
● Training and Research Centre for Women

PUBLIC ADMINISTRATION, MANAGEMENT AND MAN-POWER DIVISION

● Public Administration and Management Section
● Budgeting and Financial Management Section
● Manpower Development Section

STATISTICS DIVISION

● General Economic Statistics Section
● Demographic and Social Statistics Section
– African Census Programme
● Data Bank

POPULATION DIVISION

● Population Planning and Policies Section
● Fertility and Mortality Studies Section
● General Demography Section

Centres. It has been effective in calling groups of African states together, getting them to agree to the merits of a currency clearing house or a technical centre, and assisting in the creation of such an enterprise, gaining member government support, and finally playing the midwife role at the time of birth and early infancy in the life of the organization or mechanism. Frequently the ECA continues to support, supervise, or serve as a technical assistance agency to the institutions.

In addition, the ECA has been an effective catalyst and midwife to complex, long-term efforts to improve continental infrastructure, without which interstate communications and developments of all sorts would continue to be handicapped. Be it the Trans-African Highway or Pan-African Telecommunications, the ECA has played an important role nursing these enterprises through financial, technical, and political crises.

Adedeji and others rightly recognized that the African development efforts were handicapped by a lack of data, both numerical and non-numerical. One of Robert Gardiner's earliest efforts at the ECA was to generate statistical data for the African continent. However, throughout the 1960s and 1970s there had been virtually no effort to collect non-numerical data, to analyse them, store them, disseminate them, and have them easily available for retrieval by governments and international agencies. When Adedeji assumed office he made the establishment of a Data Bank at the ECA one of his highest priorities. In 1979 a feasibility study was mounted by the ECA as organizer, with the collaboration of the IDRC, UNDP, UNESCO, the UN-DIESA and the OAU, and financed by the Canadian IDRC. The study proposed the development of a Pan-African Documentation and Information System (PADIS), a recommendation accepted by the ECA Conference of Ministers at its 1980 meeting. The UNDP, the IDRC, and the African Development Bank joined as partners, along with the ECA itself, to fund the first phase of the project. It is estimated that the PADIS project will, during the next ten years, require 160 million US dollars to fully establish an integrated regional, sub-regional, and national network, and to train the necessary personnel. It will have to develop common standards, methodologies, manuals, and other tools for use by all participants in the system, while maintaining international norms, standards, and guidelines so the data can be integrated and used internationally. The development of a Pan-African Documentation and Information System or the construction of the Trans-African Highway are obviously costly and complex operations.[11] Yet, most agree that this sort of infrastructure will lie at the heart of African development in the years to come. These are but illustrations of the very useful role that the ECA has been playing and continues to play as a catalyst and facilitator of regional and sub-regional development. The pay-offs for this sort of work frequently are long-term, indirect, and often not easily traceable to the original facilitator. However, in the 23 years of its existence, the ECA has played a very important and frequently unsung role in these types of activities.

Conclusion

The ECA's organizational weaknesses have been persistent and its organizational ideology has often been fuzzy. It has steered an uncertain course in its efforts to define itself within the context of its dual mandate. The ECA has been both influenced by and has influenced the ideological, theoretical, and institutional contexts of regional and sub-regional organizations and strategies in the field of regional economic cooperation and integration. Thus it has shared the early euphoria and the ever-increasing cynicism about the speed and ease with which an underdeveloped continent could be developed.

As Adedeji so often points out, the situation in Africa is getting more serious. A growing population, shortages of food, manpower, and infrastructure, are problems with no easy solutions. The ECA, both as an arm of the UN and as an African regional mechanism, has at best had only a modest impact on reducing underdevelopment. But, as I hope this discussion has demonstrated, the ECA has been and remains a viable instrument at the service of the international community, the African regional and sub-regional institutions, and individual African governments. The ECA is in a dialectical relationship with its environment: the more seriously are the ECA's capacity and potentials taken, the more easily will its clients invest it with the resources with which to operate more effectively. The higher are its clients' demands and expectations, the more likely will it be that changes will be undertaken to sharpen the ECA's functions and the quality of its work. Looking at the past, one realizes that the ECA, while performing far short of needs and hopes, has nevertheless played an estimable role in regional developments on the continent. One can only hope that in the future self-reliance as a theme and pragmatism as a method will continue to foster African regional cooperation, and that the ECA will play the role of a catalyst within the context of a more sharply focused and higher quality organizational work output. For the moment, the ECA continues to merit the close attention of students of African development, since it continues to be a vital part of the African organizational map.

NOTES

1 UN Document E/CN.14/424, United Nations Economic Commission for Africa, pp. 3–4.
2 Isebill V. Gruhn, *Regionalism Reconsidered: the Economic Commission for Africa*, Westview Press, Boulder, Colorado, 1979.
3 Philippe Schmitter, 'A Revised Theory of Regional Integration', *International Organization*, XXIV, 4 (1970).
4 For examples of various theories and case studies reflecting the evolution of these ideas, see: Isebill V. Gruhn, 'Functionalism in Africa: Scientific and Technical Cooperation', unpublished PhD dissertation, University of California, Berkeley, 1967; Abdul Jalloh, 'The Politics and Economics of Regional Political Integration in Central Africa', unpublished PhD dissertation, University of California, 1969; Joseph Nye, *Pan-Africanism and East African Integration*, Harvard University Press, Cambridge, Mass., 1965.
5 See Gruhn, *Regionalism Reconsidered*, especially Chapter 2.
6 *Ibid.*, references throughout the book.
7 *Ibid.*, pp. 100–3, and Fernando Henrique Cardoso, 'The Originality of the Copy: The Economic Commission for Latin America and the Idea of Development', in A. Rothko Chapel Colloquim, *Toward a New Strategy for Development*, Pergamon Press, Oxford, 1979.
8 See, for example, summaries in *West Africa*, 7 May 1979; 20 August 1979; 12 January 1981.
9 *West Africa*, 20 August 1979, pp. 1501–3.
10 Plan of Action for the Implementation of the Monrovia Strategy, UN Document E/CN.14/781, Economic Commission for Africa, 1980.
11 *SADEX*, iii, 2, March/April 1981 contains good discussion, summaries of speeches, etc., regarding PADIS (Pan-African Documentation and Information System).

4 The Organization of African Unity

K. MATHEWS

Introduction

In May 1983, the Organization of African Unity (OAU) completes two decades of its existence as an African continental organization. However, during the past 20 years, the OAU has utterly failed to come to terms with the vital problems affecting the future of the continent. Africa today is a continent in crisis.[1] As one United Nations Document points out: 'Twenty years after the majority of African countries have acceded to political independence, the African continent is facing the decade 1980–1990 seriously handicapped by its underdeveloped condition.'[2] The economic and social position of most African countries is indeed abysmal. Although over 10 per cent of the world's total population lives in the 50 countries of Africa, her share in world industrial output is less than 1 per cent. Of the 31 poorest countries in the world 20 are African. The continent has the world's lowest per capita income, with only ten states, including the oil producing countries, exceeding $300 per annum.

At the same time, never before have the security and sovereignty of the Africa countries and the unity of the continent been so seriously threatened as in the early 1980s. Africa has become the theatre of an intense superpower rivalry in recent years. This trend can be expected to get worse since the conservative Reagan administration assumed power in Washington in early 1981, at a time when the Soviet Union is in so effective a position to challenge Western imperialism.

How has the OAU been able to assess correctly the nature of the present predicament and condition of Africa and prepare its members to face up to the danger of being divided and set against one another by the manoeuvrings of the superpowers? Has the OAU been able to provide a suitable framework for effective co-operation among the peoples of Africa and help them achieve the much needed economic and political results? These are some of the questions which we propose to analyse in this chapter in the light of the historical evolution of the OAU and of the present realities and contradictions prevailing in Africa.

Certain contradictions and realities in fact make the OAU unique among present-day regional international organizations. First, the OAU with its present membership of 50 countries is the largest of such organizations, yet it remains the poorest and weakest among them. Second, though one of the newest among regional organizations, the OAU remains the most traditional in structure and orientation. Further, despite the absence of any big power domination of the system, the operational context of the OAU is much more international than that of other regional organizations such as the Organization of American States (OAS) and the Arab League. These factors have considerably influenced the evolution and operation of the OAU in the past two decades of its existence.

The background

The strengths and weaknesses of the OAU are related among other things, to its origins and background. The birth of the OAU in the year 1963, (called Africa's Unity year) marked an historic step in the evolutionary growth of pan-Africanism,[3] symbolizing a manifest movement towards unity among the states on the African continent. The need for African unity has emerged as self-evident and arguments in its favour are legion. As Diallo Telli, the former Administrative Secretary-General of the OAU pointed out, pan-Africanism was born out of complete alienation, physical exploitation and spiritual torment. Started in the Americas as pan-negro nationalism by persons like Booker T. Washington, W.E.B. Du Bois and Marcus Garvey, the pan-African movement gradually initiated a struggle for the breakdown of colonial power and the establishment of independent African government in its stead. By 1900, African nationalist intellectuals were also chafing under the effects of the colonial system. The two World Wars provided considerable impetus to African nationalism. After the Second World War, the centre of gravity of the pan-African movement shifted from the Americas to Africa. There was an ever-increasing demand for self-determination in Africa in the post-Second World War period. The racial, ideological and political dimensions of pan-Africanism came to be expressed through the demand that the political, economic and cultural domination of Africa by Western imperialism be ended and independence granted to the African peoples. The historic fifth pan-

African Congress which met in Manchester in 1945, categorically declared among its resolutions:

We are determined to be free ... We demand for black Africa autonomy and independence so far and no further than it is possible in this one world for groups and peoples to rule themselves subject to inevitable world unity and federation ... We affirm the right of all colonial peoples to control their own destiny. All colonies must be free from foreign imperialist control whether political or economic.[4]

The African nationalist movement and its leaders began to demand the liberation of the entire continent from foreign domination and white minority rule. In the continental phase of development of pan-Africanism in the 1950s and 1960s, African leaders realized that after independence regional co-operation would be essential to the utilization of the continent's vast potentialities and the protection and preservation of freedom. The independence of Ghana on 6 March 1957 marked the beginning of sustained activities at the diplomatic level to secure closer cooperation between African states. More importantly, Kwame Nkrumah, one of the most outstanding leaders of pan-Africanism and the first President of Ghana, pledged to work toward the liberation of the rest of the continent. Furthermore, since 1957 pan-Africanism became the tool of African leaders and heads of state, and in addition gained the support of the majority of their peoples who stood behind conscious foreign policies. At the same time, the more Africa became divided into numerous sovereign states, the more conflicting approaches and policies to African unity came to dominate the African international political arena.

In April 1958, President Kwame Nkrumah, the new uncrowned head of the pan-African movement, called the first Conference of Independent African States (CIAS)[5] in Accra, Ghana, to discuss problems of common interest. In their resolutions, the participating states proclaimed their solidarity with the dependent peoples of Africa as well as the right of all nations to safeguard their independence, sovereignty and territorial integrity. An important political decision at this conference was the recognition of the Algerian National Liberation Front (FLN) as the legitimate representative of Algeria, and the recognition of the right of the Algerian people to independence and self-determination. At the time, Algeria was still engaged in her war for independence from France.

It is pertinent to note that the resolutions passed at the conference made no mention either of the creation of a United States of Africa or of the eradication of the colonial boundaries – two of the persistent aims of the pan-African movement until the Manchester Conference in 1945. However, some of these issues were taken up at the first All African People's Conference (AAPC), also held in Accra, in December 1958.[6] The two main purposes of the conference were to give encouragement to nationalist leaders in their efforts to organize political independence movements, and to plan strategy for a non-violent revolution in Africa. There was much preoccupation with the question of the acquisition of political power by Africans throughout the continent and the avoidance of 'balkanization'. The atmosphere at the conference was highly political and the conference deliberations and resolutions dealt with questions of imperialism and colonialism, racism, frontiers and federations, tribalism and tribal institutions and the establishment of a permanent organization. The conference among other things, endorsed pan-Africanism, the desire for unity among African peoples and the need for the creation of a commonwealth of free African states. The conference also decided to establish a permanent, professionally staffed secretariat in Accra. It also supported the desire for various parts of Africa to form regional groupings of states.

Between 1958 and 1960, there were several attempts to bring about African unity at regional and local levels. For example, on 1 May 1959 Ghana and Guinea announced that the two countries had formed a Union, with a common national flag and anthem, common citizenship and an open invitation to other African states to join. On 30 May 1959 four French-speaking States – Ivory Coast, Upper Volta, Niger and Dahomey (now Benin) – set up the Conseil de l'Entente. The association appeared to be looser than the Ghana-Guinea Union, but it was to prove more long-lived.

At the same time, particularly from 1960 onwards, when an increasing number of African states became independent and began to assert themselves on the African political scene, the questions of leadership of the pan-African movement, personal rivalries and ideological differences came clearly to the forefront. Approaches and attitudes differed with regard to the ends to be achieved and the means to be adopted. Two groups representing the two approaches to pan-Africanism and political questions came to dominate the African scene. First, the moderates including Ivory Coast, Nigeria and most French-speaking countries advocated a gradualist, functionalist approach to African unity and the formation of a loose association of states. Second, the radicals, led by Kwame Nkrumah of Ghana and Sekou Touré of Guinea, pleaded for a political union and the creation of a strong United States of Africa. These two approaches dominated political developments in the following years.

The second All African Peoples Conference, held in Tunis from 25 to 30 January 1960, clearly demonstrated in a heightened form some of these basic differences.[7] At the second Conference of the Independent African

States (CIAS), held in Addis Ababa in June 1960,[8] the incipient ideological cleavages became a violently open split, particularly over the question of political union and personalities. However, the majority agreed that pan-Africanism was the only solution to the problems of Africa, even though the groups differed widely as to the methods and means of achieving the objective. The Nigerian rejection of Ghana's radical proposal for a political union of African states as premature and unrealistic marked the beginning of concrete divisions between the radicals and the moderates. African political leaders were now clearly ranged against one another. There was an increasing danger that these divisions could become permanent. The Congo crisis (1960–63)[9] added a new dimension to the conflicting African political diplomatic scene. Differences among African leaders persisted with regard to attitudes and policies towards the crisis. These differences later converged in a concrete form with the formation of the Brazzaville, Monrovia and Casablanca groups.

The formation of the so-called Brazzaville group (named after the meeting place of the group in December 1961) was an achievement of the moderate group of states. The meeting had been initially summoned by Ivory Coast in Abidjan in October 1960 to discuss the Algerian crisis. The 12 member states of this group, namely Congo (Brazzaville), Cameroon, Central African Republic, Chad, Gabon, Mauritania, Upper Volta, Malagasy Republic, Senegal, Ivory Coast, Niger and Dahomey (now Benin) formed a new organization known as the Union Africaine et Malgache (UAM) thus creating a new power bloc in African politics to safeguard their interests in dealing with other states. On the Algerian question, the group decided to mediate between Algeria and France. The Malagasy Republic even regarded the Algerian issue as an internal affair of France! On the Congo question, the group backed Kasavubu against Lumumba and urged mediation in the crisis. As for Mauritania, the group supported her application for UN membership against Morocco's claim that Mauritania was part of Moroccan territory.

The formation of the Brazzaville group evoked immediate reaction from the other camp. As a reaction to the sponsorship of Mauritania by the Brazzaville group, Morocco convened another conference in Casablanca in January 1961, which was attended by Morocco, Ghana, Guinea, Mali, the United Arab Republic (UAR), Libya and Algeria. The group came to be known as the Casablanca group. Its members signed an agreement known as the African Charter which came into force on 7 January 1961. On the question of Congo, the group supported Lumumba. On African unity, it recommended the creation of an African Political Union, a joint African High Command, and an African Common Market. The restrictive nature of membership and the revolutionary orientation of the Casablanca conference represented the thinking of the radical group of pan-Africanists.

In May 1961, on the joint initiative of President Houphouët-Boigny of Ivory Coast, President Tubman of Liberia and President Senghor of Senegal, a bigger gathering of 19 independent African states comprising the 12 members of the Brazzaville group plus Liberia, Nigeria, Somalia, Sierra Leone, Togo, Ethiopia and Libya, took place in Monrovia (Liberia) to discuss African issues and the ways of consolidating African unity. With the exception of Libya, the Casablanca group of states, though invited, decided not to attend the meeting. The Monrovia Conference thus became the gathering of an enlarged Brazzaville group, namely of all UAM countries plus the states outside the Casablanca group. Understandably, it took a distinctly different stand on African Unity from the Casablanca group. The conference declared:

The unity that is aimed to be achieved at the moment is not political integration of sovereign states, but unity of aspirations and of action considered from the point of view of African social solidarity and political identity.[10]

The conference issued a declaration of non-interference in the domestic jurisdiction of African states. Obviously, this did not apply to territories under colonial rule. The next meeting of the Monrovia group was held in Lagos (Nigeria) from 25–30 January 1962, with the Casablanca group again boycotting it. The Monrovia group accepted the idea of cooperation among African states, but rejected immediate political union or the leadership of any one country.

Thus during the period immediately preceding the establishment of the OAU in 1963, the African political scene was generally dominated by splits, conflicts and cleavages, despite occasional attempts at compromise. By the end of 1962, however, the tension between the two opposing blocs had somewhat subsided. The independence of Algeria in 1962 and the admission of Mauritania to the UN removed two specific sources of dispute. The efforts of neutral states such as Ethiopia also helped to create an atmosphere favourable to reconciliation. Moreover, the general anxiety to bring all independent African states into a pan-African forum and the strong common desire to eradicate imperialism, colonialism, racialism, apartheid and the white minority regimes, helped to bring about a rapprochement among the conflicting groups. This led to the convening of the historic Summit Conference of 31 independent African states in Addis Ababa from 15–25 May 1963, which founded the OAU.

The Addis Ababa compromise and the founding of the OAU

The drafting of the Charter of the OAU at the Addis Ababa Conference in May 1963 was not an easy task for the 31 states represented. As Modibo Keita, President of Mali stated:

To convene in a conference at a round table thirty-one African states still completely involved with that ardent nationalism which led them a few years ago to independence, to organize a co-operation between countries like ours that are firmly attached to their recently won sovereignty, will be hailed as an event in the history of the world.[11]

The acrimonious debates at the conference[12] clearly reflected conflicting attitudes on basic issues and different approaches to African unity. There was the federal approach of Kwame Nkrumah and the Casablanca group which sought the immediate creation of a Union Government of African States. Another was the gradualist-functionalist approach supported by most of the so-called Monrovia group, including the regionalist approach advocated by President Nyerere and most of the East African countries.

President Nkrumah put forward a strong federalist position when he argued:

African Unity is above all a political Kingdom which can be gained by political means. The social and economic development of Africa will come only within the political Kingdom, not the other way round. The United States of America, the Union of Soviet Socialist Republics, were the political decisions of revolutionary peoples before they became mighty realities of social power and material wealth.[13]

His advocacy of an 'all-embracing African High Command' was also aimed at maintaining non-alignment by ending the system of military pacts with former colonial powers and at maximizing the power of African states. Nkrumah's latest book, *Africa Must Unite*, was published just in time for the Conference and was being distributed among the delegates. His position at the conference was unequivocal and well-known.

The gradualist-functionalist group, which was in a majority at the conference, vehemently opposed Nkrumah's federalism. President Tsiranana of the Malagasy Republic summarized the pluralist position when he stated:

We intend to conserve the total sovereignty of our states ... I should underline that our adhesion means by the same token a rejection of a formula for a Federation of African States because federalism presupposes the surrender of a large part of national sovereignty. Similarly, we would reject a confederal formula seeing that the authority we superimpose on the states might impose demands which would be unacceptable for certain of us.[14]

President Bourguiba of Tunisia was equally blunt when he stated at the conference: 'Speaking for ourselves, we prefer to *see things as they are.*

We hardly know each other and we have barely had time to draw up an inventory of the things which bring us together and those which divide us.'[15] Even some radical states like Modibo Keita's Mali joined energetically in the defence of existing national frontiers. Modibo Keita said: 'The colonial system divided Africa, but it permitted nations to be born. Present frontiers must be respected and the sovereignty of each state must be consecrated by a multilateral non-aggression pact.'[16] The Prime Minister of Nigeria, A. A. Tafawa Balewa, again voiced the moderate view when he stated:

If we want unity in Africa, we must first agree to certain essential things. The first is that African states must respect one another. There must be acceptance of equality of all the states. No matter whether they are big or small, they are all sovereign and their sovereignty is sovereignty.[17]

Many leaders doubted (and realistically so) whether the African states would be prepared to surrender their recently acquired sovereignty to a central government. They felt that such a momentous decision should be reached only at the end of a process of evolution, beginning with less binding forms of association. It was also doubtful whether any far-reaching arrangement for unity would gain the support of the people in the various countries.

The advocates of functionalism and regionalism at the conference believed that this approach would favour cooperation and contribute to the flowering of African continentalism. Many felt that regional arrangements had an important role to play in the development of Africa and that it would be necessary to create new regional groupings to cover the continent with machinery for harmonious cooperation. It is easier, they argued, for countries combined in a regional unit to harmonize their economic and social policies within the framework of joint programmes. President Nyerere of Tanzania was an ardent advocate of regional functionalism[18]

Briefly, at the conference, the Casablanca group failed to convince the members of the Brazzaville-Monrovia groups (who commanded the majority) of the urgent need for the immediate political unification of Africa. Nkrumah's total commitment to pan-Africanism and his analysis of the African condition seemed to have been rejected. The overwhelming preference was for a very loose organization and limited forms of cooperation. In short, far from supporting the 'African personality', the choice was clearly made in favour of the 'national personality' of African states. This is clearly reflected in the OAU Charter drawn up at the Addis Ababa conference.

Nevertheless, the conference resolutions on colonialism, apartheid and racialism reflected unity over the revolutionary spirit of the Casablanca group. All agreed on the urgency of terminating colonialism. Some even declared that the independent African countries could not contemplate union without first liberating the colonized territories in Africa. President Ben Bella of Algeria made a memorable declaration saying: 'so let us agree to die a little, or even completely, so that the peoples still under colonial domination may be freed and African unity may not be a vain word'.[19] On the strength of such feelings, it was generally agreed to set up funds and facilities for the training of the liberation movements. The conference, besides recommending diplomatic and economic sanctions against Portugal and South Africa, also established a Co-ordination Committee for the Liberation Movements in Africa (popularly known as the 'Liberation Committee'), then consisting of nine states, namely Ethiopia, Algeria, UAR, Uganda, Tanganyika, Guinea, Congo (now Zaire), Senegal and Nigeria.[20] With headquarters in Dar es Salaam (Tanzania), the Liberation Committee was to be responsible for coordinating assistance to liberation movements and for managing the newly created Special Fund for Liberation. The Liberation Committee was to become the directing centre of military operations, aimed at overthrowing the white minority regimes in southern Africa and speeding up the total liberation of the African continent from the remnants of colonialism and racialism. The conference further resolved to buy arms for the freedom fighters and give them all necessary training in camps to be set up in various independent African countries. It also decided to launch a full-scale guerilla war against colonial and white minority regimes. This aspect indicated the success of the Casablanca group at the founding conference. However, the OAU Charter drawn up at the conference reflected a compromise in favour of a weak and loose organization. The draft on which the Charter was drawn up was prepared by Ethiopia, itself a member of the moderate Monrovia group.

The OAU Charter
The purposes of the OAU as stated in Article II(1) of its Charter are:
a) to promote the unity and solidarity of the African states;
b) to coordinate and intensify their cooperation and efforts to achieve a better life for the peoples of Africa;
c) to defend their sovereignty, their territorial integrity and independence;
d) to eradicate all forms of colonialism from Africa; and
e) to promote international cooperation, having due regard to the Charter of the United Nations and the Universal Declaration of Human Rights.
Article II(2) sets out the ways in which the above ends would be achieved. The signatories pledged themselves to 'coordinate and harmonize their

general policies' through cooperation in the political, diplomatic, economic, communications, health, sanitation, nutritional, scientific and technological spheres as well as cooperation in defence and security. More importantly, the member states, in pursuit of the above purposes, pledged their adherence to seven principles, which are stipulated in Article III of the OAU Charter, namely:

a) the sovereign equality of all member states;
b) non-interference in the internal affairs of states;
c) respect for the sovereignty and territorial integrity of each state and for the inalienable right to independent existence;
d) peaceful settlement of disputes by negotiation, mediation, conciliation or arbitration;
e) unreserved condemnation, in all its forms, of political assassination as well as of subversive activities on the part of neighbouring states or any other state;
f) absolute dedication to the total emancipation of the African territories which are still dependent; and
g) affirmation of a policy of non-alignment with regard to all blocs.

It is interesting to note here that of the seven basic principles, four are clearly in defence of sovereign rights of member states insisted on by the Monrovia group. The very first principle on the sovereign equality of member states was a rejection of the pan-Africanist contention that there were too many unviable and unjustifiably small sovereign states in Africa. Only two principles seem to be concessions to the Casablanca group. These were the dedication to liberate the dependent territories and the declaration of adherence to the principle of non-alignment. The principle of non-alignment has anyway been embraced by most African countries as best serving their national interests. In the context of the East-West conflict, the African states saw non-alignment probably as the only course to afford them room for manoeuvre. It is significant to note that the word pan-Africanism does not appear even once in the whole Charter. In the same way, reference to political union is avoided entirely in consonance with the rejection of Nkrumah's proposal.

The assiduity of the founding fathers to protect both sovereignty and equality reflected the main arguments during the debates on African unity at the founding conference. It is significant against the background of the Congo crisis – the most important problem faced by the African countries in 1963 – that the founders of the OAU should insist on the principle of non-interference in the internal affairs of states. Besides, on 13 January 1963, just a few months before the Addis Ababa Summit, President Sylvanus Olympio of Togo had been assassinated in a *coup d'état*. Whether justifiably or not, Ghana was suspected of having had a hand in the affair. As the first assassination of an incumbent African head of state, the event sent shock waves throughout the continent. It will also be recalled that there were several disputes over the harbouring of exiles in neighbouring states. Under these circumstances, it was not surprising that one of the OAU Charter principles should seek specifically to make member states refrain from political assassination or subversive activities.

Membership of the OAU is open to all independent African states (Article V). However, membership is not binding. Under Article XXII, any state may withdraw from the organization and its withdrawal takes effect one year after a written notification has been sent to the Administrative Secretary-General.

The structure of the OAU
As indicated in the Organization Chart of the OAU (Fig. 4.1), four main organs were created under the Charter, namely:
a) The Assembly of Heads of State and Government;
b) The Council of Ministers;
c) The Secretariat;
d) The Commission of Mediation, Conciliation and Arbitration.

The Assembly of Heads of State and Government is 'the supreme organ' of the OAU (Article VIII). Its functions are mainly to discuss matters of common concern with a view to coordinating and harmonizing the general policy of the Organization. In addition, it reviews the structure, functions and acts of other organs and specialized agencies. However, it is clear that this organ is intended to be essentially a deliberative one. All resolutions and decisions at the Assembly are made by a two-thirds majority (Article X). The purpose of the Assembly is to provide a forum of discussion, not to execute decisions. The resolutions of the Assembly are not legally binding. In this lies the main weakness of the OAU.

The second main organ is the Council of Ministers charged with the preparation of the conferences of the Assembly, implementing the decision of the Assembly and coordinating inter-African cooperation (Article XII). Made up of the foreign ministers of member states, the Council cannot be in continuous session. It ordinarily meets only twice a year. Consequently, it finds it hard to ensure implementation of decisions. Therefore, there is no doubt that the OAU needs a more stable executive body.

The General-Secretariat of the OAU in Addis Ababa is headed by an 'Administrative Secretary-General' appointed by the Assembly. At the Addis Ababa Summit, the Heads of State were particularly anxious to curb the powers of the top official of the Organization. Accordingly, the

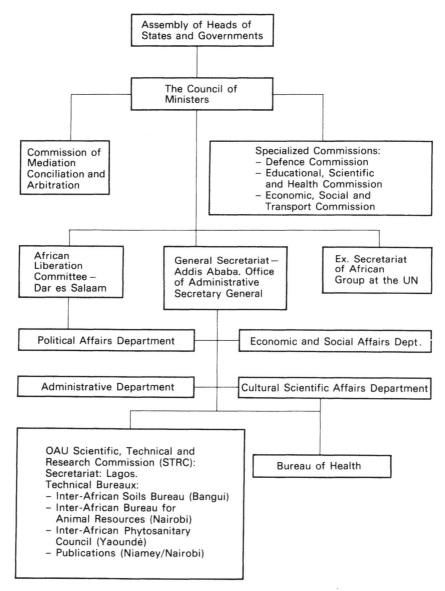

Fig. 4.1   The organization chart of the Organization of African Unity

Secretary-General is merely an administrative officer without any political role or functions (Article XVIII). He could, however, be a very useful coordinator was he allowed to attend *ex-officio* the meetings of the Assembly, the Council and the Commissions. Being denied this opportunity, which would permit him to become fully aware of what goes on in the meetings of the Organization, the Secretary-General cannot play a more constructive role in coordinating the activities of the OAU. This weakens even further an already loose organization which needs revitalization and effective coordination of its activities.

The Commission of Mediation, Concilation and Arbitration is set up under Article XIX as an organ to facilitate peaceful settlement of disputes among OAU members.[21] According to Article XIX,

Member states pledge to settle all disputes among themselves by peaceful means and, to this end, decide to establish a Commission of Mediation, Conciliation and Arbitration, the composition and conditions of service of which shall be defined by a separate protocol to be approved by the Assembly of Heads of State and Government. The said Protocol shall be regarded as forming an integral part of the present Charter.

Accordingly, a separate Protocol of Mediation, Concilation and Arbitration was drafted and adopted by the Assembly of Heads of State and Government held in Cairo in July 1964. The Protocol consists of 33 articles divided into six parts dealing with the structure and functions of the Commission. The Commission is not a judicial organ neither does it have any powers of sanction. It operates in the spirit of the Charter by encouraging cooperation. In fact, as we shall see later, it has never undertaken successfully the settlement of any dispute.

In addition to the Commission of Mediation, Conciliation and Arbitration, under Article XX, five other specialized Commissions[22] were established, namely:
a) The Economic and Social Commission;
b) The Educational and Cultural Commission;
c) The Health, Sanitation and Nutrition Commission;
d) The Defence Commission;
e) The Scientific Technical and Research Commission.
However, in November 1966, the above five were amalgamated into three commissions as follows:
a) The Economic and Social Commission also in charge of Transport and Communications;
b) The Educational, Cultural, Scientific and Health Commission;
c) The Defence Commission.
   Briefly, the organs created by the OAU Charter, though inadequate in

themselves, provide opportunities for cooperation between African states in both the political and technical fields. However, the extent to which the obligations of the Charter can be translated into action and the role the organs can play will greatly depend upon the manner in which the practice of the Organization develops. The record of the OAU has much to tell in this matter.

The record of the OAU

Evaluating the record of the OAU for the past two decades is not an easy task, considering the vast and complex field of activities it has been engaged in as a continental organization. But this record shows that the organization has today undoubtedly more to show on the debit than on the credit side.

The OAU is a collection of some of the poorest, politically and socially fragmented nations in the world, plagued today by the ills that affected most of the developed nations over a hundred years ago. Most of the OAU member states have only recently acquired their independence and are still, at the economic and military levels, dominated by imperialism. Inevitably, and in varying degrees, the governments of these countries are influenced by considerations of prudence in their dealings with countries that give them moral and material aid. This is true as much of those countries supported by the United States and her allies as of those supported by the Soviet Union and her allies. Indeed, penetration by superpowers is itself one of the most serious causes of division among African countries, but one has to emphasize here that such penetration is also a product of African economic backwardness and military weakness.

As noted earlier, the OAU Charter proclaims African non-alignment[23] on East-West issues and at international forums. However, the extent to which the OAU members can follow a collective policy of non-alignment depends on their ability to limit their individual dependence for development and security on foreign powers, as well as on their ability to reduce cleavages and tension among themselves.

An overall assessment of the performance of the OAU cannot fail to give some credit to the Organization, despite its many glaring weaknesses. Its major merit lies perhaps in its continued existence in the midst of innumerable failings and divisions. Over the years, there has arisen a tradition in the OAU by which differences between the African states are not allowed to wreck the unity of the Organization. This unity has, of course, been threatened often, but the threats have never been allowed to go over the brink to destroy the Organization. This has meant that the

OAU has often taken virtually no action at all (for example, on the Nigerian civil war or the Shaba crises in Zaire) rather than press for an issue which could disrupt the unity of the continent. Some regard this kind of unity as of a dubious value. I think, on the contrary, that an openly disunited continent which does not even have a forum in which the differences can be brought out on the surface would be an unmitigated disaster because it would open the continent to the intrigues of imperialism even more than is the case now.

To elaborate and elucidate this, it may be useful to focus our analysis on the role of the OAU in some vital areas of its concern and activity, such as the questions of decolonization, the maintenance of peace and security in Africa, world diplomacy, and intra-African economic cooperation.

The OAU and decolonization

As noted earlier, the only issue on which there existed unanimity at the founding conference in Addis Ababa in 1963 was the question of liberation of the rest of dependent Africa. In fact, the liberation and decolonization of Africa, particularly southern Africa, has been the central theme and perhaps the only force that has kept the OAU united. One of the major purposes laid down in Article II(1) of the OAU Charter is 'to eradicate *all* forms of colonialism from Africa'. Besides, one of the main principles of the OAU in Article III is 'absolute dedication to the *total* emancipation of the African territories which are still dependent' (emphasis added). To realize these objectives the founding conference resolved to establish the OAU Liberation Committee (ALC), with headquarters in Dar es Salaam, to coordinate the policies of various African countries in the liberation of Africa. The conference also established a Special Fund to be contributed to by member states to supply the necessary practical and financial aid to the various African liberation movements.

We must, however, distinguish between two phases of the struggle against '*all* forms of colonialism'. One, the anti-colonial and anti-racial phase, is the struggle against the remaining pockets of European colonial rule in Africa. The second, the anti-neo-colonial phase, is the struggle against continued domination and exploitation of Africa by imperialist countries. We shall here deal with the first phase only.

It goes without saying that liberation is the task primarily of the oppressed and exploited peoples themselves. in the final analysis, for example, it was the people of Mozambique, Angola, Guinea-Bissau and Zimbabwe who liberated themselves from colonial racial minority rule. But what role has the OAU as a regional organization played in this struggle? One might distinguish the following six forms of assistance given by the OAU to national liberation movements either through its Liberation Committee, the 'front-line' states of southern Africa, or individual members.

Ideological support
Despite differences about strategy and tactics, there is not a single OAU member that has not supported the right of nations to freedom from colonial oppression. This may seem too obvious a point, but it is significant that not even the most reactionary state in Africa can justify the continuation of direct political control of colonial powers over any part of Africa.

Diplomatic support
Diplomatic support includes action within such forums as the UN, the non-aligned group of nations, and the Commonwealth, as well as through bilateral diplomatic relations.

Material support
Material support is in the form of arms and equipment for the soldiers and food, clothing, shelter, educational books, etc, for the civilians. The Liberation Committee of the OAU has a budget for such support, and though members have often defaulted in paying their share of the budget, there has always been a hard core of supporters whose contributions to the sustenance of the struggle must not be underrated.

Providing military bases for training and operations
These provisions must be distinguished from the above because only a few member states can provide a rear base for the freedom fighters. Countries such as Tanzania, Zambia, Botswana, Angola and Mozambique have made enormous sacrifices in providing facilities which have often made them targets of military reprisals by the colonial and racist regimes of South Africa (and until recently Rhodesia).

Negotiating with imperialist countries
Though such negotiations may fall under the second category above (diplomatic support), we treat it separately, because, with the more or less formal recognition by the OAU and the world at large of the 'front-line' states, this function has acquired a special significance in the whole strategy of the OAU toward the conduct of anti-colonial struggle.

Fostering unity within the liberation movements

This has probably been one of the most important and at the same time the most difficult task of the OAU. The task of keeping rival liberation movements together in a united front against the common enemy. It has been one of the most important and difficult tasks because division within the liberation movements is precisely what creates the basis for imperialist manoeuvres, as the history of the struggles in Zimbabwe has amply demonstrated.

Without concrete analysis of each situation in its specificity, it is difficult to be precise about the role of the OAU since each situation has been so different that it is difficult to generalize. For example, the problems that beset Angola were very different from those that faced Mozambique. In both, the liberation movements were split but in Mozambique the division was healed at an early stage, while in Angola the divisions still persist. In the same way, Zimbabwe had become a veritable battleground for rival movements fostered and encouraged by imperialism. In Zimbabwe, the formation of the Patriotic Front (PF) in 1976 comprising Mugabe's Zimbabwe African National Union (ZANU) and Nkomo's Zimbabwe African People's Union (ZAPU) and the recognition and support extended to it by the OAU, was a crucial step in the development of the struggle leading to Zimbabwe's ultimate independence in April 1980.

Liberation through dialogue or armed struggle?

Here, it is pertinent to point out that the debate that rocked the OAU and threatened its unity in the late 1960s and early 1970s – whether liberation has to be achieved through dialogue or through armed struggle – has definitely receded into the background. The Lusaka Manifesto of 1969, which urged 'the resistance movements to use peaceful methods of struggle even at the cost of compromise in the timing of the change' (Article 12) may have served the unity of the OAU in placating its more moderate members, but it certainly displeased the liberation movements themselves. In any case, the situation changed rapidly, and by October 1971 the OAU took the line in the 'Mogadishu Declaration', that 'there is no way left to the liberation of Southern Africa except armed struggle'.[24] This debate has now receded into the background because there is general consensus that while armed struggle is the principal means, it must be accompanied by negotiations whenever it is opportune to do so. Reflecting this changed orientation in the strategy of liberation, the Dar es Salaam Declaration of 1975 stated:

The liberation of those areas still under colonial and racist domination can be achieved either by peaceful means or by armed struggle. As it was clearly stated in the Lusaka Manifesto, we would prefer to achieve our objectives by peaceful means if that were possible. But whether the solution take the form of intensified military confrontation or negotiations would entirely depend on the response of the racist and colonialist regimes.[25]

Thus, certain victories have been scored by the OAU even if at times it looked as if the members would get at each other's throats and split the Organization. But there are forebodings that grave dangers lurk ahead despite successes in Angola and Zimbabwe, and the OAU may come to face its hardest time yet on the Namibian and South African questions. It is to the credit of the OAU and the 'front-line' states that, despite divisions amongst them, they have been able to maintain a degree of unity against imperialism.

The OAU and maintenance of peace and security in Africa

Perhaps nowhere else is OAU's weakness more clearly exposed than in matters relating to the maintenance of peace and security in Africa. At the founding conference of the OAU in 1963, the African leaders showed a great awareness of the various security concerns with which the OAU would have to deal. Attention was indeed given to the potential conflicts arising out of boundary and territorial disputes, refugee problems, charges of subversion, non-recognition of governments coming into power by *coups d'état* as well as extra-regional aggression, and the need for collective action against the remnants of colonialism.[26]

The OAU is an instrument for conflict management among its members, not for collective measures against any of them or against an outside aggressor. The OAU is entrusted with no disciplinary power over any offending member. It is only a coordinator of African policies on regional problems but not a defence alliance. Article II(c) of the OAU Charter proclaims, as one of the main purposes of the Organization, the defence of its members' sovereignty, territorial integrity and independence. It requires member states to co-ordinate and harmonize their general policies regarding defence and security, and provides for the establishment of a Defence Commission. But these provisions have not been accompanied by any collective security treaty, like the Arab League Collective Security Pact of June 1950. In fact, the OAU Charter contained no provision for collective security to the effect that member states are legally obliged to come to the assistance of other members in the event of aggression.[27]

Subsequently, an attempt was made to set up a military wing of the OAU through the creation of an African Defence Organization (ADO). ADO held its first ordinary session in December 1964 in Addis Ababa and the second in Freetown, in February 1965. Unfortunately, nothing came out of these attempts. Later, in August 1970, the OAU Council tried to reactivate the Defence Commission composed of defence ministers or chiefs of staff of member states, with a new mandate of 'concentrating on the growing threat from Southern Africa.' As before, the scheme never materialized for a variety of reasons, the most important being the inherent military weakness of most African states. In 1977, William Etekei, the Administrative Secretary-General of the OAU, made a proposal for the creation of a pan-African force to cope with the worsening conflict situation in Rhodesia, but in vain. At the 15th Summit of the OAU in Khartoum in July 1978, a new proposal for an OAU 'Committee of Defence' was made, but could only succeed in cataloguing possible problems in the creation of a Pan-African Defence Force. The problems of logistics, standardization of weapons and training programmes, language barriers and ideological differences among African states seemed insurmountable.

The peaceful solution of intra-African conflicts is instead a major aim of the OAU. The Mediation, Conciliation and Arbitration Commission was created to that effect. But African countries have so far declined to use a quasi-juridicial instrument for the management of intra-African disputes, preferring a more political approach. The Commission has thus been inactive to the point that suggestions were made to abolish it. In practice, attempts to solve intra-African conflicts have been mainly undertaken by the two major political bodies of the Organization: the Assembly of Heads of State and the Council of Ministers. The Assembly's function has been either to endorse mediation efforts by individual African presidents or to create *ad hoc* committees for that purpose. Through its special sessions, the Council of Ministers was particularly active in the management of intra-African disputes in the early years of the OAU. Out of eight special sessions held during the first ten years of the Organization, six took place between November 1963 and December 1965.

The record of the OAU in the solution[28] of intra-African disputes was initially promising. The Organization managed to arrange a cease-fire in the Algerian-Moroccan border dispute in 1963, to replace British with African troops in Tanzania after the army mutiny in that country in 1964, and even to improve relations between Ghana and its neighbours on the issue of subversion in 1965. But following its inability to play any meaningful role in the Congo crisis and its total impotence in dealing with the Unilateral Declaration of Independence in Rhodesia, the OAU retreated more and more into inactivity while superpower influence on the continent spread. As shown in the following outline of major intra-African conflicts since the creation of the OAU (Table 4.1), during the late 1960s and throughout the 1970s the Organization played practically no role not only

Table 4.1. *Outline of major intra-African conflicts (1963–81)*

Conflict	Issue	Role of OAU	Outcome
1 Algeria–Morocco 1963–5	Territory	Legitimize cease fire, aid communications and provide neutral site for leaders' meeting	Bilateral settlement
2 Dahomey–Niger 1963	Territory	None: UAM handled	Settled (UAM help)
3 Ethiopia–Kenya–Somalia: since 1964	Territory	1964 order cease fire; 1967 provide neutral site; 1973 establish a good office – Committee – etc.	Ongoing
4 Ghana–Upper Volta 1964–5	Territory	1964 conciliation; 1965 provide forum; pressure on Ghana	Settled (Ghanaian withdrawal)
5 Equatorial Guinea–Gabon 1972	Territory	Assist negotiations, create commission to define border	Quiescent (settlement pending)
6 Ghana–neighbours	Subversion	1965 attempt mediation	Settled (conflict ended with Ghanaian *coup*)
7 Rwanda–Burundi 1966–73	Subversion	1966 legitimize Mobutu mediation; 1973 establish Mediation Committee	Quiescent
8 Tanganyika (internal) 1964	Army mutiny	Legitimize Nyerere's actions and troops loans. Replace British peace-keeping	Settled
9 Ghana–Guinea 1966	Subversion/ seizure of diplomats	Inquiry by council of ministers, pressure on Ghana by Assembly	Settled
10 Guinea–Ivory Coast 1966–7	Subversion/ seizure of diplomats	Legitimize Tubman's initiatives	Settled
11 Guinea–Senegal since 1971	Subversion	1971 establish Mediation Commission	Settled
12 Tanzania–Uganda 1972	Subversion	1973 provide neutral site for leaders, assist Somalia mediation efforts	Settled (reconciliation)

Conflict	Issue	Role of OAU	Outcome
13 Congo 1964–5	Civil war	Attempt conciliation. Attempt to limit external involvements	Settled (military victory)
14 Nigeria–Biafra 1967–70	Secession	Support Federal government, attempt conciliation	Settled (military victory)
15 Sudan 1964–71 (internal)	Secession	None	Settled (some assistance from Ethiopia)
16 Burundi 1964–7 (internal)	Ethnic strife	Minimal, legitimize government actions	Ongoing
17 Kenya–Uganda	Territory	Attempt conciliation	Settled
18 Angola 1975–6 (internal)	Civil strife	Special OAU Summit	Settled (military victory of MPLA)
19 Western Sahara (Morocco–Mauritania) 1976–81	Territory	Attempt conciliation	Ongoing
20 Zaire 1977–8 (internal)	Civil strife/ subversion	Discussion	Settled, outside OAU
21 Egypt–Libya	Territory	Attempt conciliation	Bilateral settlement
22 Chad 1977–81 (internal)	Civil strife etc.	OAU discuss, November 1981 create peace-keeping force	Ongoing
23 Upper Volta–Mali 1977	Territory	Conciliation, OAU commission	Settled
24 Sudan–Ethiopia 1977–80	Territory	OAU Commission	Ongoing
25 Benin–Gabon 1977	Territory	Attempt conciliation	Settled bilaterally

Table 4.1. (*continued*)

Conflict	Issue	Role of OAU	Outcome
26 Uganda–Tanzania 1978–9	Civil strife/subversion	OAU consider, but failed	Settled (military victory)
27 Liberia	Civil strife	OAU no action	Settled (military victory)
28 Gambia 1981 (internal)	Civil strife/subversion	OAU no action	Settled (military victory)

in domestic conflicts or civil wars, for which clear inhibitions existed, but also in most intra-African disputes. It was notoriously ineffective in the Somali-Ethiopian and Ugandan-Tanzanian wars, the civil strife in Chad and the Western Sahara issue.

At the 1981 OAU Summit in Nairobi, however, hopes were raised that during the 1980s the Organization may revert to the more active role of its early days. An agreement was apparently reached for a peaceful solution of the Western Sahara conflict through a referendum, though the details of the agreement were not clearly spelled out. Perhaps more significant, a decision was taken and later implemented to send an OAU peace-keeping force to Chad. If successful, these two initiatives may have heralded a new era for the OAU's role in the solution of intra-African disputes or even internal conflicts.

But, at the time of writing, events do not seem to confirm expectations. Apart from financial difficulties, the OAU force in Chad does not seem to have established the necessary climate for a long-term political solution nor even good working relations with the government of that country. The civil war continues unabated, its final outcome remaining still uncertain. Should the OAU force fail to stop the civil war and be withdrawn before achieving its overt or covert objectives, such a negative experience may prevent similar initiatives for a long time to come. The parties to the Western Sahara conflict also appear more determined than ever to seek a military solution. The unprecedented decision by the OAU Secretary-General to admit the Polisario into the Organization aroused violent protest by 18 African countries, provoking a series of boycotts and counterboycotts of OAU's meetings. Should this situation continue, the future of the Organization may be at stake. This situation is particularly ominous in view of the already controversial venue for the 1982 OAU Summit in Tripoli, Libya. In brief, the long-term effects of these two bold OAU initiatives may well be more negative than positive. If the Organization comes out weakened from these experiences and retreats into further inactivity in the matter of intra-African conflicts, superpower influence in Africa may spread even faster in the 1980s than it did in the previous decade.

Intra-African conflicts are, in fact, symptoms of a deep-seated malaise, namely the vulnerability of the continent to imperialist machinations and the impotence of the OAU in maintaining peace and security in Africa.

The question of intra-African conflicts takes us to the neo-colonial phase of African struggle against imperialist domination and exploitation of the continent. The achievement of political independence has indeed been a major step forward bringing to the fore the next phase of the struggle to win economic independence and socio-political advancement. One may ask how this is connected with the question of intra-African conflicts? Obviously, with the political withdrawal of colonial powers from Africa and the installation of independent African governments, even the inter-imperialist conflicts and rivalry in Africa can only be waged through these governments and against these governments. Thus what may appear at first sight to be a purely 'territorial' dispute between African states (e.g. in the former Spanish Sahara) or a case of rebellion (as in the Shaba Province of Zaire in 1977–8) may in fact be the manifestation of a new form of inter-imperialist rivalry. We should therefore be careful not to analyse intra-African disputes on the basis of their formal appearance only.

To assess the role of the OAU in the struggle against neo-colonialism in Africa, it would be necessary to study each situation in its specificity. At a general level, we can only make the following two observations. The first is that superpower intervention takes many overt and covert forms. The deployment of Moroccan troops to squash the Shaba rebellion is clearly a covert proxy intervention by Western imperialism, that is the use of the troops of one African state in another African state, just as in an earlier decade the United States used Thai and Philippino troops to fight its battles in an Asian country – Vietnam. The installation of the present government in the Comoro Islands by 'Colonel Denard' and his band of mercenaries is another case of covert intervention by French imperialism. On the other side, the use of Cuban troops to squash the democratic aspirations of the oppressed nationalities in Ethiopia and Eritrea, despite its revolutionary veneer, is no less a covert intervention by another superpower in the struggles of the people of Africa. Even the Nigerian civil war, which at first sight appeared to be a tribal war, was a war in which imperialist superpowers fought through proxies to protect or advance their own interests[29]

The second observation relates to the role of the OAU in alerting members about these overt and covert forms of superpower interventions that either initiate or compound intra-African contradictions. The usual reaction among OAU members is to see the mote in the other's eye while not seeing the beam in one's own. Thus Angola could accuse Zaire of the presence of French troops in its territory, and be accused in turn of depending on Cuban troops.

The economic and military stakes in Africa are too high for either superpower to quit Africa. Hence, we are likely to witness an intensification of superpower confrontations on the continent which would variously appear as a 'border problem', or a problem of 'subversion' or a 'territorial' problem or one of incipient or actual 'civil war' or an ethnic war. This then is the greatest danger that lurks in Africa. At the moment, the OAU can only reflect the general weakness of its membership.

The OAU in world diplomacy

By the diplomatic role of the OAU in international relations, we mean the African impact on world affairs through the diplomatic efforts of African states. This would require us to deal with African states' impact on crucial world problems such as disarmament, development, the new international economic order, exploitation of the seabed and other resources of the ocean, protection of the environment, treatment of refugees, and other world social and economic issues. One could also refer to more specific non-African political problems such as the Afghan, Cambodian and Palestinian issues or the question of the unification of Korea.

But to summarize Africa's role in world affairs very briefly, one would simply say that Africa has brought to the fore, probably more sharply than any other region in the world, the problems stemming from racialism, colonialism and underdevelopment. It has brought to the struggle of the oppressed peoples a certain degree of militancy and urgency. Though Africa has not come up with any major radical departure from the past, the democratic and nationalist aspirations of the oppressed masses the world over have received a major thrust forward with Africa's entry into the arena of world diplomacy. But while African diplomacy has been effective in radicalizing the struggle against colonialism, racialism, and underdevelopment, it has been markedly less effective on other world issues of the day such as disarmament, ecology (even if the headquarters of the

UN Environment Programme is in Nairobi), or the exploitation of the resources of the ocean.

If one were to isolate Africa's impact on the structure and role of the system alone, the role of African diplomacy becomes even clearer. There is no doubt that it was the impact of the African states that resulted in the formal amendments of the UN Charter, enlarging the membership of the Security Council from 10 to 15 and the Economic and Social Council from 18 to 54, as well as other bodies of the UN.

The growing importance attached by the UN system to economic issues has also come mainly as a response to demands of African countries. The expansion of the UN role in this field is evidenced in the various United Nations Conference on Trade and Development (UNCTAD) conferences, particularly the 4th UNCTAD conference in Nairobi in May 1976 and the fifth in Manila in May 1979. The African members of the UN have thus been spearheading in recent years the Third World struggle for the establishment of a New International Economic Order through the UN, starting particularly from the fourth Non-Aligned Summit Conference in Algiers in 1973 in the wake of the oil crisis and carried through in three special sessions of the General Assembly of the UN (6th, 7th and 11th, in 1974, 1975, and 1980). The OAU members have been playing a very significant role in this crucial field.

The African impact on the UN is also evident from the efforts in recent years at restructuring the economic and social activities of the UN system to make them more coherent, effective and responsive to the needs of a new international economic order. The appointment in July 1978 of an African economist, Kenneth Dadzie of Ghana, as the Director-General for Development and International Economic Cooperation[30] is only a reflection of the special role of Africa in this field. Recently, the unanimous nomination by the 18th OAU Summit in Nairobi (July 1981) of Tanzanian Foreign Minister, Salim A. Salim, as the African candidate to the post of Secretary-General of the UN to succeed Kurt Waldheim clearly reflected the claim of the special role of Africa in the UN. It is no wonder that the Africans rightly argued that Western Europe has had three UN Secretary-Generals, Asia one, and that it was now their turn.

In addition, the OAU members have also made a considerable impact on the non-aligned conferences. The third and fourth non-aligned summits held in Lusaka in 1970 and in Algiers in 1973 were predominantly African conferences focusing on African problems. Much of the time and energy at these conferences was spent in legitimizing African positions on liberation struggles in southern Africa and decolonization generally. The major theme that emerged from these conferences was the idea of Third World economic cooperation against the economic and political dominance of the rich North. Similarly, the fifth and sixth non-aligned summits held in Colombo in 1976 and Havana in 1979 attested to this concern. At the recent conference of the non-aligned foreign ministers in Belgrade in September 1981 (to celebrate 20 years of the movement), problems such as the liberation of Namibia, the problem of apartheid in South Africa and Third World economic cooperation dominated the discussions.

The OAU and intra-African economic cooperation
Compared with the progress made by the OAU in the fields of decolonization, global diplomacy and with the success of its international campaign against apartheid, its performance in the vital field of Africa's economic development has been utterly disappointing. At the founding conference in 1963, special emphasis was placed on economic cooperation as an approach to African unity. As we noted earlier, Nkrumah's political approach to African unity was rejected as unrealistic. At the time, emphasis was also placed on regional economic groupings which President Nyerere of Tanzania regarded as the stepping stones towards African unity.

One of the OAU's main objectives, laid down in Article II of the Charter, includes a duty on the part of OAU members 'to coordinate and intensify their cooperation and efforts to achieve a better life for the peoples of Africa', and 'to cooperate in the fields of transport, communications, health, sanitation and nutrition as well as science and technology'.[31]

The history of the OAU in the field of economic cooperation has been one of ineffectiveness and indifference. A number of factors could probably be mentioned as contributing to the OAU's weak performance on the economic front. First of all, the OAU was intended mainly as a political organization, and it has survived largely because of the unanimous stand of its members on decolonization and apartheid. Secondly, the backwardness and dependent nature of African economies equally contributed to the ineffectiveness of OAU action in the area. Thirdly, when the OAU came into existence in 1963, the UN Economic Commission for Africa (ECA), an economic institution established in 1958, was in an incomparably better position to take initiatives on African economic problems, and it indeed took full advantage of this. A possible duplication of efforts in the economic field was solved by the usual OAU policy of 'leaving it to the ECA'.[32] During the early years of its work at least, the impression was created that African economic problems were really none of the OAU's business. Economic issues prominently featured for the first time on the OAU agenda at the Kinshasa Summit in 1967,[33] when the OAU Administrative Secretary-General, Diallo Telli, submitted a detailed report on African economic cooperation and demanded action. In order to improve the economic situation of the continent, the establishment of an African common market and the development of regional economic groupings were suggested.

Since 1967, the OAU has been showing increasing interest in economic matters culminating in the calling of a special OAU summit on economic issues in Lagos in April 1980. The OAU summit in Algiers in September 1968 for example, explicitly recognized that 'economic integration of the African continent constitutes an essential prerequisite for the realization of the aspirations of the OAU'.[34] The competition between the OAU and the ECA in economic matters was reduced following the acceptance by the ECA in 1969 of the primary responsibility of the OAU for cooperation between African states under the terms of Article II of the OAU Charter. Further, a resolution adopted by the OAU summit in Addis Ababa in 1970 attempted to rectify the omission in the OAU Charter of clear guidelines determining OAU's responsibilities in economic and social matters.[35] The cooperation between the OAU and the ECA has also increased and several major conferences have been held in the 1970s to discuss economic matters. In 1971, the ECA conference of ministers in Tunis adopted a resolution (218(X)) entitled 'Africa's strategy for Development in the 1970s'. In May 1973, the OAU, ECA, and the African Development Bank (ADB) jointly held the African Ministerial Conference at Abidjan, Ivory Coast, on 'Trade, Development and Monetary Problems'. The report of this conference formed the basis of the OAU 'African Declaration on Cooperation, Development and Economic Independence' which was adopted by the 10th OAU summit in 1973. This document set out the basic principles of collective and individual action by all African countries on cooperation, development and economic independence. It set out guidelines on a wide range of issues, from human and natural resources, to relations with other regions of the world, the emphasis being on the promotion of joint efforts. This conference was also instrumental in harmonizing the views of African countries on the forthcoming negotiations with the European Economic Community for the adoption of the Lomé Convention.

In December 1976, the Extraordinary Meeting of the OAU Council of Ministers meeting in Kinshasa, Zaire, adopted the well known 'Kinshasa Declaration' which, among other things, recommended the establishment of an African Economic Community. The target of economic integration, according to the document, should be achieved within a period of 15 to 25 years.

The conference also asked the Secretary-General of the OAU together with the Executive Secretary of ECA to give priority in their research programmes to the details of establishing an African common market. The 14th Summit of the OAU Heads of State in Libreville (Gabon) in July 1977 endorsed the Declaration. In February 1979, the OAU and ECA organized a colloquium in Monrovia (Liberia) on the future development prospects of Africa towards the year 2000. Some of the major conclusions of that symposium formed the basis text of the book: *What kind of Africa by the Year 2000?*[36] – a book which was to prove influential subsequently. Most of the recommendations therein were incorporated in the famous 'Monrovia Declaration' adopted at the 16th Summit of the OAU held in Monrovia, in July 1979. The declaration commits the African countries to follow guidelines and adopt measures aimed at promoting national and collective self-reliance in social and economic development. The document stresses that African countries should strive for the integration of their economies, a step that would pave the way for the eventual establishment of an African Economic Community.

The Monrovia (1979) Summit also decided to hold an Economic Summit of the OAU in Lagos (Nigeria) in April 1980. The Lagos Summit adopted the 'Lagos Plan of Action for the Implementation of the Monrovia Strategy for the Economic Development of Africa.'[37] This document has proved to be of considerable interest in Africa and the world. The programme of work of the OAU based on the Lagos document was adopted at the 18th Summit of the OAU held in Nairobi, Kenya in June 1981.

The Lagos document set out comprehensively the actions which African countries should take at the regional, sub-regional and national levels in order to achieve economic integration of the continent by the year 2000. In many cases, timetables for the achievement of the targets were included.[38] Briefly, all the measures aimed at creating the African Economic Community, which the Lagos Plan of Action expects should be set up by the year 2000. During the first decade, action will concentrate on establishing and strengthening sub-regional economic communities. In the second decade, the sub-regional economic communities will establish closer ties among themselves in view of achieving continental integration.

But to what extent are African countries determined to implement these objectives? Experience shows that there is often a lack of commitment and political will to make adjustments and evolve compromises to translate rhetoric into reality. The problems of African unity are too numerous. The ideological divisions between the OAU members, for example, have made close cooperation between capitalist and socialist oriented economies virtually impossible. However, it is encouraging to see that African leaders have at last responded to the gravity of the African situation. Whatever the outcome of these plans, the Lagos summit of 1980 has created a new awareness of the appalling economic conditions in the vast majority of African countries.

Problems and prospects

The above survey of the structure and performance of the OAU shows that the Organization has not been very effective as a regional arrangement. Perhaps it may not be incorrect to say that at the time of its establishment in 1963 the OAU 'bit off more than it could chew'. It loudly proclaimed the institutional realization of African unity when all that existed was a general belief in the necessity of inter-African cooperation.

As already noted, despite its large membership, the OAU is institutionally weak and commands very modest resources and capabilities. The total annual budget of the OAU, after two decades of its existence, is only around US$12 million, an insignificant amount for a continental organization.[39] The OAU has also been plagued by recurrent arrears of payment by its members. The OAU has only a very small and weak administrative apparatus with an 'administrative' Secretary-General, who is at best a dignified clerk without any political role or relevance, unlike the UN Secretary-General.

In the years following independence and the birth of the OAU, the climate of cooperation existing in the pre-independence period in Africa has progressively deteriorated. The spirit of pan-Africanism which led to the formation of the OAU in 1963 has gradually declined. Today, except for the few days spent at the OAU summits (if they attend at all), most African heads of state spend their time in promoting narrow national interests at the expense of the spirit of pan-Africanism. The present division of Africa into small and largely unviable nation states means inevitably that Africa will drift apart unless definite and deliberate counteracting steps are taken.

Neither the OAU as an organization nor its member-states have taken definite and deliberate counteracting steps against these narrow nationalisms. Instead, some African leaders boycott OAU summits or even threaten to quit the OAU because of selfish national interests. Here, among others, one may mention Morocco's threat in 1980 to withdraw from the Organization if the OAU were to accept Western Sahara as a member.

Over the years, the newly independent African states have become more keen on exercising fully their newly won sovereignty and could not tolerate any infringements on it. The immediate preoccupations of these states have been the accelerated struggle for national identity, the struggle for consolidation of internal political power and gaining political influence in relation to their neighbours. Consequently, there seems to be little time and energy left for such remote concerns as the OAU.

At the same time the frequent military coups and civil strifes in many African states[40] have turned the interest of most African states from foreign policy to domestic affairs. This phenomenon may also explain the usual poor attendance of heads of state at successive OAU summit conferences. For example, at the 13th Summit of the OAU in Port Louis (Mauritius) in 1976, only ten of the 48 heads of State participated. At the Kampala summit of the OAU in 1975, the then Nigerian President, General Gowon, was forced to make an embarrassing exit from the conference when informed of the overthrow of his regime in Lagos. Thus, a marked preoccupation with domestic problems has become a dominant feature of the African political scene, which has in turn adversely affected the fate of the OAU.

Another reason for the weakness of the OAU is the persistent ideological conflict between its more radical and conservative members. In fact, ideology has been playing an extremely crucial role in African domestic and international relations. The struggle between the radicals and moderates which dominated the founding conference of the OAU in 1963 has continued to affect every aspect of the work of the OAU in the later years. The success of the conservatives at the founding conference in 1963 was also responsible for the weak role of the OAU in African affairs. At the 1971 summit of the OAU, even the principle of universality of membership of the OAU was attacked over the dialogue issue.[41] Furthermore, the ideological divisions between OAU members have made close cooperation between capitalist and socialist oriented economies virtually impossible. This has also affected the working of regional economic groupings in Africa. The economic relations between Tanzania and Kenya is a clear case in point.

Another basic problem hindering unity and solidarity among African states is the persistent problem of border disputes among them. One of the principles of the OAU is the 'respect for the sovereignty and territorial integrity of each state' (Article II(1)). But because of the arbitrariness of the colonial boundaries which the African states had to inherit at the time of independence, this principle has not been well-observed by member countries. At the Addis Ababa conference in 1963, the leaders of Africa were fully aware of the inner contradictions in the state system that they had inherited as a colonial legacy, but they were divided on how to solve the contradictions. On the one hand, the movement for continental unity brought together states with varying colonial experience under a common cause. On the other, the urge in each state to keep intact the colonially inherited territory and possibly recover those portions which by accident of history had been lost to other neighbouring states, introduced within the continent a situation seemingly irreconcilable with the larger theme of African unity. On the question of boundaries, the OAU had adopted the principle of *uti possidetis* i.e., 'member states should respect the borders existing on their achievement of national independence'. The OAU however, does not have the physical or moral power to enforce its principles. That is why when it comes to border disputes, narrow national interests always override the OAU principle, as illustrated by a study of various border disputes in Africa.[42]

The above analysis amply supports the view that the OAU, if it is to live up to the high expectations for which it was founded in 1963, needs urgent reform and revitalization. Many Africans now rightly think that the OAU should not remain riveted to a Charter drafted two decades ago under circumstances profoundly different from those of today. The African states, despite the difficulties encountered since independence, have developed considerably, while the OAU has not grown along with them. The OAU Charter needs to be re-examined in the light of new developments. The OAU was in fact born before the real problems of independence had begun to reveal themselves. It is pertinent to note that none of the seven paramount principles of the OAU Charter under Article III is concerned with the many vital problems of economic and social development.

The OAU Charter, for instance, does not contain any provision for the protection of the rights of the African masses. Significantly the OAU Charter starts with the words: 'we, the Heads of African State and Government', and evidently the emphasis in 1963 was on the state rather than the people. As President Nyerere of Tanzania, one of the founding fathers of the OAU, has pointed out, the OAU Charter spoke for the African peoples still under colonialism or racial domination, but once the countries emerged to nationhood, the Charter stood for the protection of their heads of state and served as a trade union which protected them. In other words, the OAU appears to be an institution of the African heads of state, by the heads of state and for the heads of state. This probably explains the utter lack of popular debate on and enthusiasm for the OAU.

The Addis Ababa conference in May 1963, which met in the shadow of the assassination of Sylvanus Olympio of Togo in January of that year, went so far as to include in its seven principles an explicit declaration of 'unreserved condemnation, in all its forms, of political assassination as well as subversive activities on the part of neighbouring states, or any other states.' (Article III(5)). However, in Africa today, there is more need to protect the African masses from the atrocities and violence of their Heads of State than vice versa.[43] The horrible experience of Uganda under Idi Amin, that of the Central African Republic under Jean Bedel Bokassa, and of Equatorial Guinea under Macias Nguema etc, have in recent years generated a new awareness of the need for protection of the human rights of African peoples. It is encouraging to note that since 1979 when the three above African tyrants fell, the OAU has been taking certain initiatives in this area. At its 16th Summit in Monrovia in July 1979, the OAU for the first time decided to draft an African Charter of Human Rights and Rights of People. The proposed Charter, that provides for the creation of a commission to investigate human rights complaints, was approved in January 1981 at the meeting of African Justice Ministers held in Banjul (Gambia). To enter into force, it has to be ratified by the OAU members. Combined with the Lagos Economic Summit (April 1980), the stand of the OAU on human rights will mark in some ways a definite turning point in its history.

It is increasingly obvious that if the OAU is to survive as a truly continental Organization, capable of facing the crucial problems of Africa, it has to accommodate the concept of politico-economic union somewhat along the lines advocated by Kwame Nkrumah. The arguments as to whether this is to be achieved through a merger of regional unions or by the creation of central institutions such as an African High Command, an African Monetary Union, an African Common Market, and similar other bodies with executive powers, will no doubt continue. But irrespective of the approach chosen, what matters is that the resulting arrangements be capable of meeting the political and economic needs of the continent. In short, the time has come to give the OAU 'teeth' and to make it a positive instrument that can shape the destinies of the African peoples.

It is clear that the OAU lacks both the power and the means to play even the moderate roles assigned to it by the founding fathers in 1963. Many African leaders still voice their discontent, saying that the OAU is not strong enough to perform the roles assigned to it, forgetting that they themselves have preferred not to equip it with the necessary means and machinery. It is pointed out in OAU official circles that there exists a general sense of frustration, a feeling that there is too much talking and too little action. As one OAU official put it: 'we have a grand design, but nobody is paying attention to it'.[44]

However, despite its weaknesses and failures, the OAU remains an essential instrument, if not for solving those issues that divide African countries, at least for harmonizing their positions on the few issues that unite them. Whatever its weaknesses and shortcomings, the OAU provides the general institutional framework within which continental interaction in Africa takes place. It also provides a device for replacing and superseding the erstwhile bilateral pattern of African international relations with multilateral, continental media for promoting coordination and cooperation among its members and resolving the numerous problems facing them. The OAU also serves as the collective voice of the African states in various international organizations, and acts as a link between the African regional system and the international system as well as other competing regional systems. This notwithstanding, it is to be emphasized that if the OAU is to survive and prosper, it is essential that African leaders rethink and decide to equip the organization with the necessary powers and mechanism. This calls not only for a change of attitudes, but also for positive action to strengthen the Organization by improving its present constitution and functioning style.

The need for a thorough reappraisal of the OAU's structure and performance has long existed. The OAU Charter, the result of a flabby compromise in 1963 that left the new Organization hopelessly emasculated, calls for a fundamental revision.[45] In this regard, the 1976 report and the recommendations of the 'Turkson Committee[46] on the structural reform of the General-Secretariat of the OAU could provide a useful starting point. This report proposed the establishment of an Assembly for Development Cooperation – that is, an Economic Summit of the OAU. Among other things, the report also recommended the strengthening of the role of the 'Administrative Secretary-General' of the OAU, including a new designation: 'Secretary-General'. In order to play a more effective role in the affairs of the Organization, he will no longer be confined only to 'implementing resolutions of the Council of Ministers and the Assembly of Heads of State and Government.' He will also be expected to initiate various political moves on behalf of the OAU as well as negotiations between its members, and to take an active part in them on a par with the chiefs of the negotiating teams of member states concerned. Besides, the OAU should also have a full-time executive organ to implement decisions and resolutions.

Conclusion

Briefly, there exists a definite need for positive action for a stronger OAU, equipped politically and militarily to guarantee the security of the continent and the fundamental rights and welfare of the African masses. Politically disunited and militarily defenceless in a ruthless world, Africa with her enormous reserves of natural resources holds out an open invitation to international adventurism, a second Berlin. The struggle against neo-colonialism in Africa is likely to be much more disruptive of African unity than the struggle against colonialism and racialism. Much of this struggle will take the form of intra-African disputes, though lurking behind these disputes are likely to be the hands of one or the other superpower. Unless the masses of Africa become politically conscious of the lurking dangers and demand that their leaders preserve the independence and integrity of the African continent as a whole, we shall witness not only an inevitable polarization of African states as between the superpowers, but also the collapse of the Organization of African Unity, the only hope of the African peoples to develop their continent and its resources for themselves.

NOTES

1 Oginga Odinga, 'Africa: A Continent in Crisis', *Africa Now* (London) October 1981, pp. 93–4. Also Y. Tarabrin, 'Problems of Africa in 1980s', *International Affairs* (Moscow) June 1981.

2 UN Doc. A/S-11, 25 July 1980, p. 12.

3 For details see: Adekunle Ajala, *Pan-Africanism: Evolution, Progress and Prospects*, André Deutsch, London, 1973; I. Geiss, *The Pan-African Movement*, Methuen, London, 1974; Colin Legum, *Pan-Africanism: A Short Political Guide*, Praeger, New York, 1962; V. B. Thompson, *Africa and Unity: The Evolution of Pan-Africanism*, Longman, London, 1969.

4 Resolution passed by the 5th Pan-African Congress, Manchester 1945.

5 The CIAS took place in Accra from 15 to 22 April 1958 with delegates from independent African States including, Ghana, Ethiopia, Liberia, Morocco, the Sudan, Tunisia, and the UAR.

6 This conference took place from 8 to 13 December 1958, with delegations from a total of 28 independent and dependent African countries participating.

7 For details see, Chimelu Chime, *Integration and Politics Among African States*, Scandinavian Institute of African Studies, Uppsala, 1977, pp. 140–70.

8 *Ibid.*

9 For details see, H. T. Alexander *The African Tightrope*, London, 1965; Rajeshwar Dayal, *Mission for Hammarskjold: The Congo Crisis*, Princeton, 1961, and Crawford Young, *Politics in the Congo*, London 1965.

10 Quoted in Chime, *Integration and Politics*, n. 7., p. 164.

11 Quoted from Michael Wolfers, *Politics in the Organization of African Unity*, Methuen, London, 1976, p. 41.

12 Two important conferences preceded the signing of the OAU Charter on 25 May 1963: They are, (1) The Preparatory Conference of Foreign Ministers from 15 to 23 May; and (2) The Summit Conference of Heads of State and Government, from 23 to 25 May 1963.

13 Quoted from Chime, *Integration and Politics*, n. 7, p. 185.
14 *Ibid*, p. 188.
15 *Ibid*, p. 189 (emphasis added).
16 *Ibid*, p. 192.
17 *Ibid*.
18 For a comparative study of Nyerere and Nkrumah on the question of pan-Africanism, see O. Agyeman, 'The Osagyefo, the Mwalimu and Pan-Africanism', *Journal of Modern African Studies*, xiii, 4 (1975).
19 Quoted in Chime, *Integration and Politics* n. 7, p. 197.
20 The membership of the Liberation Committee was subsequently increased. Currently there are 21 members of the Committee, namely, Algeria, Angola, Cameroon, Congo, Egypt, Ethiopia, Ghana, Guinea, Guinea-Bissau, Liberia, Libya, Mauritania, Morocco, Mozambique, Nigeria, Senegal, Somalia, Tanzania, Uganda, Zaire and Zambia.
21 T. O. Elias, 'The Commission of Mediation, Conciliation and Arbitration of the Organization of African Unity', *British Year Book of International Law*, xl, (1964), pp. 331–54.
22 Colin Legum, 'The Specialized Commissions of the OAU', *Journal of Modern African Studies*, ii, 4 (1964).
23 Article II(7) of the OAU Charter.
24 Wolfers, *Organization of African Unity*, pp. 200–2.
25 Quoted from N. M. Shamuyarira, *Documents and Speeches on O.A.U. Strategy for Liberation of Southern Africa*, Department of Political Science, University of Dar es Salaam, 1975 (mimeo).
26 CIAS/Plan/2/Rev 2. Resolutions adopted by the First Conference of Independent African Heads of State and Government, Addis Ababa, May 1963.
27 For details on this subject see, T. A. Imobighe, 'An African High Command: The Search for a Feasible Strategy of Continental Defence', *African Affairs*, lxxix, (1980), pp. 241–54.
28 See Mathews, R. E. 'Inter-State Conflict in Africa: A Review', *International Organization*, xxiv, (1970); see also David Mayers, 'International Conflict Management by the Organization of African Unity' *International Organization*, xxviii, (1974). The first eight special sessions of the Council of Ministers referred to in the text were motivated by the following conflicts or situations: the Algeria-Moroccan border dispute (Addis Ababa, 15–18 November 1963); the army mutiny in Tanzania and the Somali-Ethiopian border conflict (Dares-Salaam, 12–14 February 1964); the situation in the Congo-Zaire (Addis Ababa, 5–10 September and New York, 16–21 December 1964); threatened boycott of the Accra Summit (Lagos, 10–13 June 1965); the Unilateral Declaration of Independence of Rhodesia, Addis Ababa, 3–5 December 1965); the invasion of Guinea (Lagos, 9–12 December 1970); the Egypt-Israel war (Addis Ababa, 19–21 November 1973).
29 See Colin Legum, 'International Involvement in Nigeria 1966–1970' in Y. Tandon and D. Chandarana (eds.), *Horizons of African Diplomacy*, East African Literature Bureau, Nairobi, 1974.
30 This new post, widely seen as ranking next in importance to that of the UN Secretary-General, was created by the General Assembly in December 1977.
31 See Article II(1) and (3) of the OAU Charter.
32 For details see, B. Andemicael, *The OAU and the UN: Relations between the*

Organization of African Unity and the United Nations, Africana Publishing Company, New York, 1976, particularly see Chapters vii to xi, pp. 194–253.

33 For details see, Zdenek Červenka, *The Unifinished Quest for Unity: Africa and the OAU*. Julian Friedman, London, 1977, particularly Chapter x, pp. 176–89.

34 *Ibid*, p. 180.

35 *Ibid*, p. 181.

36 OAU, *What kind of Africa by the Year 2000?*, Institute of International Labour Studies, Geneva, 1979.

37 See OAU, *Lagos Plan of Action for the Economic Development of Africa 1980–2000*, Institute of International Labour Studies, Geneva, 1981.

38 For details see *Africa* (London) No. 106, June 1980.

39 The Annual budget of the OAU during the first decade of its existence varied between $2.5 million to 4.5 million.

40 See Ruth First, *The Barrel of a Gun*, Allen Lane, London, 1970; and J. M. Lee, *African Armies and Civil Order*, London, 1969.

41 For details see, Yash Tandon, 'The O.A.U. and the Principle of Universality of Membership', *The African Review* (Dar es Salaam) i, 4 (1972).

42 For details on this issue see Carl C. Widstrand (ed.), *African Boundary Problems*, Scandinavian Institute of African Studies, Uppsala, 1969.

43 See Ali A. Mazrui, 'Rights of States or of People – Where should the OAU Focus?', *New African* (London), August 1977, p. 779. Until 1979, only with reference to refugees did the OAU show a concern for the respect of human rights in independent African countries when, in 1969, it adopted the Convention for the protection of African refugees.

44 Quoted by Richard Fredland, 'The OAU After Ten Years: Can it Survive?', *African Affairs*, lxxii, (1973), p. 309.

45 Article XXXIII of the OAU Charter provides that: 'This Charter may be amended or revised if any member-state makes a written request to the Administrative Secretary-General to that effect; provided, however, that the proposed amendment is not submitted to the Assembly for consideration until all the Member States have been duly notified of it and a period of one year has elapsed. Such an amendment shall not be effective unless approved by at least two thirds of all the Member States.'

46 This Committee consisted of nine countries namely, Algeria, Cameroon, Ghana, Guinea, Egypt, Nigeria, Senegal, Tanzania and Zaire. The Committee's report is entitled 'Report of an Ad-hoc Committee on Structural Reform of the OAU General Secretariat', known in OAU Circles as the 'Turkson Report' after its Chairman, Ambassador Yaw Turkson of Ghana.

5 The African Development Bank and the African Development Fund*

FRANCIS WODIE

Introduction

After independence the African states were immediately and directly confronted with many economic problems. Their development difficulties were compounded by the small size of national markets and their narrow financial basis. Endowed with externally directed economic structures inherited from colonization, the African states were further exposed to the uncertainty of foreign markets outside their control. Such anomalies were supposed to disappear with independence.

But despite political autonomy, attention remained oriented toward the outside world and this attitude led certain states to rely on outside help for development. Besides being insufficient, as was later recognized, foreign aid engendered economic and political controls incompatible with the exercise of full sovereignty. Other African states conscious of the danger of such a policy, tried to internalize the solutions to their economic and social problems. While facing these uncertainties, the African countries progressively acknowledged the necessity of intra-African cooperation eventually leading to economic integration. In effect, the fragmentation of the African continent does not seem to favour the development of the African states. Sharing resources could possibly be a remedy to this situation.

It was in this context and supported by such demands that the African Development Bank (ADB) came into existence. The project germinated at the African Peoples' Conference held in Tunis in 1961 in the form of

* The English version of this chapter, prepared by Burney Medard, is relatively more extensive than its French original, notably part II. Reference to the specific powers of the organs of the ADB and ADF, the system of weighted voting, the data and tables on the origin and allocation of the resources of the two institutions, have been added by the editor.

an African investment bank. Moving in this direction, the Executive Director of the Economic Commission for Africa, Mr Robert Gardiner, proposed the idea of an ADB. A preparatory commission was formed to examine the economic, political and legal implications of such an enterprise.

The project met with the misunderstanding and apprehension of certain non-African states who considered it much too ambitious. The creation of an African continental bank should have been preceded and prepared for by the establishment of regional banks. African continentalism, it was said outside Africa, should begin with regionalism. The creation of African regional banks seemed to these states a necessary step towards the establishment of an African continental development bank.

However, the idea of a continental bank received enthusiastic support from the majority of the African states. The project was examined at the founding conference of the Organization of African Unity in May 1963 at Addis Ababa. The decision was then made to create the ADB the exact organization of which was turned over to specialists. Consequently, negotiations soon started and led to the conference of Khartoum where on 4 August 1963 the creation of the ADB was agreed upon. Drawing inspiration from the treaty establishing the International Bank for Reconstruction and Development and that creating the Inter-American Development Bank, the Agreement setting up the ADB made it appear as much as an international organization as an international financial institution.

According to the preamble of the Agreement, the creation of the ADB was motivated by the desire to reinforce African solidarity through economic cooperation among African states and by the need to improve the efficient use of African natural and human resources, thus stimulating economic development and social progress in the region. Through the ADB, the African states intended to mobilize and utilize African economic and financial resources for the benefit of Africans. The Bank should have been the favoured financial instrument for the development of Africa and as such should have remained in the hands of Africans. Membership of the Bank was to be precluded to non-African states and its activities were to be restricted to Africa.

Such an international institution which proposes to internalize the requirements and the means of economic development and social progress, introduces in the African context a distortion between the African international order and the internal order of African states, for most of the member-states of the ADB opt for the exogenous model of development, largely open to foreign investments and outside initiatives. To the external orientation of the domestic structures of finance would have corresponded the internal orientation of this external (inter-African) structure of finance which is the ADB; a contradiction hard to overcome. By shutting out foreign capital, the ADB wants to lessen the effect of the excessively extroverted national structures of African countries.

Could this break between the domestic and the international level within the region be more than euphoric? Outwardly oriented at the domestic level, attention constantly turns towards the exterior on the inter-African level, underlining that what is international reflects what is national. Progressively, outside influences penetrated the domain of economic and financial cooperation organized by the ADB. Either because one could not or did not know how to mobilize resources sufficiently or because these resources proved to be insufficient in the face of the immense needs, the ADB had to resort to external participation in its activities. To safeguard the African character of the Bank and its operations, the external orientation took the form neither of an increase of capital stock by non-African contributions nor of a subscription of shares by non-African countries. Under the provisions of Article 8 of its Charter,[1] the ADB formed a Special Fund through contributions by non-African states. The creation of the African Development Fund (ADF) and its organization was the object of the Agreement signed on 29 November 1972 in Abidjan. This Agreement linked the ADB to 13 states of America, Europe and Asia.

As specified in Article 2 of its Charter, the purpose of the ADF is to help the Bank to contribute more effectively to economic and social development of the members of the Bank and to promote intra-African economic cooperation and trade. The Fund procures means to finance, at favourable terms and conditions, the realization of projects which are of prime importance to development and which stimulate it. This is the peculiarity of the ADF, legally dissociated from the ADB.[2] Endowed with an international legal personality which reinforces its autonomy, the ADF nevertheless remains linked to the ADB in a way that makes both of them appear in certain aspects as two international organizations in one, and in other regards as two complementary financial institutions. These two aspects will be discussed in turn.

The ADB and the ADF, two international organizations in one

The ADB and ADF are two international organizations in that they regroup states through international agreements. Established by two different treaties and formed by states which are not identical from one organization to the other, the ADB and the ADF show in this way their autonomy. However, as a partner to the treaty creating the ADF, the

ADB is tied to this institution by links which group the two organizations together and give unity to the two institutions.

The autonomy of each organization

The autonomy of the ADB and the ADF can be clearly seen from the respective Charters, membership, and competence of the two organizations. The Agreement creating the ADB was adopted by the representatives of 33 African states on 4 August 1963 at Khartoum. As specified in Article 63, the Agreement remained open for signature by these states until 31 December 1963. Article 64 required the original signatories to deposit their instruments of ratification or acceptance with the Depositary before 1 July 1965. According to Article 65, the Agreement could not have entered into force before 12 signatory governments representing at least 65 per cent of the authorized capital stock of the Bank had deposited their instruments of ratification or acceptance. But whatever the date of these ratifications or acceptances, the Agreement should have not entered into force before 1 January 1964. Emanating from this treaty and organized by it, the ADB as a subject of international law concluded on 29 November 1972 with 13 non-African states[3] the Agreement creating the ADF. It is thus by two distinct legal paths that the ADB and the ADF acquired their international legal personalities. The Agreement creating the ADF was not a simplified arrangement since Article 55 submits it to ratification, acceptance or approval by the signatories. As an international act, the Agreement creating the Fund was not an inter-state act. The approval of this Agreement by the ADB was the responsibility of the Board of Governors of the Bank, according to Article 29 of its Charter which stipulates that all powers of the Bank are vested in the Board of Governors. While the Charter of the ADB is silent on the right of states to formulate reservations, the Agreement creating the ADF recognizes in Article 58 the right of the parties to formulate reservations or an interpretative declaration at the time of depositing their instruments of ratification, acceptance or approval. These acts, which limit or modify the scope of the obligations undertaken can only refer to the immunities and privileges granted to the Fund and its agents on the territory of member states. The treaties creating the Bank and the Fund make them open organizations according to terms which highlight the specificity and the autonomy of each of the two institutions.

Concerning the ADF, a state which is not a founding participant may become a participant, according to Article 3 paragraph 3 and Article 57 paragraph 2, by signing the Agreement and by depositing with the Bank an instrument of ratification, acceptance or approval which becomes effective on the date of the deposit. Membership in the ADF is open to member-states of the United Nations and any of its specialized institutions or the International Court of Justice. By this provision, as its original composition shows, the ADF loses its African specificity, though its operations retain their African vocation. All independent states could become members of the Fund. The very terminology underlines the specificity and the autonomy of each organization. A state is a participant in the Fund, while it is a member of the Bank. In contrast to the Fund, the Bank remains in every way an international regional or continental organization open only to independent states from the African continent and the African islands, as specified in Article 3 of the Agreement. African countries other than the original signatories of the Agreement can accede to the Bank upon acceptance of the Agreement, as stipulated in Article 64, paragraph 2. In such cases the Board of Governors fixes the exact date when membership becomes effective. Acquired in this way, membership in the Bank or participation in the Fund could be lost temporarily or permanently.

Loss of membership could only come through a voluntary act on the part of the member. The state participant in the Fund or the state member of the Bank wishing to withdraw from them sends a written notice to this effect to the principal office of the institution concerned. The notice cannot take effect less than six months after its reception. No exclusion procedure was provided for nor organized by the constitutive treaties.

The state ceasing to be a member of the Bank 'remains liable for its direct obligations to the Bank and for its contingent liabilities to the bank . . .' (Article 45, paragraph 1). The state that loses its membership in the Bank logically has to fulfil the obligations undertaken while still a member. Following the same logic, the state which ceases to belong to the Bank also ceases to incur liabilities with respect to loans and guarantees entered into thereafter by the Bank and to share either in the income or in the expenses of the Bank.

The withdrawal of a state does not affect the capital of the Bank, which 'shall arrange for the repurchase of its shares as part of the settlement of accounts with that state . . .' (Article 45, paragraph 2). The state which ceases to be a participant in the Fund must, according to Article 39, fulfil all financial liabilities to the Fund, whether as a participant, borrower, administrator or under any other title. An arrangement must be reached between the state and the Fund to settle the accounts. Whatever the circumstances, the state which ceases to be a participant is relieved of all further obligations to the Fund when its withdrawal becomes effective. The Agreement creating the Fund contains provisions to cover a situation where the Fund and a given state cannot settle a dispute among themselves. Any conflicts born from this situation between the Fund and the state are submitted to a procedure of arbitration. The dispositions of the charters of both organizations are silent on the law that should be applied in such a situation.

Applying to two international legal personalities, the state and the Bank, the state and the Fund, the rules must be based on international law, through which the international personality of both institutions will be recognized and respected. Article 31, paragraph 2 of the Agreement creating the Fund specifies that this is an entity legally independent and distinct from the Bank. Created by two treaties, that is by two international legal acts, the Bank and the Fund are endowed with their own organs through which they express their own personality from that of the states *ut singuli* and realize their objectives. Article 50 of the treaty creating the Bank provides that, in order to fulfil its purpose and functions, the Bank possesses full international personality. Therefore, it is entitled to conclude agreements with member-states and non-member-states as well as with other international organizations.

The legal personality of the Fund is separate from that of the Bank. Born from two treaties, both institutions constitute on the international level two distinct entities. Article 42 of the Agreement creating the Fund specifies that it possesses full legal personality and particularly the capacity to contract, acquire and dispose of movable and immovable property. All those acts which do not exceed the legal powers of the Fund cannot be ascribed either to the participant states or to the Bank. Such acts are imputable to the Fund which is responsible for them. It is even said that the Agreement creating the Fund appears as an act not implicating *(res inter alios acta)* the member-states of the Bank, though the Bank itself is a party to the treaty.

Although formally correct, this view should be qualified. It would be difficult to consider the members of the Bank as non-parties to a treaty to which the Bank is a party. Member-states of an international organization could not be considered as third parties to agreements passed by such an organization. The principle of the absence of third party effects of treaties does not hold in such cases. The problem was examined and incorrectly solved to our mind by the International Court of Justice when it judged that member-states of the League of Nations could not make use of the mandate which links this organization to South Africa. We are instead of the opinion that the acts of an international organization affect both the interests and the rights of its members.

As to the competence or powers of these two institutions, their constitutive treaties specify that the detailed list of functions spelled out in the text is not exhaustive. It might even be said that the Fund and the Bank exercise the competence stated and implied by their goals and the need to implement them effectively. Here the idea of implied competence of international organizations is introduced. This principle could be accepted as a general principle in the law of international organizations, including regional organizations.

Recognized as international organizations, the Bank and the Fund are granted immunities and privileges normally attached to this type of institution. The immunities provided for in the constitutive treaties and specified in the headquarters agreement are of two types: those benefiting the international organization as subject of international law and those concerning the officers and employees of the Bank and the Fund. In this way the property, archives and assets of the Fund and the Bank cannot be seized. The Governors, the Directors and their Alternates, the officers and employees of the Bank and the Fund enjoy privileges and immunities in the performance of all their official duties. These immunities are attached to the function and not to the person of the officers or employees of the two organizations. Based on the function, the immunities may be waived in the interest of the organization. The waiving of immunities is at times optional when it is justified by the interest of the organization, and at other times compulsory when it aims at ensuring the normal course of justice. In either case the waiving of immunities is carried out on behalf of each organization by the competent authority, namely the Board of Directors or the President. Immunity from jurisdiction becomes operative *ratione materiae* and recalls the distinction introduced by the international doctrine concerning the state between a situation where the state is acting *jure imperii* and a situation where it intervenes *jure gestionis*. As specified in Article 43 of the Agreement creating the Fund and Article 52 of the Charter of the Bank, both organizations cease to enjoy immunity from the legal process in cases arising out of the exercise of their borrowing powers. Could the explanation of this derogation be found in the commercial nature of the act accomplished by the international organization? Having lost the immunities, the organization – the Fund or the Bank – may be brought before the competent courts. The right to bring such action against the Fund or the Bank is open only to non-member-states (Bank) or non-participants (Fund). The member-states or the participant states and their representatives must have recourse to internal law procedures provided for in the constitutive treaties. As a result, the immunity from jurisdiction entirely ceases in certain cases only with regard to third parties. It remains valid in the case of members or participant states.

What has been discussed in the previous pages proves the autonomy of the ADB and the ADF. At the same time, it suggests the existence of links uniting them. Party to the Agreement creating the Fund, the Bank was tied to this institution from the very beginning. What follows will show that the unity of the two institutions prevails over their autonomy.

The unity of the two organizations

The unity of the two institutions is symbolized by the joint use of the same headquarters. The inviolability of the headquarters thus applies as much to the Bank as to the Fund. This situation is of great advantage to the Fund as no headquarters agreement has been reached between the Fund and the host country. But, even more relevant, between the two institutions exists an organic, structural and functional relationship.

The member-states of the ADB are automatically qualified as members of the ADF. Consequently, the African states as members of the Bank participate directly or indirectly in the activities of the Fund and can be considered indirectly as parties to its constitutive treaty. As already mentioned, Article 2 of the treaty creating the Fund states that its goal is to help the ADB to contribute more effectively to the economic and social development of its members and to promote intra-African economic cooperation and trade. These provisions underline the solidarity of the two institutions and the unity of purpose which must guide their activities. However, it is on the level of their organizational pattern, their officers and representatives that this unity is the most obvious and best structured.

Article 20 of the Charter of the ADB specifies that the president of the Board of Governors of the Bank is automatically president of the Board of Governors of the Fund. The president of the Bank is automatically president of the Fund. He is elected by the Board of Directors of the Bank from among the nationals of member states according to the procedure determined by the agreement creating the Bank. The president, elected for a renewable five-year mandate, ceases to exercise his functions regarding the Bank and the Fund, if the Board of Directors of the Bank so decides by a two-thirds majority of the total voting power of the members. The president is the legal representative of the Fund and the Bank and the head of personnel of the Bank. He presides over the boards of directors of the Bank and the Fund. This results in joint administration and responsibility between the two organizations. That the two institutions have the same head can only reinforce the unity of action of the members.

The Board of Governors of the Fund holds all powers just as all powers are vested in the Board of Governors of the Bank. While retaining full authority over any delegated matter, the Board of Governors of the Bank is allowed by Article 29, paragraph 2 of the Agreement to delegate to the Board of Directors all its powers except the power to: (a) decrease the authorized capital stock of the Bank; (b) establish or accept the administration of Special Funds; (c) authorize the conclusion of general arrangements or agreements for cooperation with non-members of the Bank; (d) determine the remuneration of directors and their alternates; (e) select outside auditors; (f) approve the General Balance Sheet and Statement of Profit and Loss of the Bank; and (g) exercise such other powers expressly reserved to the Board of Governors in the Agreement. Between the two boards of governors exists an organic and functional relationship. The participating states (in the Fund) not members of the Bank have logically separate Governors. But this should not affect the unity which exists or should exist between the Bank and the Fund. This unity between the Bank and the Fund reappears as the Governors and the Alternate Governors of the Bank are automatically and respectively Governors and Alternate Governors of the Fund. In addition to their organic unity of composition, the two Boards of Governors also hold joint sessions. The annual meeting of the Board of Governors of the Fund takes place at the same time as the annual assembly of the Board of Governors of the Bank.

With respect to the composition of the Board of Governors of the Fund, it may be noted that the personality of the member-states of the Bank did not fade behind that of the Bank which legally was the only party to the Agreement creating the Fund and consequently member of the Fund. Each member-state of the Bank has a Governor and a Alternate Governor in the Fund just as in the Bank. From a legal point of view, the composition of the Board of Governors of the Fund could have been slightly different. The Governors of the Fund could have or should have been considered as the representatives of the Bank *in corpore*. If this point of view had been adopted, the number of Governors representing the Bank in the Fund would no longer have corresponded to the number of Governors of the member states of the Bank. Certainly it was for practical reasons that the present solution was adopted.

The Board of Directors of the Fund exercises the same functions as the Board of Directors of the Bank, namely the functions of preparation of the work of the Board of Governors, plus its own peculiar functions as those functions delegated to it by the Board of Governors. As specified in Article 32 of the Agreement, the Board of Directors is responsible for the conduct of the general operations of the Bank, in particular: (a) the election of the President; (b) the preparation of the work of the Board of Governors; (c) the decisions concerning particular direct loans, guarantees, investments in equity capital and borrowings of funds by the Bank; (d) the determination of the rates of interest for direct loans and of commissions for guarantees; (e) the submission of accounts for each financial year and an annual report for approval to the Board of Governors at each annual meeting; and (f) the determination of the general structure of the services of the Bank. Being in continuous session at the principal office of the Bank, the Board of Directors of the Bank is in many ways that of the Fund. The Board of Directors of the Bank is composed of nine members. The function of a Director is incompatible with that of a Governor or an Alternate Governor. Elected for three years by the Board of Governors from among the nationals of member-states of the Bank, the Directors and their Alternates can be renewed in their functions. The ADF has instead a Board of Directors of 12 members of which six come from the Board of Directors of the Bank, the six others being designated by the non-African States participants in the Fund. Here too the organic unity of the two institutions is ensured.

But if the composition of the organs of the two institutions shows some slight differences, the unity of officers and staff is complete, and the ADF has no officers and staff of its own. Article 30, paragraph 4 of the Agreement creating the Fund provides that the President manages the current business of the Fund using when necessary the officers and staff of the Bank as well as its organization, services, and premises in order to manage successfully the current business of the Fund. It should be specified in the light of these statements that officers and staff of the Bank do not have double functions, Bank officers and Fund officers. They are only Bank officers acting, in certain circumstances and under the responsibility of the President, on behalf of the Fund. It is only this analysis which explains and justifies the terms of Article 31 of the Agreement creating the Fund by which the Fund reimburses the Bank the exact cost of using the services of the officers and staff of the Bank. This reimbursement is effected on the basis of an intervening arrangement between the Bank and the Fund. It is within these structures that the Bank and the Fund show the other aspect of their personality: their financial complementarity.

The ADB and the ADF, two complementary financial institutions

The ADB and the ADF are legally distinct financial institutions, yet their objectives are the same. The goal of both is to mobilize resources from within and outside Africa to contribute to the economic development and social progress of member states individually and jointly. However, the degree of underdevelopment of African states varies and the stages and priorities of development are such that it was judged wise to model action on demands. Therefore, two financial institutions were created which, while pursuing the same goals, retain their specificity.

The treaty establishing the ADB adopted on 4 August 1963 endowed the Bank with an original capital stock of 250 million units of account (UA)[4] divided initially in 25 000 shares of a par value of 10 000 UA each. The ordinary capital resources of the Bank include the authorized capital stock, funds raised by the Bank through borrowings, funds received in repayment of loans and income derived from such loans. As at 31 December 1979 the available resources of the Bank[5] amounted to over 900 million UA of which roughly 300 million was represented by paid up shares by the African member-states and 600 million came from the Bank's borrowings[6] on the international, notably Western European, money market. As is the case with other financial institutions of this kind, the ADB has adopted a system of weighted voting based on quotas. The voting power of the members of the Bank is thus related to the amount of their subscriptions.[7] Nigeria, the major contributor to the Bank with a subscription of 16 900 shares equivalent to 42 250 000 UA or 14 per cent of the paid up shares of the Bank, enjoys 17 505 votes or almost 13 per cent of the total voting power of members. At the other extreme, countries like Cape Verde, the Central African Republic, the Comoros, Djibouti, Guinea-Bissau and the Seychelles, each subscribing to only 200 shares equivalent to 175 000 UA or 0.17 per cent of the resources of the Bank, can cast only 825 votes each or 0.60 per cent of the total voting power of members.

The ordinary capital resources of the Bank should be distinguished from the special resources which are to be set aside to create Special Funds. Article 11 of the Agreement establishing the ADB states that 'the ordinary capital resources of the Bank shall at all time and in all respects be held, used, committed, invested or otherwise disposed of, entirely separate from special resources. Each Special Fund, its resources and accounts shall be kept entirely separate from the other Special Funds, their resources and accounts.' As at 31 December 1979, apart from the ADF, the resources of the existing Special and Trust Funds[8] amounted to over 90 million UA.

On the basis of Article 8 of the Charter of the Bank and in conformity with the provisions noted above, the ADF was endowed with its own resources which do not constitute capital stock. The subscribing states are not the same in the Bank and in the Fund. By its own subscriptions, the Bank also contributes to the resources of the Fund. These subscriptions remain special resources separated from the ordinary resources of the Bank. As at 31 December 1979, following two general replenishments, the subscribed resources of the Fund had gone up from the original 135 million in 1973 to 950 million UA, of which 619 million had already been paid up. The Fund also follows the system of weighted voting. But to safeguard the African character of the Fund, the ADB, contributing only 21 500 000 UA or less than 2.5 per cent of the resources of the Fund has been granted 1000 votes or 50 per cent of the total voting power of all participants.[9] The single largest contributor to the resources of the Fund is Japan, with an amount of almost 178 million UA and 202 votes or 10 per cent of the voting power of all participants. Six countries of the European Economic Community provide jointly close to 300 million UA and enjoy 304 votes or 15 per cent of the total voting power. Among the other participants, the major contributors are Canada with 135 million UA, Sweden with 69, Norway with 52 and Switzerland with 50 million UA.

The Fund like the Bank can borrow to increase its means of intervention. But while the Bank can borrow freely on the world market, the Fund can only accept loans made available at favourable conditions. It does not contract loans on any market nor participate as borrower, guarantor or otherwise to the selling of bonds on any market. The ADF in fact is expected to procure the means of financing at favourable conditions the realization of objectives which present unique importance for regional and sub-regional development and stimulate it. The difference in the functioning of the two institutions can be seen here. The ADB functions according to the principles and procedures governing the activities of any regional or international financial institution. The Bank provides without discrimination loans to member-states and their institutions according to these principles and takes into account the credit-worthiness of the bor-rower and the profitability of the project to be realized. Authorized loans are of two types: some specific for a particular project, others global for national or regional financial organizations. The Bank tends to favour investments in the private sector and to stimulate private initiative and enterprises. The interest rates applied by the Bank are also close to those prevailing on the international market. The ADF as an alternative makes available at favourable conditions special loans to member-states in extreme financial needs. Such loans aim at improving the living conditions and productive activities of the least favoured sections of the population. The decision to lend takes into account the social character of the project. As a matter of priority, loans are advanced for development programmes in the sectors of agriculture, health, education, roads and public utilities. The regional and sectoral distribution of the resources of the ADB and the ADF is given in Tables 5.1 and 5.2.

Table 5.1. *Comparative regional distribution of ADB and ADF loans*
(ADB, 1967–79; ADF, 1974–9)

	Projects (number)		Loans (million UA)		Percentage share of loans	
	ADB	ADF	ADB	ADF	ADB	ADF
East Africa	63	51	238	261	29	39
Central Africa	39	28	156	126	19	19
North Africa	41	12	175	53	21	8
West Africa	73	52	261	228	31	34
TOTAL	216	143	830	668	100	100

Source: African Development Bank and African Development Fund, *Annual Report 1979*, pp. 29, 80.

Table 5.2. *Comparative sectoral distribution of ADB and ADF loans*
(ADB, 1967–79; ADF, 1974–9)

	Projects (number)		Loans (million UA)		Percentage share of loans	
	ADB	ADF	ADB	ADF	ADB	ADF
Agriculture	35	52	145	244	17	37
Transport	57	38	211	184	25	28
Telecommuni-cations	14	1	56	2	7	0.30
Power and electricity	33	2	139	15	17	2
Water supply and sewerage	26	26	108	105	13	15.70
Industry and development banks	49	3	161	15	20	2
Education and health	2	21	10	103	1	15
TOTAL	216	143	830	668	100	100

Source: African Development Bank and African Development Fund, *Annual Report 1979*, pp. 29, 80.

As at 31 December 1979, the two institutions had jointly committed funds for the value of almost one and a half billion UA: 830 million by the Bank during its 13 years of operation and 668 million by the Fund in its first six years of operation. The Bank has obviously not yet played a major role in development financing in Africa. But if one looks at recent trends, the future role of the Bank is more promising. The amount of loans committed and disbursed by the Bank in 1977–9 was almost twice as much as during its previous ten years of operation.[10] The proposed opening of the Bank to non-African states may further enhance the financial position of the Bank. In any case, judging from its relatively good start, the Fund is likely to master in the long run greater resources than the Bank. The data also show the Fund's deeper involvement in the least developed regions of the continent. East Africa with its high share of Africa's least developed countries received 39 per cent of the Fund's resources as against only 8 per cent for North Africa, considered a relatively more developed part of the continent. The tables equally confirm the sectoral complementarity of the activities of the two institutions. Agriculture, education and health account for less than 19 per cent of the Bank's loans as against over 52 per cent of the Fund's loans.[11] By contrast, the Fund invests less than 5 per cent in telecommunications, power and industry combined, sectors which absorb 43 per cent of the Bank's resources. Only for transport and water supply do the two institutions allocate more comparable percentages of their resources: 38 per cent by the Bank and 43 per cent by the Fund.

The ADF, following the example of other international organizations, distinguishes three categories of beneficiary states, on the basis of their respective level of economic development: (a) countries with a GNP per capita inferior or equal to US$280; (b) those between US$281 and US$550; and (c) those with a higher per capita income. The countries in category (a) have the highest priority in the allocation of loans by the Fund; those in category (b) have access under certain conditions to the Fund's loans; and countries in category (c) have in theory no access to the Fund's resources. It is a similar idea which guides the recognition on the universal level of the category of the Least Developed of the Developing Countries.

As noted earlier, the Bank generally provides loans at market conditions, while the Fund does not charge interest. Loans made available by the Fund are subject to an overhead administrative commission of 0.75 per cent. The period of loan repayment to the Bank is normally between five and 20 years. Loans repayment to the Fund is spread over a period of 50 years with a grace period of ten years. The grace period may vary depending on the nature of the operations undertaken. *Mutatis mutandis*, from a functional point of view the ADF is to the ADB what the International Development Association (IDA) is to the International Bank for Reconstruction and Development (IBRD).

In addition to this ordinary function of financing operations, a function common to the two institutions, the Bank can in theory guarantee loans made by other financial institutions. The responsibility of the Bank would thus be committed in case the principal debtor is found defaulting. But the ADB does not seem to be in a haste to undertake this type of operation.

To sum up, if their respective operations are conceived and accomplished differently, yet the two institutions are guided by the same objectives. The specific character of the respective operations of the Bank and the Fund aims at reinforcing their complementarity and making the development effort and regional cooperation in Africa more effective. The Fund and the Bank are instruments of development for their African member-states and their operations on the territory of a member can be undertaken only with the consent of that state. Both organizations are basically composed of African states. Even if the Fund includes participants from Europe, America and other parts of the World, its functions and activities are restricted to Africa. According to Article 14 of its constitutive treaty, the Fund finances only projects and programmes aimed at promoting economic and social development on the territory of members of the ADB. In the same way, the Bank can only finance operations undertaken by a member state or by an agency located on the territory of that state. What is important here, it would seem, is less the nationality of the company than its contribution to the development of the member state of the Bank. By concentrating their activities on African territory, both institutions contribute in their own ways to the development of this continent.

Development is not to be considered as an isolated national undertaking. The development effort must have a regional character and encourage projects of this type. The two institutions give priority to financing projects which are an integral part of national, regional or sub-regional programmes. The Bank and the Fund favour development projects and programmes involving two or more member-states and likely to promote continental or sub-continental cooperation. The Bank and the Fund also provide technical assistance to their member-states and participate in pre-investment operations.

To prevent straying from the objectives and assure proper utilization of resources for development and intra-African cooperation, the Bank and the Fund have established similar procedures for the control and evaluation of the use of allotted funds. Article 17 of the Agreement creating the Fund is particularly explicit on this. It requires the Fund to undertake a full and continued assessment of the progress of projects, programmes and activities financed by the Fund, so as to help the Board of Directors and the President to appreciate the efficiency of the Fund in the realization of its objectives.

Finally, the fact that all operations are undertaken and all decisions made by the Board of Governors and the Board of Directors, organs in many ways common to the Bank and the Fund, greatly encourages and develops cooperation and interaction between the two institutions.

Conclusion

The Bank and the Fund are two original African institutions which propose to contribute, principally through African resources, to the development of Africa. However, from the start, the Bank came up against the general context of the extroverted orientation of development in Africa and the insufficient financial resources within the continent. The needs were so immense and the means so meagre. Cooperation with regional or universal organizations, such as the Arab Bank and the IBRD, and the help offered by these organizations did not give as much satisfaction as had been hoped for. Progressively, African governments accepted the idea of making financial demands on the outside world by opening the Bank to the participation of non-African states. To support this position, reference was made to other regional development banks such as the Inter-American Development Bank. This proposal was partially realized with the establishment of the ADF. But this was only the beginning of a new trend.

In 1975, President Labidi again brought up the idea of opening the Bank to non-African states in order to revitalize this institution which had begun as an exclusively African institution. Nigeria, which wanted to maintain the African vocation of the Bank, opposed this initiative vigorously. Understandably, it may have been feared that the initiatives and the operations of the Bank would be taken out of African hands. Through the Bank, the instrument of development, Africa should have instead taken responsibility for itself. Opening the Bank to other states was to confirm to a certain extent the idea that Africa was incapable of solving her economic and social problems and reducing its underdevelopment by itself.

A certain number of member-states of the ADB, whose economy was propelled from abroad through the injection of private foreign capital, continued to believe that this was the only road to development. This attitude had its influence on the orientation of the Bank. At Libreville in

1978 a resolution in nine points was adopted to regulate the opening of the ADB to non-African states. The purpose of this resolution was to maintain the African vocation of the Bank in spite of this opening. To preserve this vocation, the resolution declares that the headquarters of the Bank must remain in Africa, namely be located in an African member-state. Further, the resources of the Bank could only be used for the benefit of African states. The Bank must remain under the direction of an African. The new Board of Directors composed of 18 members should have 12 African Directors. The African member-states should retain at least two-thirds of the votes, while the non-African member-states should not have more than one-third of the votes. Important decisions should be taken by a qualified majority. The granting of loans should never be guided or influenced by political considerations. But all these legal precautions will be of little help in the face of the mounting economic difficulties which led to the opening of 'the dam'.

The economic difficulties are real. The Bank borrows on the international financial market at about 15 per cent, while it lends to member-states at 9 per cent approximately. This can be financially catastrophic. However, must one always look abroad for solutions to internal problems? This is both an economic and political issue. The attitude which diverts attention from Africa also makes Africa persistently look for external help. In 1979, at the meeting in Abidjan the amendment 0 779 was made to the constitutive treaty thus allowing the ADB to open its capital stock to non-African states. This proposal needs to be accepted by member-states.[12] Three 'loud voices', Algeria, Nigeria and Libya opposed, wisely perhaps, this proposal which could make the ADB dependent on non-African states. One of the states, Algeria, 'practising what she preached', evaluated the resources expected to be raised from such an opening and made a pledge to supply them to the Bank. However, the reasoning behind this proposition did not shake the determination of those in favour of the opening. The problem has not only an economic but also a political dimension.

This is the challenge facing the ADB: how to find the important financial support needed for the development of Africa, while preserving its own African identity and vocation.

NOTES

1 By the terms of Article 8, 'the Bank may establish, or be entrusted with the administration of Special Funds which are designed to serve its purpose and come within its functions. It may receive, hold, use, commit or otherwise dispose of resources appertaining to such Special Funds.'

2 Here we must distinguish the ADF from the Nigerian Trust Fund (NTF). Although created and organized in 1976 by an international agreement linking the Bank and Nigeria, the NTF has no legal personality. The resources put at the disposition of the Bank by Nigeria are directly managed by the Board of Directors of the ADB. Its resources which amount to a renewable 100 million dollars have independent book-keeping. All operations under the NTF require the approval of the Nigerian State.

3 The 13 original signatory states of the Agreement creating the ADF are: Belgium, Brazil, Canada, Denmark, Finland, the Federal Republic of Germany, Italy, Japan, Netherlands, Norway, Sweden, Switzerland and the United Kingdom. Spain who participated in the founding conference did not sign the Agreement until 1 March 1973. On 29 March 1973, Yugoslavia also signed the Agreement. As at 31 December 1979, the number of participant non-African states had risen to 21 with the addition of Argentina, France, Kuwait, Saudi Arabia, the United Arab Emirates and the United States of America.

4 The unit of account is equivalent to 0.88867088 gramme of fine gold. Until 1971, this corresponded to one US dollar. In 1979, it was equivalent to 1.3 US dollar.

5 African Development Bank, *Annual Report 1979*, pp. 62–5.

6 Most of the borrowings are in the form of Euro-credits (some 400 million UA) or Bonds in Deutsche Marks (about 90 million UA) repayable within a period between five and ten years at an interest rate varying between 7¾% per cent and 15 per cent. An amount of about 28 million UA was provided by the governments of Canada, Sweden and Austria at no interest and repayable within 50 years with a grace period of ten years.

7 African Development Bank, *Annual Report 1979*, pp. 64–5.

8 As at 31 December 1979, the following Special and Trust Funds were in operation:
  Nigeria Trust Fund (76.4 million UA);
  Staff Provident Fund (2.9 million UA);
  Arab Oil Fund (11 million UA);
  Special Relief Fund (176 thousand UA); and
  Mamoun Beheiry Fund (4 thousand UA).

9 African Development Fund, *Annual Report 1979*, p. 105.

10 African Development Bank, *Annual Report 1979*, p. 30.

11 Dependency theorists could however easily interpret this complementarity between the Bank and the Fund, in particular the Fund's greater concern with the social character of a project, as an attempt by non-African states dominating the Fund to perpetuate the existing North-South division of labour by giving less support to more productive activities, notably in the industrial sector.

12 The proposal was accepted while this book was being printed.

6 OCAM: one scene in the drama of West African development

R. A. FREDLAND

Introduction

Robert Wood, in an article in the *Virginia Journal of International Law*, reminds us of Harold Lasswell's enumeration of individual values: power, wealth, well-being, enlightenment, skill, affection, respect, rectitude.[1] In the process of political organization man has sought to fulfil, maximize, and preserve these values, in some hierarchical order. In 1960, when 12 former French colonies as well as five other areas emerged upon the African political scene as independent entities, dichotomous perceptions of how Lasswell's values might be met were given impetus. On the one hand there was France, a major power of declining greatness dominated by an imperious leader. On the other hand there was the emerging continent of Africa with only five previously independent sub-Saharan states at the opening of 1960[2] but with 17 additional states added during that benchmark year.[3]

The process of independence manifested in the creation of Africa of over 50 states supports Wood's contention that there is 'strong evidence in the international arena of a "will to fragmentation" because of diverse cults, incompatible notions of justice, the will to power.'[4] The post-Second World War creation of over 100 sovereign states is at once evidence of the 'will to fragmentation,' but at the same time provides evidence that the concomitant 'will to power' is thwarted by the relative fragility of so many small states. The desire for autarky – one aspect of power – is clearly frustrated by smallness.

Just as the historical process of socio-political organization has led from the nuclear family to the tribe, the city and finally to the nation-state, so the universal search for security has led small states, particularly in Africa, to extend that search for forms of organization by which they could gain strength *vis à vis* the older, more powerful industrialized states. In West Africa this has taken the form of economic groupings. (See Table 6.1.) These have been highly dynamic organizations centred upon French-speaking states with irregular participation by English-speaking neighbours.

Even prior to the independence surge of 1960, there were incipient organizations, e.g., the Equatorial Customs Union (UDE), the West African Customs Union (UDEAO), and the Conseil de l'Entente (Table 6.1). Exercising the first blush of independence meant, inter alia, that the constraint of cooperation in a centralized economic organisation was intolerable in spite of both good intentions and the apparent need for means of maximizing small-state economic power in a dynamic world then dominated by bipolar pressures.[5] So, while states were individually interested in development and modernization in various forms, there was an overarching felt need for the exercise of political sovereignty, even at the expense of economic improvement if that meant policy constraints. As Wood points out, reality is not something to be discovered but it is a construct of the mind; what is valuable at one time need not be so at another.[6] Only after the felt need for the complete exercise of sovereignty had been satisfied could the cost of cooperation be realistically evaluated.

At the same time that the new states of Africa and elsewhere were aggressively exercising their newly-acquired sovereignty, however, another process was well under way. In Europe, among the oldest organized societies from the perspective of international relations, there was a remarkable movement toward economic cooperation that would prove to be unique in its impact upon the internal policies of the participating states. The evolution of the European Economic Community demonstrated a trend contrary to Africa's rush to independence: economic integration. Responding to another kind of empirical reality, economic and other aspects of interdependence, the European states, urged on by the United States, set about minimizing sovereignty and worked to maximize cooperation in several selected areas.[7] These simultaneous, though geographically separated, processes established the parameters of the exercise of sovereignty in the mid-20th century. Reflecting on the processes which have resulted from the two ends of that conceptual continuum, it appears two decades later that the Europeans were clearly further along the developmental track than the Africans. The European Economic Community, though experiencing internal strains as it moves toward increasingly intricate cooperative ventures, has become the model for many other regions as they aspire to similar levels of development and cooperation.

Table 6.1. *Economic groupings in West Africa*

Organization	Founding date	Members*
Mali Federation	1958–60	12, 17
Ghana–Guinea Union	1958–63	9, 10
Conseil de l'Entente	1959	11, 14, 20, 1, 19
UDE (Union Douanière Equatoriale)	1959	3, 4, 5, 7
UAM (Union Africaine et Malgache)	1961	2, 1, 11, 14, 20, 13, 17, 19, 3, 4, 5, 7, Malagasy Republic
OAMCE (Organisation Africaine et Malgache de Coopération Economique)	1961	Same as UAM
UMOA (Union Monétaire Ouest Africaine)	1962	1, 11, 13, 14, 17, 19, 20
UAMCE (Union Africaine et Malgache de Coopération Economique)	1964	1, 13, 19, 12, 10, 5
OCAM (Organisation Commune Africaine et Malgache)	1965	1, 2, 3, 4, 5, 7, 11, 12, 13, 14, 16, 17, 19, 20, 21, Mauritius, Malagasy Republic
UDEAC (Union Douanière et Economique de l'Afrique Centrale)	1965	2, 3, 4, 5, 7
UDEAO (Union Douanière des Etats de l'Afrique de l'Ouest)	1966	1, 11, 12, 13, 14, 17, 20
UEAC (Union of Central African States)	1968	4, 21
OERS (Organisation des Etats Riverains du Sénégal)	1968	10, 12, 13, 17
OMVS (Organisation pour la Mise en Valeur du Fleuve Sénégal)	1972	12, 13, 17
CEAO (Communité Economique de l'Afrique de l'Ouest)	1974	11, 17, 12, 14, 20, 13,
ECOWAS (Economic Community of West African States)	1975	1, 8, 9, 6, 10, 11, Liberia, 12, 13, 14, 15, 17, 18, 19, 20

*1. Benin (Dahomey), 2. Cameroon, 3. Central African Republic, 4. Chad, 5. Congo (République du Congo), 6. Equatorial Guinea, 7. Gabon, 8. Gambia, 9. Ghana, 10. Guinea, 11. Ivory Coast, 12. Mali, 13. Mauritania, 14. Niger, 15. Nigeria, 16. Rwanda, 17. Senegal, 18. Sierra Leone, 19. Togo, 20. Upper Volta, 21. Zaire (République Démocratique du Congo).

But, as Ramamurthi observes, 'The important question . . . is not whether they will be initiated but what happens to them after their creation.'[8]

The highly volatile African setting with new groupings appearing regularly during the decade of the 1960s has passed on to more stable organizations now seeking means for genuine development within the constraints of the relative poverty Africa endures. One significant step along this path was the African and Malagasy Common Organization (Organisation Commune Africaine et Malgache, OCAM).

The earlier naivety-cum-political euphoria which led to frequent and ineffective alignments has been tempered, as observed by O'Leary:

Rather than observing the necessity, and therefore the inevitability of natural economic and technological forces, the new political economy emphasizes the critical importance of the framework of international political relations in structuring and regulating the market relations of states.[9]

That is to say, the developing states of Africa did not emerge into an international system which could be characterized as a *tabula rasa*. There was an international political and economic system in place which was not of their making, but also not susceptible to their manipulation. The implicit choice presented them was to either adapt or suffer the consequences. In their process of adaptation, it has been only reasonable for the inherently weak states to attempt to gain as advantageous a position as possible from which to confront the existing political-economic system.

The Origins of OCAM

The French-speaking states of Africa were particularly vulnerable to the existing infrastructure because of their lack of preparation for independence coupled with the French-dominated infrastructure elements which they retained upon independence, e.g., communications links and central bank operations through Paris.[10] The 1956 *Loi-Cadre* established by France assured similar government in each territory. The African states recognized, as Wionczek points out, that leaving production allocation to the free market would be the equivalent of concentrating development in the more advanced countries.[11] In order to be competitive, even in an inherently uncompetitive situation, the African states recognized the need to collaborate in meeting the challenges of international economic activity. As O'Leary puts it: Third World mercantilism is the result of seeking security and control of destiny in a world of 'political economy increasingly seen as uncontrollable.'[12] Differing perspectives were noted by Onwenu: 'while France views cooperation and association with her former colonies as enlargement of France, all of those former colonies view French cooperation as an economic compromise and an economic opportunity. . . .'[13] Gould points out that 'wherever there is a need to control the mobilization and distribution of resources some form of organization will be utilized.'[14] Viewed from the perspective of French interests in her former colonies in West and Central Africa, OCAM became a means for this control more subtle than the overt institutional management which occurred in financial, defence, and foreign policy arrangements created before independence but continuing beyond.

Substantive political ties had been established among Niger, Upper Volta, Dahomey,[15] Mauritania, Senegal and Mali as they met in 1958 at Bamako in the Federalist Conference and Dakar less than a month later. From those contacts emerged the Mali Federation consisting of Mali and Senegal which lasted until late 1960.[16] Several conferences among French-speaking states occurred in 1960 and 1961 concomitant with the independence wave. From these there evolved the Union Africaine et Malgache, established in late 1960. This spawned Air Afrique, a joint venture international airline, in March, 1961. Later that same year the Organisation Africaine et Malgache de Cooperation Economique (OAMCE) was established along with a defence agreement (Union Afrique et Malgache de Defense, UAMD) and a cooperative agreement for communications (Union Africaine et Malgache des Postes et Telecommunications, UAMPT).

At another level the newly-independent African states were aligning and realigning within the context and constraints of the then pervasive Cold War mentality as well as the ideal of pan-Africanism which was being enthusiastically espoused by the Ghanaian President, Kwame Nkrumah, particularly since that country's independence in 1957. Following the break-up of the short-lived Mali Federation in August 1960, and the abortive Ghana-Guinea Union of African States (December 1960), there was established the Afro-Malagasy Economic Cooperation Organization (AMECO) which was the concrete manifestation of the 'Brazzaville Group', taking its name from a 1960 meeting in the capital city of the former French Congo.[17] The eruption of total disorder in the former Belgian Congo offered opportunities for alignment with the leading factions there: the leftist Prime Minister, Patrice Lumumba, and the more conservative Joseph Kasavubu, President. Unhappy with the Brazzaville Group's support of Kasavubu, Ghana, Guinea, Mali, Morocco, and Egypt along with the Algerian FLN and Libyan delegations met in Casablanca and, inter alia, expressed support for Prime Minister Lumumba. These two groups tended to represent the left and right of African international politics in the early 1960s. With Lumumba's death in 1961 their raison d'être disappeared and they disbanded after the founding of the Organization of African Unity (OAU) in 1963[18]

Less ideological was the Monrovia Group,[19] a result of Liberian President Tubman's efforts to form a pan-African organization. Twenty states, but not the five Casablanca members, met in early 1962. A remarkable aspect of this meeting was its bicultural constituency: both English-speaking and French-speaking states participated. One principle agreed upon was the creation of a 'consultative inter-African and Madagascaran organization.'[20]

On the other hand, the very sinews which link the French-speaking states serve to sever ties with English-speaking states. The 'real obstacle to West African unity' concealed by the Casablanca-Monrovia cleavage, Williams suggests, 'is simply the British and French heritages . . .'[21] The cultural differences between the educated elites in these groups are far more significant, he maintains, than the superficial ideological rhetoric from Casablanca states and Monrovia states. '*Négritude* seems to have far less *political* content for men like M. Senghor than "the African personality" has for Dr. Nkrumah . . .'[22] He concludes: to see these groupings as 'East versus West' or the beginnings of a new Scramble for Africa 'is to pin already shoddy labels onto a new continent.'[23] History has confirmed this judgement; even groupings among culturally similar states (e.g., the East African Community and several versions of West African unity – see Table 6.1) have failed, and as this is written, the OAU experiences serious disagreements. While remnants of Cold War issues have intruded in these organizations, local differences have been far more important in the failure of regional groupings to coalesce and provide a strong basis for cooperation.

These regional, sub-continental groupings were all superseded, in structure if not in spirit, by the creation of the OAU in 1963. The OAU was primarily a political institution which came into being as the practical manifestation of Nkrumah's dream of a pan-African United States of Africa.[24] Červenka attributes four attitudes to the founders: a) an all-encompassing political declaration, b) a loose association similar to the Organization of American States, c) a mechanism for increased economic cooperation, and d) the Ghanaian desire for political unity.[25] There was no expectation that in the near future the OAU would evolve into a regional economic organization precluding regional arrangements which might prove desirable among sub-regional groupings. As a matter of fact, this was articulated by OCAM's then-President Leopold Senghor of Senegal when he argued that, 'thenceforth, the major task of OCAM would be to create a Central and East Africa of small economic communities of

Francophone states, communities which will be the first steps toward the large groups of East and West Africa.'[26] However, unlike the United Nations Charter, no provision for sub-regional organizations is made in the OAU Charter. The spare document only provides for the most essential details of operation.

For one major regional grouping, the OCAM Charter[27] is terse in its statement of objectives. The second and third articles cover the points:

Article 2. The OCAM is based on the solidarity of its members. In the spirit of the Organization of African Unity, its purpose is to strengthen cooperation and solidarity between the African and Malagasy states in order to accelerate their economic, social, technical, and cultural development.
Article 3. For this purpose, the Organization shall seek to harmonize the action of the Member States in the economic, social, technical, and cultural fields, to coordinate their development programs, and to facilitate foreign-policy consultations between them, with due respect for the sovereignty and fundamental rights of each member state.[28]

When the meeting of the UAMCE (Union Africaine et Malgache de Cooperation Economique) transformed itself into OCAM in 1965 there was only slight conceptual movement from a 'purely economic, technical, and cultural organization'[29] to the organization depicted in the above quotation – a continuation of the Monrovia mentality. In the March 1963 UAM meeting, alternative models were proposed: some members favoured the Entente approach to unity with emphasis on economic and technical cooperation. Presidents Senghor and Youlou, on the other hand, proposed greater emphasis on political as well as economic questions.[30] It was clear that of the two contending schools of thought, functionalism prevailed. The evolution from the Brazzaville grouping through the alphabet organizations of OAMCE, UAMD, UAM to OCAM represented a setting out of identification on at least two axes: the extensivity of regional grouping and the intensivity of objectives. It was clear that the OAU was not going to bring about a united Africa within the political lifetime of any French-speaking African leader as it was also clear that the economic future of these states was tied closely to France, a circumstance which precluded fruitful integrative activities with English-speaking states.

International political and economic realities faced by the new West African states included the following:
– no state was capable of being a substantial international power because of impotence largely as a result of small size,
– great power domination of the international political/economic system was not to be undone easily, if at all;
– political realities prevented substantial integration of the several states;

- the apparent benefits of some form of cooperation were greater than the perceived costs;
- maximal expectations in the economic realm would be limited by the modest level of development and the constraints of their national products;
- there was an international division of labour which was disadvantageous to them.

This led implicitly to behaviour which would enable them to overcome their problems within the politically-tolerable realm of costs. As suggested by Belassa and Stoutjesdijk, there were four options available to them: a) to work within their respective national frameworks, b) to pursue regional integration, c) to increase their trade with developing countries in other regions, or d) to participate in the existing international division of labour[31]

As Nye points out, the developing countries, particularly in the early and mid-1960s, were too politicized to consider fully the potential of integration.[32] Green and Seidman were optimistic regarding both the necessity of and the potential for African unity because of the adequacy of natural resources. The needs they saw included industry which achieved economy of scale, comprehensive planning, and the bargaining power which resulted from unity.[33] Trade, as Wionczek points out, 'needs to be more promoted than freed.'[34] Williams reported that in 1961 intra-African trade constituted only 1 per cent of all African trade, demonstrating a substantial potential under proper circumstances[35]

As economic reality supplanted political aspirations, functional organizations emerged. For example, both the Chad and Senegal River basins were organized for development purposes.[36] Irrigation, flood control, salt water barriers, and improved river travel are the purposes of the two organizations reported in 1979 at the conclusion of a decade and a half of study. However, by 1981, while the cost has increased but the same purposes remained, suspicions were reported by a development official: 'It's a ploy by the French and West Germans to revitalize their construction industry by using Arab money.'[37] Even the most basic development efforts can be seen to be tied into industrialized powers' economic objectives.

The West African Monetary Union continued through the period to provide a stable, French-based currency system for seven states (see Table 6.1) which reflected the overriding need for political aspirations to give way to economic necessity.[38] Gould evaluates international organization, such as the monetary union, ambivalently. 'On the one hand purposeful organization can result in unintended consequences, particularly long-term structuring.'[39] The organization is, in Gould's term, 'a part of the global structure for the purpose of altering the interaction matrix.'[40] On the other hand, Gould cites Galtung's point that international organizations act as media which allow elites in developing states and in the power centres to prolong patterns of dependence and inequality between and within developing states.[41]

OCAM in action

The immediate predecessor organization to OCAM was UAM – the Union Africaine et Malgache, established at a conference in Yaoundé in 1961 with, ultimately, 14 members. The membership consisted of the 12 states of the former 'Brazzaville' group plus Togo and Rwanda. The Brazzaville-UAM grouping represented the conservative, French-speaking position in contrast to the more strident positions taken by the 'Casablanca' group.[42] Its purpose was harmonious political and economic relations. However, as President Senghor of Senegal observed at Bangui, March 1963: 'As great as it is, ours is only a regional organization of the continent. Once again the objective remains the same: to build together the whole continent . . .'[43] Moving beyond rhetoric, specific common institutions were established, e.g., Air Afrique, UAMPT, Union Africaine et Malgache de Défense, and OAMCE, all of which came into being in 1961. DuBois commented in 1963 that its functional approach '. . . enabled this organization to achieve more concrete progress than any other African grouping in establishing viable technical agencies.'[44]

Still, UAM was not free of the political dichotomies which had come to characterize African post-independence politics. The meeting of March 1963, removed the organization's Secretary-General, Albert Tevoedjre, because some member-states found him too zealous an advocate of African unity.[45] DuBois further reported that a long-standing dilemma which has confronted all regional organizations also beset the UAM: Should the emphasis be on technical cooperation as the route to unity as favoured by the Entente states, or should Leopold Senghor's advocacy of political unity be the dominant path?[46] One other problem which the dissolution of the organization rendered moot was membership for non-French-speaking Somalia.

With the demise of the UAM in 1963, the door opened for yet another successor organization, this time it was the short-lived UAMCE, Union Afro-Malgache de Coopération Economique, later transformed during a conference at Nouakchott into OCAM. The non-revolutionary nature of the Brazzaville states' policies and the continuity of purpose prompted *Pravda* to observe that Nouakchott was located in France.[47] Its specific, conservative objectives included: a) how to consolidate, b) how to deal

with Ghana's subversive activities among her neighbours, c) how to meet
the threat from Communist China, and d) how to achieve peace in the
Congo (Zaire).[48] The African international political climate can better be
understood when one recalls that 1963 was also the founding year of the
pan-continental OAU. While the calls of Nkrumah and others for a united
Africa had borne no fruit, the creation of the OAU at least resulted in a
single organization which claimed as members all the independent states
of black Africa.[49] The impetus to establish functioning regional organizations was strong, but it was apparent that such mundane activities as
postal unions, mutual defence arrangements, and cooperation in research
would not likely come soon at the continental level, if ever. UAM did take
the step of dissolving its UN mission, ceding its material to the OAU.[50]
Consequently, the simultaneous emergence of the OAU and UAMCE-
OCAM was not an indication of rivalry but rather a striving for common
goals, on a grand, political level in the former case and on a more functional
level in the latter.

At its formation it was observed that the 'fastest moving African
international group' was the UAM. The impetus credited with stimulating
the organization was the desire of French-speaking Africa to resolve the
Algeria revolution, but it was also suggested that the 'underlying factor
is economic. Both Guinea and Mali have found that no amount of Eastern-
bloc friendships can alter the fact that the West has more to offer them,
in aid, in trade, in capital investment.'[51]

With the dissolution of UAM, its specialized agencies – Air Afrique,
UAMCE, UAMPT, and UAMD – remained. UAMCE was to be the
overarching mechanism for cooperation. However, at the scheduled date
for the foreign affairs ministers' meeting to sign the new charter, only ten
states were represented in Nouakchott. Consequently, it was decided only
to initial the charter and reconsider. It was, after all, 'little more than a
paper organization.'[52] UAMCE President Daddah of Mauritania convened
a conference of heads of states at Nouakchott in February, 1965, at which
it was agreed to establish yet another umbrella organization, OCAM,
which would absorb UAMCE and assume responsibility for the specialized
agencies. It was further agreed that this would be within the framework
of the OAU and that the malaise of the OAU would be diagnosed[53]

The establishment of OCAM concomitant with the OAU despite the
euphoric spirit of the times should have suggested to objective observers
that the only possible path would be downhill; the realities of the age were
such that great accomplishments by a group of developing states with no
industrial or mineral base were unlikely. Their expressed objectives of
working within the context of the OAU, reinforcing cooperation and

solidarity among themselves and speeding up political, economic, social, technical, and cultural development were logical and reasonable. It was simply that any expressed enthusiasm for such goals would likely – and in the case of OCAM did – raise expectations to unattainable levels. And so while OCAM was initiated with a strong rhetorical boost, necessary productivity was unavailable. Still, it was adjudged to be a 'remarkably effective organization' given its successful establishment of a regional industrial programme, an airline, shared educational institutions, and a joint telecommunications system.[54] The lack of political will, opportunity, or perhaps adequate external threat prevented the full accomplishment of perceived potential.

It has been observed that not every religion requires a god, but all religions require a devil. If that be so, OCAM was endowed with the devil of President Nkrumah in Ghana, and so long as he pursued – or was perceived to pursue – subversion in West Africa there was a rallying point for OCAM. The elusive 'gods' of social development or reinforced solidarity among the members would remain distant no matter what transpired; they were definitionally unattainable for there was always more or better social development or solidarity to be attained. But the devil manifested in President Nkrumah was real, present, and destructible. So, perhaps the decline of OCAM came about as much as a result of the overthrow of Nkrumah as any other single factor. Had he continued in power, the rationale for OCAM would have been much more pressing and immediate.

The regional enthusiasm was reflected in proposals such as the idea of dual citizenship for all nationals of OCAM members proposed by President Houphouet-Boigny of the Ivory Coast (it was to be studied), or the suggestion that this organization was 'a stepping stone toward pan-Africanism.'[55] Regularly at the conclusion of speeches during conferences the cry was: 'Vive l'OCAM! Vive l'unité de l'Afrique!'

Consistent with French President de Gaulle's aggressive Francophilisme, a proposal appeared in the December 1966 edition of *Nations Nouvelles* proposing 'Francophonie', a 'cultural community' of French-speaking states throughout the world. Including such unlikely French-speaking locales as Louisiana in the United States and even Venezuela, Ethiopia and Norway as locations where French is an 'obligatory foreign language', the community was proposed. 'Francophonie is defined as a culture – that is, as a white system of intellectual and moral values.'[56] Philip Allen addresses the ulterior motive of the African states in supporting Franco-phonie: It would afford an opportunity to sustain ties with the Maghreb states. However, he observes, the concept represents 'more a pattern of behaviour than an organization.'[57] Even though the French see themselves having one of the four or five great civilizations founded on unity of language, and even though 24 states were included in the proposal, no more than 0.1 per cent of the world's population thinks in French.[58] President Senghor was authorized at this organizing conference to travel throughout Africa to 'take a sounding' regarding the proposed Francophone commonwealth.[59] Senghor and President Bourguiba of Tunisia, the co-author of the proposal, outlined steps to the commonwealth, e.g., an African council on higher education, interparliamentary meetings, and a franc zone. Though President de Gaulle was reported to be unenthusiastic about the idea, his Minister of State for Foreign Affairs, Jean de Broglie was reported as observing that France would 'naturally take a general position of sympathy and interest, without, however, departing from its care to avoid arousing unfriendly criticism.'[60] At least two conferences did transpire: the 'First Conference of Wholly or Partially French-Speaking Countries' in Niamey, February 1969, followed by the 'Conference of Francophone People' there a year later.[61] With the passing of General de Gaulle and the appearance of divisive and pressing international issues, the concept of Francophonie was pushed from the agenda of urgent items.

Table 6.2 indicates the membership of OCAM. Fourteen heads of state plus representatives of Rwanda and the Congo Republic ratified the OCAM Charter in a meeting at Tananarive, 27 June, 1966.

The following brief excerpts from the OCAM Charter indicate its proclaimed purpose as well as clearly indicating its members' limited expectations:

Art. 3:   The Organization shall seek to harmonize the action of the Member States in economic, social, technical, and cultural fields ... and to facilitate foreign policy consultations between them ...

Art. 5:   Conference of Chiefs of State ... shall be the supreme authority ...

Art. 7:   The Conference shall meet once yearly ...

Art. 9:   Any decision ... shall be binding ...

Art. 15: The ... Organization shall have an administrative general secretariat with its headquarters in Yaoundé ...

Art. 17: [The Secretariat] shall supervise the activities of joint enterprises, in particular, the multinational airline ... and the Union Africaine et Malgache des Postes et Télécommunications.

Art. 20: [The budget] shall be maintained by the contributions of the Member States, to be fixed on the basis of the net amount of their respective operating budgets.

As observed by Allen, OCAM was not a simple substitute for the French *Communauté*: 'Gossamer though it sometimes seems, OCAM offers a way of attaining some of the goods of independence without sacrificing the benefits of continued specialized dependence on the former metropole.'[62] Madagascar promptly found OCAM, however, to be expensive, top-heavy,

Table 6.2. *OCAM membership*

State	Date entered	Date withdrew
Benin (Dahomey)	February 1965	—
Cameroon	February 1965	1 July 1973
Central African Republic	February 1965	—
Chad	February 1965	3 July 1973
Congo	February 1965	22 September 1973
Gabon	February 1965	September 1976
Ivory Coast	February 1965	—
Madagascar	February 1965	4 August 1973
Mali	February 1965	1973
Mauritania	February 1965	9 July 1965
Mauritius	January 1970	—
Niger	February 1965	—
Rwanda	February 1965	—
Seychelles	1977	1977
Senegal	February 1965	—
Togo	February 1965	—
Upper Volta	February 1965	—
Zaire	May 1965	19 April 1972

and excessively ceremonial.[63] While on the one hand the implicit purpose of such a regional organization was to enhance independence, underlying OCAM was an implicit acquiescence in French domination in important areas of activity – as Allen observes, France was recognized as essential, but not adequate.[64]

Aside from the pre-existing agreements establishing Air Afrique and the postal and telecommunications union, the Charter, as can be seen from the salient excerpts above, clearly reflected a remarkably low level of consensus, even for a large number of newly-independent states, particularly in the light of the predecessor organizations which existed during the process of aggregating interests. While it is usual for international organizations to express vague objectives in their basic documents, the nebulous nature of OCAM as read in its Charter is striking. Nonetheless, there is still the opportunity for frustrated expectations among the citizenry who have rapidly rising visions of an improved life – and which they may expect the organization to further.

OCAM's Secretary-General observed in 1972 that OCAM had three advantages other international organizations lacked: a) OCAM had first-hand information about international problems; b) it facilitated coordination of the positions of its members; and c) it augmented their weight in the process of decision.[65] Viewing this observation in the light of the licence normally taken by diplomats, it is clear that even the organization's chief executive had little expectation of great accomplishments. Rather, as Secretary-General Kane observed, the organization can be expected to 'agitate to weave a veritable net of reciprocal interests' which each state is able to get something out of.[66] Nowzad points out that there is a basis for industrial development in West Africa.[67] A large aggregate population and a low gross national product suggest at least the potential for a more viable market if organized regionally rather than individually. The small populations of several West African states further suggest that larger-scale markets must be achieved if substantial development is to be expected.

The most significant international role OCAM filled during its early stages was involvement in the Congo civil war. After deploring problems confronting the OAU, OCAM expressed the sentiment that continuation of the problem in the Congo was a permanent danger to the OAU's existence 'considering foreign covetousness which is growing in Africa' and recommending 'prudence and vigilance' to all.[68] The organization advocated aid to the legal government, a position which aligned the members with the West and against radical and revisionist regimes in Africa and elsewhere. An unsuccessful effort was made to resolve the Nigerian-Biafran war.

One of the most visible technical aspects of OCAM was L'accord Africaine et Malgache sur le Sucre, a sugar marketing agreement signed in October 1966. This had the effect of creating a price support system within a common marketing area. The net effect, however, was for exporting states to subsidize sugar purchases by poorer neighbours because of the requirement of satisfying community needs at an agreed-upon price. Unhappiness with this led in 1973 to the withdrawal from the sugar accord of Zaire, Madagascar, Cameroon, Chad, Mauritania, and Congo.[69] Obviously there were differing opinions, for the Secretary-General reported at the June 1972 session: 'The accord has functioned not without difficulties . . ., but one can say that all in all it has given satisfaction to all the parties.'[70]

The zenith of the organization was symbolically recorded in a full-page advertisement in the *New York Times*, 4 February, 1973. There a large map of Africa with political boundaries was shaded to indicate the 13 current members. Reporting on the 1972 summit meeting in Lomé, much was made of the election of President Senghor. But its inherent weakness was also apparent: 'The OCAM States are among the most important world producers of sugar, peanuts, tropical woods, copper and manganese.'

Table 6.3. *Institutions associated with OCAM*

African and Malagasy Bureau of Legislative Studies
African and Malagasy Coffee Organization
African and Malagasy Institute of Applied Economics and Statistics
African and Malagasy Institute of Architecture
African and Malagasy Institute of Bilingualism
African and Malagasy Office of Industrial Property (OAMPI) (1962) Yaoundé
African and Malagasy Sugar Agreement, Fort Lamy
African and Malagasy Union of Development Banks (UAMBD) (1961)
African and Malagasy Union of Posts and Telecommunications (UAMPT) (1961)
African, Malagasy and Mauritania Cultural Institute (ICAM) Dakar
African Institute on Information (IAI) Libreville
Air Afrique (1961)
Architectural Institute (1973)
Center for Training of Cadres
Conference on Statisticians
Council on Administration of Information (1972)
Governmental Experts of OCAM on the Problems of Film Production
Institute of Sciences and Veterinary Medicine (EISMV) (1973) Dakar
Inter-State School of Engineers of Rural Equipment (1972) Ouagadougon (also
    known as The School for Engineering and Agricultural Equipment) (EIER)
Jurist Experts
Merchant Fleet (1973)
Organization for Meat Marketing, Niamey
Organization for the Development of Tourism in Africa (1973)

All these are primary products, and all are available not only from neighbouring African states but also from several other locations.

On the other hand, the intentions of OCAM were realistic: a plan to allocate at least one new regional industry to each of the OCAM member states. Had adequate resources been available, and had interested industries appeared at the appropriate times this modest goal might have been achieved. But political problems arose which precluded the organization's furthering even such a reasonable and potentially realistic goal.

An impressive array of institutions either pre-existed or were created or proposed during the existence of OCAM. A partial list is given in Table 6.3 (founding dates and sites are indicated where known).

Air Afrique was the most successful subsidiary of OCAM. With 11 founding member-states in 1961, it antedated both UAM and OCAM.

Despite its success, it was also clearly evident that there was a substantial degree of French control. Each founding member-state owned 6 per cent of the company with the remaining 34 per cent owned by the Société pour le Développement du Transport Aérien de l'Afrique (SOUDETRAF) which, in turn, is owned 25 per cent by the French government.[71] Internal airlines of the member-states are also owned one-third by SOUDETRAF. The organization which manages the airports in the member-states, the Agence de Securité de la Navigation, is owned half by France and half by the member-states.[72] During the decade of the 1960s, the airline's employees grew from 200 in number to 4000; gross income from US$8 million to US$80 million. Both economic and political problems beset the airline. First, claims against member-states rose from US$4.6 million in 1966 to over US$14 million by 1972. At the same time, the management reported political interference in the airline such as the unpaid use of planes to transport government officials, as well as increasing domination by Senegal and the Ivory Coast[73]

Along with the growing regional consciousness during this period came a students' organization, MEOCAM (Mouvement d'Etudiants de l'Organisation commune Africaine et Malgache), which was established in 1967 in Niamey with representatives of nine states present. It was noted that student unions in French-speaking Africa were under the control of the extreme left and students were urged to 'regroup at the OCAM level and effectively oppose their straying and brain-washed comrades who would like to prolong a situation in which Africa would have nothing to gain.'[74] Headquarters were established in Abidjan along with a centre in Paris.

A standard institutional device for economic cooperation is a postal and telecommunications union. OCAM's version, the Union Africaine et Malgache des Postes et Télécommunications (UAMPT), was established in September 1961, even before the organization itself was created. It has continued to this day.

As retrenchment dominated the political needs of OCAM, the then new Secretary-General Kane, reported at one official meeting that the plans for OCAM were as follows: (a) international negotiations, (b) product accords, (c) transport and telecommunications, (d) economic regulation, (e) training, and (f) banks.[75] Kane went on to suggest that OCAM would serve as intermediary with UN bodies and even represent such non-member-states as Burundi, Mali, Mauritania, and Somalia.

As with many bureaucratic institutions, the initial enthusiasm of its creators has been dissipated by subsequent demands, e.g., the transformation of the world economy in the mid-1970s. African crises such as the Tanzanian overthrow of Idi Amin's Ugandan regime, the rise of Libyan power, lack of resolution of the Namibian independence process, civil war in Zimbabwe, the Sahelian drought, conflict in the Western Sahara, and numerous other political conflicts and economic problems have occupied the OCAM members leaving its maintenance much in the hands of its staff. Several indications of pessimism were evident in OCAM's periodical *Chronique Mensuel* for August-September, 1974: there was an editorial which suggested that OCAM's detractors were waiting for the organization to fail but it concluded that this was a new stage, one of renewal. The commentary went on to complain that certain member-states appeared to consider OCAM their exclusive property monopolizing the organizations on their territories and hoarding the posts.[76]

As the Foreign Minister of Congo (Brazzaville) observed after his government had decided to retain its OCAM membership: OCAM should not become a political body; it was there that the least chance of unity would be found.[77] While it did not become a political body *per se*, manoeuvres of members into and out of the organization constituted politicization of a type inevitable during the first flush of independence in Africa. This finally led to the 1977 summit meeting's renunciation of a political activity.[78] But by then (after several months of postponement) the decision was too late and OCAM had shrunk to its current nine members.

Differences of objectives and perspective led to substantial conflict by 1974. Problems included 'growing alienation between states of West Africa and those of Central . . . Africa . . .'[79] Cameroon and Chad had withdrawn from Air Afrique, Zaire had diverged from the paths taken by many of the members, President Houphouët-Boigny's dialogue with South Africa alienated most members, differing levels of development, the success of the Entente, and the expulsion of West Africans by Zaire in 1971 all contributed to strains within OCAM.

According to DuBois, the participants in the 1972 conference simply avoided discussion of the divisive issues because it 'was in no one's interest to see it fail.'[80] While OCAM was saved in 1974 through the efforts of President Bokassa, and the headquarters was moved from Yaoundé to his capital of Bangui, it was not possible for the organization to prevent its inevitable decline. The election of President Habyarimana of Rwanda as President and its final heads of state meeting in Kigali signalled the transformation of OCAM from a French-speaking institution into an amorphous form which was not expected to adapt. The defection of OCAM's core members to the newly-organized West African Economic Community (CEAO) in 1974 offered further evidence, if such was needed, of new responses to newly-perceived policy objectives.[81]

Consideration of OCAM, and particularly its demise, must be conjoined with the activities of the European Economic Community (EEC), most especially the Yaoundé and Lomé agreements. The favoured access to both EEC markets and development assistance superseded the French relationship which had been at the heart of OCAM foreign relations at its founding.[82] That created the economic reality which circumscribed the functioning of OCAM. But also one must consider the theoretical context. Let us consider the latter first.

Ake observed, the '. . . degree of cultural homogeneity is the most important determinant of the level of political integration. However, it is possible for a political system to achieve a level of integration quite out of proportion to its cultural homogeneity.'[83] The political will that has kept the EEC alive has not been present to the necessary extent elsewhere, particularly not among newly-independent states.

It is argued by at least one observer that the Lomé agreement is actually a neocolonialist continuation of European economic domination. Dolan explains in detail the elements of his argument while allowing that the Lomé agreement is, at least, an improvement upon the Yaoundé agreement.[84] To the extent that OCAM participates in the Lomé-inspired trading arrangements it continues to reinforce French and European domination of long-standing trading patterns. On the other hand, if there is no viable alternative, such an arrangement may indeed be desirable.

A 1973 drop in sugar prices made it undesirable and economically impossible for states to adhere to the OCAM sugar accord. This served as justification for the withdrawal of several states and the ultimate abandonment of the agreement by the organization in 1977.[85] By 1979 the two most successful integrative efforts, Air Afrique and the postal union, were excluded from the organization.

The achievements of OCAM: an assessment

While OCAM is extant at the time of writing, it has been eclipsed by events, perceptions, and needs. The post-Second World War framework of international cooperation has proven to be inadequate to the needs of all participants, most particularly primary-producing agricultural states. But no creative alternative has been found to replace it. So, from the level of the UN, through regional and continental organizations, the organization of the peace which was the objective of world leaders at San Francisco in 1945, has been overtaken by events they only dimly foresaw. OCAM has survived to this point only because it has reflected a measure of adaptability as French-speaking states shuffled membership to accommodate new needs during the dynamic decade of the 1960s.

In evaluating the effects of OCAM on the populations of the participating states something more than the occasional pronouncements emanating from the meetings of heads of state, foreign ministers, or specialists on one field or another is necessary. The final measure of the success of a regional organization is apparent and measurable benefit for the participants. While perceived benefit or at least the absence of perceived net costs may be adequate political incentive to continue political participation, if there is no positive change in the lives of the citizens of the participating states, the organization can hardly be said to have succeeded.

Table 6.4 provides some rough data comparing OCAM states[86] with all other African states (except South Africa which would have skewed the data). There are clearly several caveats in considering this data. These are averages of averages derived from an unreliable base in many instances. The temporal limits are not derived from OCAM activities but from the

Table 6.4. *Comparison of OCAM with non-OCAM states: economic measures*

	Non-OCAM Africa	OCAM members (N=15)	All-Africa average	Line number
1978 GNP	389	298	352 (N=37)	1
1960–78 avg. per annum GNP per capita growth	1.91	1.186	1.61 (N=36)	2
Avg. annual inflation rate				
1960–70	3.03	5.47	4.02	3
1970–8	12.11	10.8	11.58	4
% change	+299.67	+97.44	188.06 (N=37)	5
% adult literacy				
1971	19.65	15.41	18.0	6
1975	35.76	19.92	28.66	7
% change	+81.98	+29.3	59.22 (N=29)	8
Life expectancy				
1978	48.69	44.40	46.95	9
1971	45.17	43.06	44.0	10
% change	+7.79	+3.1	6.70 (N=37)	11
Avg. per capita index of food production (1969–71=100)	89.27	92.80	90.7 (N=37)	12
Average annual growth rate percentage				
GDP 1960–70	4.21	3.86	4.07 (N=37)	13
GDP 1970–8	3.50	2.63	3.14 (N=36)	14
% change	−16.86	−31.86	−22.85	15
Agric. 1970–8	1.51	.967	1.28 (N=31)	16
Indus. 1960–70	8.12	9.17	8.54 (N=15)	17
Indus. 1970–8	3.26	5.75	4.27 (N=32)	18
% change	−59.85	−37.30	−50.00	19

Table 6.4. (*continued*)

	Non-OCAM Africa	OCAM members (N=15)	All-Africa average	Line number
Mfg. 1960–70	7.69	10.65	8.60 (N=13)	20
Mfg. 1970–8	3.78	3.14	3.56 (N=26)	21
% change	−50.85	−70.52	−58.60	22
Mfg. % of GDP				
1960	9.42	6.21	7.5	23
1978	10.77	11.6	10.68	24
% change	+14.33	+86.80	+42.40	25
Priv. consumption				
1960–70	3.69	4.68	4.01 (N=31)	26
1970–8	3.43	3.01	3.37 (N=36)	27
% change	−7.05	−35.68	−15.96	28
Pbl. consump.				
1960–70	11.45	14.87	12.53 (N=36)	29
1970–8	16.90	17.60	16.89 (N=35)	30
% change	+47.60	+18.36	+34.80	31
Terms of trade				
1970=100, 1960	99.74	92.47	100.88	32
1978	118	94.2	104.47	33
% change	+18.31	+1.87	+3.56 (N=32)	34
% exports primary products (incl. fuels)				
1960	89.67	95.4	92.6 (N=30)	35
1977	88.00	90.8	90.5 (N=35)	36
% change	−1.86	−4.82	−2.27	37
% exports to developing countries				
1960	23.5	21.62	21.13 (N=30)	38
1978	22.5	24.67	22.76 (N=34)	39
% change	+4.26	+14.11	+7.71	40
Secondary enrolments as % of relevant age group				
1960	4.59	1.79	3.06 (N=35)	41
1977	16.18	13.27	14.26 (N=31)	42
% change	+252.51	+641.34	+366.01	43
Debt service as % of GNP				
1970	2.09	1.19	1.67 (N=33)	44
1978	3.19	2.91	2.86 (N=34)	45
% change	+52.63	+144.54	+71.26	46
IBRD External public debt (US$ millions)				
1969	90.7	83.7	79	47
1975	94.5	312.4	92	48
% change	+4.1	+261.29	+16.46	49
As % of exports '69	86	69.6	19.3	50
As % of exports '75	95.7	84.3	24.5	51
% change	+11.28	+21.12	+26.94	52
As % GNP '69	21.04	18.2	19.9	53
As % GNP '75	24.6	24.5	25.3	54
% change	+16.92	+34.62	+27.14	55

Sources: 1960–70 data from *Africa: Economic Growth Trends* (U.S. Agency for International Development, Washington, 1972). 1970–9 data from *World Development Report 1980* (International Bank for Reconstruction and Development, Washington, 1980)

activities of the World Bank. The indicated changes are often changes in *rate*, not in the absolute measure of the phenomenon considered. Nonetheless, with these caveats entered, it is still apparent that in many significant measures of quality of life citizens of non-OCAM states on the average were better off than were the OCAM citizens in 1978.

For example, non-OCAM citizens had a GNP that was about 30 per cent higher than that of OCAM residents in 1978 (line 1). Their GNP *per capita* growth rate in the decade of the 1960s was about 40 per cent better than that of OCAM residents (line 2). Adult literacy was both substantially lower and growing less rapidly in the 1970s for OCAM residents (line 8) and their life expectancy was shorter (line 9). Their average annual gross domestic product growth rate was both lower and declining more rapidly from the 1960s to the 1970s than for non-OCAM residents (lines 13–15). Agricultural production in the 1970s grew at only about two-thirds the rate of non-OCAM states.

Depending upon whether one prefers private or public sector growth, the figures in these areas are good or bad. The growth rate of private consumption declined by over a third from the 1960s to the 1970s for OCAM states while it remained almost steady in the rest of Africa (lines 26–28). While the public consumption growth rate changed less for OCAM states, the 1970s growth rate was about the same for both groups (lines 29–30). Terms of trade for OCAM states improved only slightly from 1960 to 1978 while there was a 20 per cent improvement in other states (lines 32–34). Though debt service as a per cent of gross national product more than doubled during the 1970s, it still remained slightly behind non-OCAM states (lines 44–46), but actual debt rose dramatically compared to the rest of Africa (lines 47–55).

In several financial areas OCAM states stood out: The inflation rate in OCAM states both grew less rapidly and was at a lower level than for other African states (lines 3–5). Their level of per capita food production was slightly above other African states (line 12). The industrial sector growth rate was better throughout this entire period (lines 17–19), and the manufacturing growth rate was marginally better though it declined more from the decade of the 1960s to the 1970s (lines 20–22). There were not clear differences in primary products as percentages of exports (lines 35–37) or percentage of exports sent to other developing states, though there was a distinct increase for OCAM while there was a slight loss in the rest of Africa (lines 38–40). The rapid increase in percentage of secondary school students, 640 per cent for OCAM versus 250 per cent for non-OCAM states, still does not conceal the fact that only 13 and 16 per cent, respectively, of eligible students were in school (lines 41–43).

Table 6.5. *Haas-Schmitter Model applied to OCAM*

Model characteristics	OCAM
Background conditions	
Size of units	Small
Pluralism	Little; uniparty states, homogeneous levels of political and economic development
Elite complementarity	Given the dynamism of political development and external pressures irrelevant or dichotomous to OCAM, this is not highly developed
Conditions at time of union	
Governmental purposes	Despite expressed unanimity, many other factors intruded, competing and conflicting claims upon government attentions left little energy for OCAM
Power of union	Barely discernible
Process conditions	
Decision-making styles	Very much *ad hoc* – lack of evidence that efforts were being made to evolve a body of tradition upon which union could be built and expanded
Rate of transactions	Low level for OCAM *per se*; relations flowing through France and other organizations could conceivably have been funnelled through OCAM
Adaptability of governments	Conceivable, but this was not a high priority political goal

On balance, there is little to distinguish OCAM states from the rest of Africa on the basis of empirical data as presented here. Particularly, it does not appear that individual benefits are greater for OCAM residents. Perhaps a long-term benefit will accrue if the fruits of industrial growth are spread around equitably. The continued French domination of the economies of OCAM states leaves this in doubt, however.

At a conceptual level an evaluation of OCAM reveals even less about which to be optimistic. Taking Haas and Schmitter's model of political integration, which is also relevant to other integrative attempts, we find a decided absence of success in virtually every measure. The Haas-Schmitter categories are indicated to the left in Table 6.5; on the right is this writer's judgement about OCAM's success.[87]

Not surprisingly, on the Haas-Schmitter scale OCAM comes out poorly. There are not the requisite circumstances for effective integration in West

Africa. The fact that OCAM has survived 16 years while many similar efforts proved to be more ephemeral may bode well, not for OCAM, but for a successor organization which could emerge from the ashes of OCAM should a political thrust from a respected leader (similar to President Senghor's stalwart efforts to keep OCAM alive) coincide with a broadly perceived political need for a regional organization.

A fruitful adaptation would be to incorporate English-speaking states into future integrative efforts. Physically working around such West African states as Ghana, Sierra Leone, and Nigeria renders practical functionalism a farce. On the other hand, the recent dramatic development of Nigeria could easily mean that it would dominate any organization to which it belonged making voluntary cooperation difficult at best. If, however, it were excluded, the potential for an adversarial process of development could be counterproductive.

The new awareness of North-South issues, conflict, and dialogue has given a new focus to organizational content and context. As Shaw puts it in discussing the OAU: 'Changes in the world system as well as in the African sub-system have served to undermine the tenuous unity and to revive the factionalism that characterized the continent in the early 1960s.'[88] This, overshadowed as it is particularly at the time of writing, by threat of nuclear war, has rendered economic regional organizations in developing areas obsolete. The surge of behaviour patterns associated with independence has waned; the futility of much of the claims to independence especially in the realm of economics and finance has become apparent. The challenge now is to construct a relationship between given developing states – in the case of OCAM in French-speaking Africa – with former metropoles in a way that gives not only the appearance of integrity and sovereign exercise of power by the African state, but also acknowledges inevitable ties with France in a variety of activities.

The similarities which gave rise to OCAM – common language, common poverty, common colonial experience, and so on – also contained the elements of limited potential for the organization. For example, the potential for air travel among impoverished states, trade between states producing the same or similar agricultural surpluses, and cooperation *vis à vis* France when there are local animosities to be reckoned with have all contributed to parameters for OCAM that have limited the actual growth of OCAM as well as its potential. Despite optimism expressed by various observers,[89] the potential for such a regional organization is necessarily limited and in need of thoroughgoing transformation periodically. Perhaps the axiom of international politics that an external threat is a generator of internal cohesion can be looked to for guidance when OCAM might be stimulated to reorganize and regenerate.

Short of the coming of a day when genuine humanitarian concern will be displayed by either industrialized states for developing areas or by more developed African states for impoverished neighbours, it is unlikely that much can be expected to emerge from OCAM. Infrastructure cooperation such as posts and telecommunications, protection of industrial property, and the like are both intellectually defensible and visibly beneficial to all participants at very low cost; they are likely to continue except in the face of extreme disagreement. Trading arrangements will languish so long as industrialization eludes the member-states. Lack of contiguity is also a problem: The detachment of Madagascar and Mauritius as well as the intrusion of several English-speaking states compounds an already difficult infrastructure problem. If regionalism is to succeed, as is regularly observed, there must be the perception on the part of decision-makers that benefits of participation outweigh costs. The perceived balance sheet for OCAM is still unclear; hence the organization continues without either abandonment by its members, as was the case with the East African Community in 1977, or determined efforts to strengthen and expand its operations as has occurred in the EEC.

NOTES

1 Robert S. Wood, 'Public Order and Political Integration in Contemporary International Theory', *Virginia Journal of International Law*, xiv, (1974), p. 426.
2 Ethiopia, Ghana, Guinea, Liberia, Sudan, as well as the then-Union of South Africa.
3 From the dissolution of French Africa: Central African Republic, Chad, Gabon, Congo, Dahomey (later Benin), Madagascar (Malagasy Republic), Mali, Mauritania, Ivory Coast, Niger, Senegal, and Upper Volta. Also in that year: Cameroon, Togo, Nigeria, Somalia, and Zaire (formerly the Congo).
4 Wood, 'Public Order', p. 447.
5 See, for example, Michael F. Lofchie (ed.), *The State of the Nations; Constraints on Development in Independent Africa*, University of California Press, Berkeley, 1971, particularly Chapter 2.
6 Wood, 'Public Order', p. 425.
7 See, for example, regarding the development of the European Community, Denis de Rougemont, *The Idea of Europe*, World Publishing Co., Cleveland, 1968; Ernst B. Haas, *The Uniting of Europe; Political, Social and Economic Forces, 1950–1957*, Stanford University Press, Stanford, 1968; Howard Bliss, *The Political Development of the European Community*, Xerox College

Publishing, Waltham, 1970; Michael Curtis, *Western European Integration*, Harper and Row, New York, 1965; and for a more recent evaluation G. N. Minshull, *The New Europe; An Economic Geography of the EEC*, Hodder and Stoughton, London, 1980.

8 T. G. Ramamurthi, 'The Dynamics of Regional Integration in West Africa', *India Quarterly*, xxvi, (1970), p. 257.

9 James O. O'Leary, *Systems Theory and Regional Integration: The Market Model of International Politics*, University Press of America, Washington, 1978, p. 1.

10 See, for example, Andrew M. Kamarck, *The Economics of African Development*, Praeger Publishers, New York, 1971, especially Chapter iv; or Dennis L. Cohen and John Daniel, eds., *Political Economy of Africa*, Longman, London, 1981.

11 Miguel S. Wionczek, 'Requisites for Viable Economic Integration' in Joseph S. Nye, Jr. (ed.), *International Regionalism*, Little, Brown & Co., Boston, 1968, p. 293.

12 O'Leary, *Systems Theory*, p. 6.

13 Z. D. Onwenu, 'Economic Cooperation in Africa: Lessons for Industrialization within ECOWAS', in Vremudia P. Diejomaoh and Milton A. Iyoha, eds., *Industrialization in the Economic Community of West African States (ECOWAS)*, Heinemann Educational Books Ltd., Ibadan, 1980, p. 336.

14 Lawrence V. Gould, Jr., 'International Organization in the World System: Implications for a Multi-Level, Contextual Approach', paper presented at the International Studies Association, 1977.

15 Dahomey became Benin in 1975. During the OCAM period it was regularly referred to as Dahomey in the literature. Both names will appear here.

16 A depiction of early African regional groupings and conferences appears in I. William Zartman, *International Relations in the New Africa*, Prentice-Hall, Englewood Cliffs, N.J., 1966, pp. 18–19.

17 The Brazzaville group consisted of the twelve French-speaking sub-Saharan states – excluding the former Belgian Congo: Cameroon, Central African Republic, Chad, Congo, Dahomey, Gabon, Ivory Coast, Malagasy Republic, Mauritania, Niger, Upper Volta, Senegal.

18 Victor D. DuBois, 'The Search for Unity in French-Speaking Africa', American University Field Staff *Reports* vii, 3, (1965), p. 4.

19 The Monrovia Group: Ethiopia, Somalia, Libya, Nigeria, Sierra Leone, Liberia, Togo, Tunisia, Mauritania, Senegal, Chad, Gambia, Niger, Upper Volta, Dahomey, Ivory Coast, Gabon, Cameroon, Congo, Central African Republic, Malagasy Republic – virtually all African states outside the Casablanca group. See, for example, Colin Legum, *Pan-Africanism*, Praeger Publishers, New York, 1962, Chapter iv.

20 Doudou Thiam, *The Foreign Policy of African States*, Praeger Publishers, New York, 1965, p. 57. Discussion of the process of African groupings is found in Thiam, pp. 49–72 as well as Vernon McKay, *Africa in World Politics*, Harper and Row, New York, 1963, Chapter 7 and Legum, *Pan-Africanism*, Chapter iv.

21 David Williams, 'How Deep the Split in West Africa?', *Foreign Affairs*, xl, (1961), p. 121.

22 *Ibid*, p. 123.

23 *Ibid*, p. 127.
24 See, for example, Kwame Nkrumah, *I Speak of Freedom*, Heinemann, London, 1961.
25 Zdenek Červenka, *The Unfinished Quest for Unity*, Julian Freidman, London, 1977, pp. 2–3.
26 *Chronique Mensuel* No. 30 (June-July, 1973), p. 30.
27 The text of the OCAM Charter appears, *inter alia*, in American Society of International Law *International Legal Materials* (1967), pp. 53–6.
28 *Ibid*.
29 'From Brazzaville Twelve to OCAM', *Africa Report*, February 1968, p. 53.
30 Victor D. DuBois, 'UAM at the Crossroads', *Africa Report*, April 1963, p. 3.
31 Bela Belassa and Ardy Stoutjesdijk, 'Economic Integration Among Developing Countries', World Bank Reprint Series: Number 30, September, 1975, p. 37.
32 Joseph S. Nye, Jr., 'Patterns and Catalysts in Regional Integration', in Nye, *International Regionalism*, p. 336.
33 Reginald H. Green and Ann Seidman, *Unity or Poverty? The Economics of Pan-Africanism*, Penguin Books, Baltimore, 1968, passim.
34 Wionczek, 'Requisites for Viable Economic Integration', p. 292.
35 Williams, 'How Deep the Split in West Africa?' p. 119.
36 *New York Times*, 19 August 1979. Participants in the Senegal Basin scheme are Senegal, Mali, and Mauritania. The Chad Basin scheme includes Chad, Cameroon, Niger, and Nigeria.
37 *The New York Times*, 11 October 1981.
38 See, for example, 'West African Nations Mark Monetary Union', *IMF Survey* 1:9 (December 11, 1972), p. 144.
39 Lawrence V. Gould, 'International Organization in the World System: Implications for a Multi-Level, Contextual Approach', paper presented at International Studies Association, St. Louis, U.S.A., March 1977, p. 10.
40 *Ibid*, p. 11.
41 *Ibid*, p. 4.
42 The Casablanca group consisted of: Ghana, Guinea, Mali, Morocco, Egypt, and the Algerian Provisional Government.
43 Quoted in Diakha Dieng, 'From UAM to OCAM', *Africa Forum*, i, (1965), p. 33.
44 Victor DuBois, 'UAM at the Crossroads', *Africa Report*, April 1963, p. 3.
45 *Ibid*, p. 4.
46 *Ibid*, p. 3.
47 DuBois, 'Search for Unity', Part 1, p. 17.
48 *Ibid*.
49 See, for example, Červenka, *The Unfinished Quest*.
50 Dieng, 'From UAM to OCAM', p. 33.
51 *West Africa* quoted in *Africa Report*, October 1962, p. 28.
52 DuBois, 'Search for Unity', Part 3, p. 5.
53 This is fully discussed in Dieng, 'From UAM to OCAM'.
54 DuBois, 'Crisis in OCAM', *American University Field Staff Report*, May 1972, p. 1.
55 DuBois, 'Search for Unity', Part 1, p. 16.
56 *Africa Report*, June 1968, pp. 12–13.
57 Philip M. Allen, 'Francophonie Considered', *Africa Report*, June 1968, p. 9.

58 *Ibid*, p. 6–7.
59 *Africa Report*, 'News in Brief, October 1966, pp. 25–6.
60 *Ibid*, January 1967, p. 25.
61 *Ibid*, May-June, 1969, and May 1970.
62 Philip M. Allen, 'Madagascar and OCAM: the Insular Approach to Regionalism', *Africa Report*, January 1966, p. 15.
63 *Ibid*, p. 18.
64 *Ibid*, p. 17.
65 *Chronique Mensuel de l'Organisation Commune Africaine et Malgache*, No. 20, July, 1972, p. 3.
66 *Ibid*, p. 5.
67 Bahram Nowzad, 'Economic Integration in Central and West Africa', *International Monetary Fund Staff Papers*, xvi (March 1969), pp. 201–202.
68 *Africa Digest*, xii:5 (April 1965) p. 144.
69 *New York Times*, 13 August 1973.
70 *Chronique Mensuel de l'Organisation Commune Africaine et Malgache, ibid*, p. 5 (translated by the writer).
71 Andrew M. Kamarck, *The Economics of African Development*, Praeger Publishers, New York, 1971, p. 51.
72 *Ibid*.
73 DuBois, 'Crisis in OCAM', p. 4.
74 *Africa Report*, March 1967, p. 21.
75 Falilou Kane, address before the African Center for Education and Research for Development Administration (CAFRAD) Tangier, 27 June 1972, reported in *Chronique Mensuel* No. 30 (July, 1972).
76 *Chronique Mensuel*, No. 37 (August-September, 1974), n.p.
77 *Africa Digest*, xiii, 6 (June, 1966), p. 136.
78 Mauritania was particularly unhappy with OCAM's political overtones which she saw competing with the OAU. Reported by I. William Zartman in 'Mauritania's Stand on Regionalism', *Africa Report* xi, 1 (January 1966), p. 20.
79 Victor DuBois, 'Crisis in OCAM', p. 1.
80 *Ibid*, p. 8.
81 See *West Africa*, 28 January 1974.
82 See for example, *The Financial Times* (London), 23 March 1973, or *The Times* (London), 17 October 1973.
83 Claude Ake, *A Theory of Political Integration*, Odyssey Press, New York, 1967, p. 2.
84 Michael B. Dolan, 'The Lomé Convention and Europe's Relationship with the Third World: A Critical Analysis', paper presented to the International Studies Association, St. Louis, 1977.
85 See *African Development*, September 1973, p. 10.
86 All states that ever held OCAM membership were included in the OCAM calculations.
87 Taken from Ernst B. Haas and Philippe C. Schmitter, 'Economics and Differential Patterns of Political Integration', *International Organization* xviii, 4 (1964).
88 Timothy M. Shaw, 'Africa' in Werner J. Feld and Gavin Boyd (eds.), *Comparative Regional Systems*, Praeger Publishers, New York, 1980, p. 364.

89 Claude Ake, *A Political Economy of Africa*, Longman, London, 1981, p. 169. See also DuBois, 'Search for Unity'.

7   Competition, conflict and decline in the Union Douanière et Economique de l'Afrique Centrale (UDEAC)

LYNN KRIEGER MYTELKA

Introduction

Since the mid-1970s, African regional integrative systems have been in decline. Some have ceased to exist; others are stagnating. While a few newcomers, ECOWAS, for example, do dot the institutional landscape, progress towards the implementation of treaty provisions which would give impetus to an integration process has been slow to the point of immobility.

In this chapter an argument is advanced to explain why regional integration did not emerge as an important instrument in a self-reliant development strategy during the first two African post-independence decades. An analysis of the Customs and Economic Union of Central Africa (UDEAC) illustrates some of the main points of this argument. Here the conditions under which competitive nationalism is evoked to the detriment of industrial coordination are brought out. Highlighted, in particular, is the emphasis on trade liberalization as the engine of integration in a context shaped by the existence of market-segmenting fiscal policies and excessively generous investment codes. Under such conditions and in view of the outward-oriented pattern of production and the absence of industrial planning, it was inevitable that few benefits would be generated by the regional integration process. A declining spiral of disinterest thus resulted.

Not until efforts to restructure the international division of labour through North-South negotiations had reached an impasse[1] and pressures resulting from the global economic crisis had mounted, was a reconsideration of the role which regional integration might play in the development of UDEAC member countries undertaken.[2] A thoroughgoing reconceptualization of the integration process and its mechanisms, as this study shows, will be required, however, if UDEAC is to be reoriented to serve the goals of a self-reliant development strategy.

UDEAC: the historical background

On 23 June 1959, shortly before independence was granted to the Central African Republic (CAR), Chad, Congo and Gabon – the four members of the former Fédération de l'Afrique Equatoriale Française (AEF) – signed a convention creating an equatorial African customs union. It can with some justification be argued that the Union douanière équatoriale (UDE) was a necessary bridge between the colonial federation and a more extensive customs and economic union. By providing an institutional framework for continued association, yet granting a number of concessions to Gabon which reduced the financial burden it had shouldered under the AEF[3], the UDE helped attenuate the conflict between those leaders pressing for political unification and those who advocated a minimum infringement of national sovereignty. It also permitted the emergence of a consensus on the need to enlarge the membership of this regional economic grouping to include neighbouring Cameroon, a former UN Trusteeship administered by France and unattached to either the French equatorial or West African federations.

But far from being an innovation, the UDE also represented the continuation of pre-existing vertical ties which bound the equatorial African states as much to France as to each other. Prior agreement to ensure the free flow of capital throughout the Equatorial African region had in fact already been reached in the accords setting up the Franc Zone with its Paris-based Banque centrale des états de l'Afrique équatoriale et du Cameroun. Each of the UDE states and the Cameroon, moreover, had been persuaded by France to adopt an investment code under which foreign private investment was guaranteed against the risks of nationalization and non-transferability of profits or capital. By granting firms a special status and exempting them from the payment of corporate profits taxes, property taxes and import duties on raw materials, intermediates and capital goods used in the production process, the investment codes also guaranteed the profitability of these foreign investments. Indeed, this system of incentives induced investors to create far more capital and import-intensive import-substituting manufacturing enterprises than were warranted by the factor proportions prevalent in these countries. The conclusion of a customs union provided the conditions within which the resulting high-cost domestic production would be guaranteed a market. Oligopolistic market structures emerged and remained protected by the common external tariff, thereby permitting these high costs to be passed along to the consumers in high prices. In the absence of mechanisms to reorient extroverted productive structures and transportation links or to plan for a more equitable distribution of the gains from integration, the Union douanière équatoriale merely reinforced the dependent character of the central African economies.

On 8 December 1964 the UDE and Cameroon signed a treaty creating the Customs and Economic Union of Central Africa (UDEAC). Despite some references to the harmonization of development plans, transport and industrial policies, the UDEAC Treaty, as the UDE Convention before it, fundamentally created a customs union within which trade was envisaged as the main engine of industrial development. Both the preamble and the operative portions of the Treaty exhibit this orientation.

During negotiations leading to the creation of UDEAC, opposition to the inclusion of Cameroon as a full member had come from Chad and the CAR, neither of which had progressed far in the development of a manufacturing sector, but each of which had plans to move in this direction. Unlimited and duty-free entry of Cameroonian manufactures, to the extent that these were cheaper, would potentially frustrate their industrialization efforts. The Customs Union, set up under Article 28 of the UDEAC Treaty was thus modified to limit free trade in manufactures by the creation of a single tax system. Mechanisms to ensure that these less industrially developed countries would receive an equitable share of new investment in the region were also proposed in the Treaty.

The single tax system and the costs and benefits of regional integration

Under the single tax system set up in accordance with Articles 59 and 60 of the UDEAC Treaty, goods manufactured in UDEAC and sold in more than one of its member-states are subject to a single tax (*taxe unique*) whose rates are fixed collectively by the UDEAC Management Committee (Comité de Direction). This tax is levied to the exclusion of all import duties and taxes on goods used in the manufacturing process and all domestic taxation on the finished product.

The rate of the single tax is always lower than the customs duty which would otherwise have applied to manufactured goods traded among these countries. This is in keeping with the original conception of the single tax as a system designed (a) to stimulate industrialization by enhancing the competitive position of local manufactures relative to foreign imports through a reduction in the overall rates of taxation when compared to the common external tariff and (b) to provide each of the member-states with the possibility of recovering a certain percentage of the revenues it otherwise would have earned through tariffs imposed on third party imports.[4] The latter was particularly important as over 50 per cent of total government revenues in the UDEAC countries in the early 1960s came from import and export taxes.[5]

The 1964 Treaty made it clear that the imposition of all other duties and taxes on intra-regional imports or exports was prohibited (Article 28). The UDEAC Treaty, however, does not imply that the single tax system is a stimulant to trade and indeed it actually limits the free circulation of locally manufactured goods to only those goods which have been accepted under the single tax system. Other manufactures might, thus, be subjected, at the discretion of the importing state, to a tax equal to the rate of the external tariff and duties or such goods might be barred from sale in the local market.

In negotiations leading to the creation of UDEAC, Chadian and Centrafrican delegates argued that uniform rates of taxation under the single tax system would unfairly advantage the more industrially developed countries at the expense of the less-industrialized countries. Compensation for the unequal trade advantages which Cameroon and the Congo were expected to secure could be forthcoming, they argued, if the 'single' tax rates were allowed to vary, not only as between products but for the same products manufactured in different countries – irrespective of whether the manufacturer, generally a subsidiary of a foreign multinational firm was in fact the same. Article 62 of the 1964 Treaty grants the principle of variable single tax rates during a six-year transitional period.

To a certain extent permitting the rate of the single tax to vary had a useful role to play in this first phase of UDEAC, marked as it was by significant differences in degrees of industrialization among the member-states. An aggregate analysis of variations in the single tax rates during the first five years of UDEAC thus revealed that Cameroon and the Congo had permitted Chadian and Centrafrican industries to remain protected in their home markets by accepting that their own goods be taxed at a higher rate when sold in these inland countries.[6] Variations in single tax rates also provided additional revenue for the poorer inland states. Other mechanisms set up under the 1964 Treaty to attenuate conflict and competition among the member-states, however, were not as successful.

It was Chadian and Centrafrican anxiety about their future industrialization possibilities that led to the inclusion in the Preamble to the 1964 Treaty of a call for 'the adoption of a procedure for the equitable distribution of industrialization projects and the coordination of development programmes in the different production sectors.' Some operational substance was given to these preambular objectives in the Third Section of the UDEAC Treaty. But there, negotiators rejected a CAR proposal which would have ensured that in the interest of harmonious and balanced development, diversification and equity in the distribution of future industries be spelled out and consultation be made obligatory on the creation of a wide range of new industries. Instead, Articles 51, 52 and 53 of the Treaty made consultation obligatory only in the case of industries designed to serve the whole UDEAC market and falling, therefore, under the provisions of the single tax system. Competition between UDEAC states to attract foreign investment into new industries would thus continue and would become one of the most contentious issues within the integrative system. This occurred in spite of the subsequent adoption of a common investment *'code-cadre'*, pursuant to Article 45 of the Treaty, intended to limit competition among the UDEAC member-states by harmonizing the incentives which could be offered to investors.

While the Preamble makes clear the intention to compensate the less-industrialized member-states for their economic disadvantage and ensure, in the future, an equitable distribution of the benefits derived from the integration effort (Preamble, 1964 UDEAC Treaty), Article 38 which sets up the UDEAC Solidarity Fund makes no reference to these broader goals of equity and compensation. It does not fix a percentage of import duties or other taxes to provide an automatic source of revenue for the solidarity fund, as had been the case in the UDE. Instead, the UDEAC Council of Heads of State was obliged to determine the lump-sum contribution each country would make to the solidarity fund on an annual basis. The proceeds of this fund were distributed to the CAR and Chad on a 35:65 basis.

From the outset the process of determining the size of the solidarity fund was highly contentious as it proved exceedingly difficult to arrive at a consensus on the way that gains and losses from integration would be measured and what the contributions would thus be.[7] Repeatedly, countries were induced to contribute through appeals to solidarity but this introduced an element of uncertainty as to the size of the fund each year. In 1968 Cameroon and Congo each contributed 500 million CFA francs (F CFA), the CAR and Chad each paid into the fund some 300 million F CFA and Gabon contributed a further 250 million.

Despite the transfers effected through the solidarity fund, Chadian and CAR leaders never felt that their countries were adequately compensated for revenue losses due to trade diversion and for the limited gains they realized in the industrial sphere. To this were added conflicts over the application of Article 33 of the UDEAC Treaty which stipulated measures to prevent double taxation of imported goods transiting through a coastal state for ultimate consumption in an inland state. Given the budgetary difficulties of several of the UDEAC states such transfers were only made after considerable delay and much protest.

By 1968 dissatisfaction with UDEAC led Chad and the CAR to consider a new union with Zaire. On 2 April 1968 the Charter creating the Union des Etats de l'Afrique Centrale (UEAC) among these three countries was signed in Fort Lamy, now Ndjamena. Encouraged by concessions from other UDEAC states, notably to retain the solidarity fund and its financial transfers, and under pressure from France, however, the CAR returned to UDEAC on 9 December 1968, shortly before the denunciation of the Treaty would have become effective.[8]

Although many observers writing in 1969 predicted the collapse of UDEAC in the wake of Chad's withdrawal, the immediate reaction was rather to renew interest in strengthening the customs and economic union. Negotiations with France in 1972 led to a greater indigenization of the renamed Banque des Etats de l'Afrique Centrale (BEAC) and its relocation from Paris to Yaoundé. Several factors also convinced the UDEAC leadership of the need to revise the 1964 Treaty.

First, it had become evident that the gains from integration were limited. This led to a decision to place greater emphasis on sector planning and to create a UDEAC financing body to ensure that adequate funds for new, regionally inspired investments, would be available.

Second, trade among the UDEAC member-states had not risen significantly since 1966, the year in which the UDEAC Treaty went into effect. In fact, as Table 7.1 reveals, imports from UDEAC as a percentage of total world imports fell from a high of 4.5 per cent in 1966 to 4.1 per cent in 1969 and to a low of 2.4 per cent in 1972. Mechanisms to stimulate trade would have to be designed.

Third, problems of food production and domestic resource development also emerged during this period. In three of the UDEAC countries (Cameroon, CAR and Gabon) between 70 and 80 per cent of the active population is in agriculture and in Cameroon and the CAR agriculture contributes some 30 per cent to Gross Domestic Product. Despite the important role of agriculture in the UDEAC economies, the 1964 Treaty was noticeably silent on the need for coordination or cooperation in agriculture, forestry, husbandry or fisheries. Not until 1971 did the Council of Heads of State[9] recommend that the Secretariat investigate areas for future cooperation in the agricultural sector. When on 7 December 1974 the heads of state of the four UDEAC countries signed a revised UDEAC Treaty, agriculture took its place alongside natural resources, technology, posts, telecommunications, transportation and energy as sectors for future regional cooperation (Article 45, 1974 Treaty).

Table 7.1. *Intra-regional trade in UDEAC; 1966–77 (billion F CFA)*

	1966	1969	1972	1975	1977
Cameroon					
Total world imports	33.0	51.4	73.2	120.8	183.5
Single tax imports from UDEAC	1.1	0.6	0.4	0.1	0.8
UDEAC as a % of total	3.3	1.2	0.6	0.1	0.4
Central African Republic					
Total world imports	9.8	10.8	10.4	16.6	15.5
Single tax imports from UDEAC	1.2	1.6	1.9	2.0	2.9
UDEAC as a % of total	12.2	13.9	16.6	12.1	18.7
People's Republic of the Congo					
Total world imports	12.9	20.9	23.7	35.6	45.0
Single tax imports from UDEAC	0.2	0.6	1.1	2.7	2.5
UDEAC as a % of total	1.6	2.9	4.6	7.6	5.6
Gabon					
Total world imports	17.4	22.0	34.3	98.0	173.4
Single tax imports from UDEAC	1.0	1.9	0.2	2.6	4.0
UDEAC as a % of total	5.8	7.3	0.6	2.7	2.3
UDEAC					
Total world imports	77.6	105.2	141.8	271.2	417.4
Single tax imports from UDEAC	3.5	4.8	3.7	7.5	10.1
UDEAC as a % of total	4.5	4.1	2.4	2.8	2.4

Sources: UDEAC, *Statistiques Générales, Commerce Extérieur,* Année 1975 and *Bulletin des Statistiques Générales de l'UDEAC,* different issues.

Enlarging the scope of regional integration

In its provisions for an economic union, the 1974 UDEAC Treaty goes considerably beyond the 1964 Treaty in widening the scope of regional integration. A close reading of the Treaty, however, reveals that few new policy instruments or institutional mechanisms were created to realize these new objectives and older mechanisms were frequently weakened in the revised treaty when strengthening was, in fact, required.

Despite the call for the elaboration of medium- and long-term industrial plans for the region (Article 45: 1974 Treaty) no firm objectives for cooperation in the various sectors listed in this Article are provided and the Article is entirely silent on the question of timetables or of steps necessary to reach these broad objectives.

Fundamentally, the 1974 Treaty remains wedded to the belief that trade liberalization is the key means to bring about closer regional integration. It is curiously contrary to the centrality of trade liberalization in the UDEAC integration strategy, that the prohibition against barriers to trade under both the customs union and the single tax sections of the 1974 Treaty are considerably weaker than in the 1964 Treaty. Article 28 of the 1964 Treaty, for example, expressly prohibited the imposition of all duties and taxes on imports and exports among the member-states and Article 60 creates a single tax to replace any and all 'duties and taxes applicable to imports . . .'. In the revised Treaty, however, Article 28 merely notes that *free trade* will be in effect for all *raw materials* and *unprocessed agricultural commodities* produced and marketed within the region. As to manufactures, the illusion of free trade is replaced with the statement that 'a preferential trading regime, called the single tax system' will be in effect.

Institutionally the 1975 Treaty revisions were also disappointing. Unlike the 1964 UDEAC Treaty, the revised Treaty spells out in detail the functions of the Secretariat. In so doing, however, it confirms that the Secretariat is not an initiating body. Despite the considerable enlargement of the scope of integration in UDEAC, there was no commensurate increase in the authority or powers of initiative of the Secretariat and many of the technical posts in the Secretariat remained unfilled.

Title IX of the revised UDEAC Treaty deals with the creation of a UDEAC financing mechanism. The purposes of this bank are clearly spelled out in Article 66 of the Treaty as follows: 'to efficaciously promote the integration of the region and the harmonious development of the States of the Union, as well as to contribute to a reduction in existing disparities in development . . .'. The Banque de Développement des Etats de l'Afrique

Centrale (BDEAC) was officially launched on 3 December, 1975. Its members include the four UDEAC member-states and Chad. Its headquarters is in Brazzaville and its Director General is a Central African.[10]

The BDEAC has a total capital of 16 billion F CFA. Each of the Central African countries and the Banque des Etats de l'Afrique Centrale, the Central Bank, hold 13.1 per cent of the capital or a total of 78.6 per cent. The remaining 21.4 per cent of the capital is held by the Federal Republic of Germany (6.3 per cent), France (6.3 per cent), Kuwait (6.3 per cent) and the African Development Bank (2.5 per cent).[11]

In addition to its own capital, the BDEAC may mobilize local savings, seek external financing in the form of long-term loans or non-reimbursable grants, secure advances and refinancing from the BEAC. As to its operations, the bank may make loans, take shares of up to 10 per cent in the capital of local firms, guarantee loans and provide interest subsidies.[12]

The primary objectives of the bank are to fund 'regional integration projects' and only secondarily 'national projects', particularly infrastructural, which might contribute to the integration effort. This may apply both to the industrial and agricultural sectors: to the industrial sector, in the case of industries granted a preferential regime under the UDEAC Investment Code; to the agricultural sector, in the case of those projects which have intraregional linkages or are complementary to other regional efforts.[13] The BDEAC is thus clearly intended to stimulate new productive investment in the region and play a corrective role in altering the fundamental economic asymmetries among the UDEAC member-states. A look at the distribution of BDEAC funds in its first three years of operation suggests that it is quite far from realizing any of its objectives (Table 7.2). Not one of the projects funded is regional in nature and productive investments fall well behind those in infrastructure and in services. Even more remarkable is the distribution of these funds among the UDEAC member-states. The primary recipients were not the less-industrialized Chad and CAR but the most industrialized, Cameroon, and the wealthiest, Gabon, of the partner states.

Foreign capital and the limited gains from trade

Intra-regional trade in manufactures is governed by the operation of the single tax system and only firms which have been accepted under the single tax system may export within the region. In 1969, 105 firms were under the single tax system. Ten years later this number had risen to only 131. Whereas for the CAR, the Congo and Gabon this represented the bulk of their secondary manufacturing sector, for the Cameroon, firms covered by the single tax system constituted only 5 per cent of the paper

Table 7.2. *Distribution of BDEAC funded projects by sector and country: 1978–81 (millions F CFA)*

Project	Chad	CAR	Congo	Cameroon	Gabon	Total
Industry						
Amount	0	150	470	700	450	1 770
%						32.4
Infrastructure						
Amount	0	325	590	1 000	145	2 060
%						37.6
Telecommunications						
Amount	0	240	0	0	500	740
%						13.5
Energy						
Amount	0	0	0	0	600	600
%						11.0
Hotels						
Amount	0	0	300	0	0	300
%						5.5
Total						
Amount	0	715	1 360	1 700	1 695	5 470
%	0	13.1	24.9	31.0	31.0	100.0

Sources: BDEAC, 'Projets financées du 25 Novembre 1978 au 15 Avril 1981,' BDEAC, Brazzaville (1981).

manufacturers, 12 per cent of the rubber and plastics firms, 21 per cent of the food industries, 38 per cent of shoe and leather companies and 53 per cent of clothing and textile firms.

In 1979, 53 per cent of the single tax firms were Cameroonian, 20.5 per cent were Congolese, 13.5 per cent were Gabonese and 13 per cent were Central African. This imbalance in the distribution of single tax firms within UDEAC is attributable to the uneven pattern of industrialization already prevailing in the sub-region and unaffected by the operations of the single tax system. This conclusion is confirmed by the fact that the vast majority of these firms were created during the 1960s, many of them before UDEAC officially came into existence.

Given this uneven pattern of industrialization, production and trade in single tax products within UDEAC became highly asymmetrical. In 1969, 54 per cent of the single tax firms were Cameroonian but they produced 66 per cent of total single tax production. By 1979, although the percentage share of single tax firms had not altered, Cameroonian firms supplied 79.4

Table 7.3. *Production and trade in single tax products: 1973–9 (million F CFA)*

UDEAC	1973	1975	1976	1977	1978	First six months	
						1978	1979
1. Total production	46 846	69 084	85 691	90 810	90 551	45 250	109 308
of which domestic consumption	40 812	61 723	75 713	80 629	84 343	42 586	104 367
2. Total exported to UDEAC	6 034	7 361	9 978	10 181	6 208	2 664	4 941
3. Total exported to UDEAC as a percentage of total production	12.9	10.7	11.6	11.2	6.9	5.9	4.5

Source: Calculated from UDEAC, *Bulletin des Statistiques Générales de l'UDEAC*, No. 1–2 (1979).

per cent of total single tax production, while their share of intra-regional exports averaged 66 per cent during the 1970s. Despite these figures, it would be misleading to conclude that Cameroonian production is being stimulated by the UDEAC market. Where production of single tax manufactures has increased by 131 per cent in 1978 over 1973, the percentage which Cameroonian firms export to UDEAC has declined dramatically from 12.5 per cent in 1973 to 5.7 per cent in 1978 and reached its lowest point, 3.4 per cent, in the first six months of 1979. An increasing proportion of Cameroon's production of single tax products is thus being absorbed by the Cameroonian market. Indeed, data provided in Table 7.3 show that, for UDEAC as a whole, production of single tax goods rose steadily during the 1970s, declining only slightly in 1978 but rising again the first six months of 1979. Exports of single tax products, however, rose far more slowly and declined precipitously in 1979. As a percentage of total production, therefore, intra-regional trade in single tax products declined from a high of 12.9 per cent in 1973 to 6.9 per cent in 1978 and figures for the first six months of 1979 showed a continuation of this trend.

This decline in single tax exports as a percentage of single tax production is particularly evident among the 15 most heavily traded products, especially if we hold inflation constant by looking at quantities traded rather than prices. Thus, although the volume of beer brewed in UDEAC increased from 1.8 million hectolitres in 1976 to 2.2 million hectolitres in 1978, the proportion exported within UDEAC fell from 1.4 per cent of the total produced to 0.3 per cent over the same period.[14] Similarly exports of aluminium articles fell from 24.1 per cent of total single tax production in 1976 to 14.4 per cent in 1978. Cigarette production rose from 3533 metric tons in 1976 to 12 119 metric tons in 1978 but the proportion of total production traded intra-regionally fell from 39.3 per cent to 1.2 per cent. Cotton textile production also rose from 59.8 million metres in 1976 to 66 million metres in 1978 but the proportion traded intra-regionally fell from 12.2 per cent to 9.9 per cent. Exports of shoes fell from 7.3 per cent of total UDEAC production in 1976 to 3.9 per cent in 1978.[15]

A close look at these data reveals that these are precisely the industries in which duplication of production among the UDEAC member-states has steadily increased. How might we explain the slow growth of intra-regional trade, the decline in intra-regional specialization and the unevenness of the trading pattern? One important part of that explanation lies in the ownership structure of firms in the UDEAC region. A second essential element is the way in which the single tax system and the provisions of the UDEAC investment code interact with that particular ownership structure.

Although data on the ownership structure of single tax firms are incomplete, they nevertheless provide striking evidence of the extent to which intra-regional trade in manufactures is structured by the foreign firms which dominate the industrial sectors of the UDEAC countries. Of the 49 Cameroonian single tax firms for which data were available in 1979, 76 per cent were foreign owned. Seventy-four per cent of the 23 Congolese firms, 75 per cent of the 12 Gabonese firms and 64 per cent of the 11 Centrafricain firms for which data were available were also foreign owned.[16]

It is in this context that the single tax system in conjunction with the investment code have promoted the disarticulation of the regional economy by, *inter alia*, encouraging imports of raw materials and intermediates, rather than the use of local inputs. The extensive use of variable single tax rates,[17] moreover, has permitted foreign firms to segment the regional market into separate national markets within each of which an oligopolistic or in some instances a monopolistic market structure is created. Where inefficient production due to overbuilt plants, high import-intensity of production and wage bills inflated by excessive expatriate salaries results in high production costs, it is this segmentation effect of variable single tax rates which in the context of high external tariffs permits the foreign firm to pass along these high costs to the consumer in the form of high prices.

Segmentation of the regional market is particularly useful to firms such as Air Liquide (industrial gases), BATA (shoes), Pechiney-Ugine-Kuhlman (Aluminium) or Dollfus-Mieg (Textiles) which have already invested in duplicate plants or plan to do so in order to prevent a rival from penetrating the UDEAC market. For these firms, market segmentation can more than compensate for production inefficiencies by sales augmentation, intra-firm transfer pricing and higher retail prices.[18] Market segmentation thus becomes a vital component in the profit maximization strategy of the firm.[19]

Understandably such firms have little incentive to specialize in production but rather are induced by their dominance in each national market to reproduce the full range of products (as in the shoe industry) or brands (as in the cigarette industry) with all that this implies for economies of scale. Such firms, moreover, are resistant to efforts at regional planning which through rationalization might reduce their market share or profit margins. Where market segmentation cannot be preserved, market sharing arrangements between firms, as in the cigarette industry, or the elimination of competitors through takeovers, as in the shoe industry, may still ensure that the multinational corporation maintains its dominance within the market and hence its ability to make crucial policy decisions over what to produce, how to produce it, where to sell and at what price. Foreign ownership shaped by this particular incentive structure leads to inappropriate technological choices, low domestic value-added and limited employment generation in addition to the loss of welfare discussed above. The shoe industry will be used to illustrate these points but they could be as easily substantiated with data on beverages, cigarettes and other consumer-oriented industries.

By 1966, six foreign-owned shoe factories, two in Cameroon (Bata and Emen's industry), two in the CAR (Splendor, Moura et Gouveia) and two in the Congo (Bata, Africaplast) had located in the UDEAC region. Combined annual capacity was over 7 million pairs of shoes but production in 1966 totalled only 3.6 million pairs or about 40 per cent of capacity. All six of the firms produced plastic footwear but only four of the companies produced canvas, rubber or leather shoes. Although the latter are products for which inputs are available domestically, foreign-owned firms nevertheless actively promoted the production of plastic sandals. In 1967, production and consumption of leather and canvas shoes in Cameroon, the CAR, the Congo and Gabon was valued at 239 million F CFA, whereas production and consumption of plastic sandals totalled only 181 million F CFA. By 1971 production and consumption of plastic sandals in these four countries had risen to 620 million F CFA, an increase of 71 per cent over the 1967 figure, while production and consumption of leather and canvas shoes had fallen to 227 million F CFA, a decrease of 5.2 per cent over this four-year period.[20]

Table 7.4. *Single tax rates on plastic and leather footwear: 1979–80 (%)*

	Consumer			
Producer	Cameroon	CAR	Congo	Gabon
Plastic footwear (64.01.11)				
BATA (Cameroon)[a]	15	18	18	16
BATA (CAR)	18	13	18	16
BATA (Congo)	18	18	18	16
Leather footwear (64.02.22)				
BATA (Cameroon)	33	33	33	28
BATA (CAR)	25	33	33	28
BATA (Congo)	33	25	33	28

[a] Africaplast and Emen's Industries sell their plastic footwear in Cameroon with a tax rate identical to BATA's. In the CAR, as well, plastic footwear from these two companies is taxed at the same rate as BATA's. In the Congo and Gabon, however, the tax rate on plastic footwear from these two firms is considerably higher – 24% and 22% respectively.
Source: Supplement to the *Tarif Douanier de l'UDEAC* (1980).

In order to produce plastic footwear, foreign-owned shoe companies must import all of the moulding and extruding machinery and all of the intermediate inputs of polyvinylchloride (PVC). Although Article 7 of the Convention Commune sur les Investissements en UDEAC stipulates that firms which have been granted '*régimes privilégiés*' 'must commit themselves to using local raw materials and other local inputs in priority', the single tax system undermines this provision by permitting duty free imports of raw materials and intermediates, thus artificially cheapening the cost of imported inputs.

The differential rates of the single tax for plastic as opposed to leather footwear further distorts the decision-making environment. As Table 7.4 illustrates, the average rate of the single tax on plastic footwear in 1979–80 was 18 per cent. The average rate of the single tax on leather footwear, in contrast, was 31 per cent. A higher tax rate on leather footwear raises the price thereby narrowing the market and discouraging the use of local raw materials. By discouraging the use of local raw materials, a disincentive to intra-regional trade in leather is created and those engaged in producing hides and skins are induced to limit processing and to export. The regional

Table 7.5. *The shoe industry in UDEAC: 1978/79*

Company	Year founded	Capital		Turnover 10^6 F CFA	Domestic value added as a % of turnover	Employees
		10^6 F CFA	% Foreign			
BATA Cameroon	1961	805	67	3 500	43.4[a]	838
BATA CAR	1969[b]	150	100	600	. . .	169
BATA Congo	1965	200	100	1 966	29.2	249

	Production capacity		Capital-intensity of production[c]
	Amount	% utilized	
BATA Cameroon	6.8 m. pairs	76.5	2 198 091 F CFA
BATA CAR	1.5 m. pairs	33.3	2 192 771
BATA Congo	1.5 m. pairs	51.2	1 879 520

[a] This is the value added for the shoe branch as a whole. As other shoemakers are making leather shoes the value added would be higher, hence this figure overestimates BATA's domestic value added.
[b] BATA took over the plant from Moura et Gouveia in 1972.
[c] As measured by investment per employee.
Sources: L'Industrie Africaine en 1979 (Ediafric, La Documentation Africaine, Paris, 1980); Congo, *Recensement Industriel* (1979); Cameroun, Ministère de l'Economie et du Plan, Direction de la Statistique et de l Comptabilité Nationale, *Activités des Entreprises du Secteur Modern, Resultats du Recensement Industriel et Commercial* (1976/1977).

economy thus becomes segmented and rearticulated through vertical linkages to advanced industrial countries where imported inputs are sourced. By keeping the single tax rate on plastic footwear low and by providing foreign firms with duty free imports of the required inputs and exonerations from domestic taxation, profit margins on plastic footwear are artificially raised.

Despite the underutilization of the capacity and the relatively slow growth of the UDEAC market for footwear, in 1969 the BATA shoe company opened its subsidiary in the CAR with a capacity of 1.5 million pairs of plastic, leather and canvas shoes. Within a few years, concentration in the footwear industry became noticeable as Splendor in the CAR closed and BATA-CAR took over its only remaining rival, Moura et Gouveia. In Cameroon, although a small manufacturer of leather valises and shoes, SACC, was established in 1972, Emen's industries has shifted its production away from plastic shoes and towards knitwear and umbrellas and Africaplast has emphasized plastic articles rather than shoes in its product mix.

Table 7.5 provides data on the consequences of the inter-active effect of foreign ownership, market segmentation through the single tax system and an incentive system which cheapens capital and imported inputs. From this table it can be seen that the shoe industry is characterized by high capital- and import-intensity of production (low-value added), low utilization and employment capacity. Because the kind of import-substituting industry induced by the single tax system and investment code is import- and capital-intensive, firms have every interest in locating in coastal countries to take advantage of closeness to their overseas sources of supply. Polarization of new investment in UDEAC thus continues. The advantages of coastal countries in economic infrastructure, purchasing power, skills and resources is thus being reinforced by the operation of the single tax system and the UDEAC investment code.

Integration for self-reliance

In sum, the shoe industry illustrates the way in which the operation of the single tax system and the investment code have permitted foreign firms to shape UDEAC's industrial structures. By segmenting the UDEAC market into separate national markets, by promoting duty-free imports of capital goods, raw materials and intermediate products, by providing tax holidays and other inducements which artificially cheapen the cost of capital, the single tax system and investment code have strengthened the market dominance of these foreign-owned companies, have guaranteed their profitability, have eliminated incentives to efficient production, have promoted capital and import-intensive production and have encouraged duplication of plants and products throughout the region.

Understandably under these conditions foreign firms see little need to rationalize production or engage in intra-regional specialization. Indeed they are likely to resist attempts to allocate specializations among the member-states, for to do so may potentially incur a loss of market shares to a rival foreign firm. Efforts to harmonize production are thus undermined by actions which reinforce the nationalism of UDEAC leaders and encourage derogations from regional plans. This was not only apparent in the textile industry during the late 1960s,[21] but was also a principal factor in the failure of UDEAC industrial allocations in 1975.

This ability of multinational corporations to thwart efforts at regional industrial planning is heightened by the lack of a coherent regional industrialization strategy and by the lack of a well-functioning regional financial institution. Within UDEAC regional planning has, until now, been conceptualized as the exclusive allocation of *whole* industries to a single member-state. Such an approach tends to limit the choice to a few large-scale, capital-intensive and hence costly industries thus giving each member-state the impression of having secured a major contribution to industrial growth. To build such industries, however, requires a heavy reliance on foreign capital, technology and managerial skills, all of which provide levers which facilitate efforts by multinational corporations to undermine industrial planning and make it possible for those countries which have greater access to foreign capital to contemplate duplication of industries allocated to others.[22] In moving beyond this approach to regional planning and towards the development of sectoral programmes, which stress intra-industry specialization and promote backward and forward linkages across the region *within a single industry*, the leverage of the multinational corporations will be reduced.

To develop such an industrial programme, however, requires a secretariat general with a far larger staff and far greater authority than the present secretariat enjoys. It also implies that the Banque de Développement des Etats de l'Afrique Centrale moves away from financing national projects towards the financing of major projects inscribed in a coherent regional integration strategy and in so doing emphasizes to a far greater degree the funding of projects in the less-industrialized member countries of the region. Finally, it implies that existing instruments such as the single tax system and the investment code will be revised in such a way as to promote self-reliant development by reducing segmentation and disarticulation within the UDEAC market. For this to be effective, a new policy instrument, regional regulation of foreign capital and technology, through the creation of a Regional Investment Review Agency, will also be required. The three pillars of a reformed UDEAC, therefore, are regional planning, regional regulation and regional finance. Only by promoting such reforms will the gains from integration increase and their distribution become more equitable.

NOTES

1 For example, see Lynn K. Mytelka, 'Africa: A Raw Materials Producing Hinterland for Europe', in John G. Ruggie (ed.) *The Antinomies of Interdependence*, Columbia University Press, New York, 1982.
2 At their annual meeting in December 1980 (Brazzaville) the UDEAC heads of state requested the Economic Commission for Africa to undertake a major evaluation of UDEAC and to make recommendations with respect to its renewal.

3 In order to ensure that customs duties and taxes were properly distributed to the importing inland states, a common customs service was established in the Congo, the CAR and Chad. Given the absence of goods being moved from Gabonese ports to other UDE states (due to the lack of road and rail transportation), Gabon created its own customs service. This concession also relieved Gabon of any sizeable contribution to the Fonds de Solidarité, set up by Article 6 of the UDE Treaty 'in a spirit of co-operation and in order to take into account errors in the customs declarations'. The Fonds was fed by a 20 per cent levy on import duties and taxes collected by the common customs bureaux only. *Convention portant organization de l'Union douanière équatoriale* in *Journal Officiel de l'A.E.F.*, Brazzaville, 30 June 1959.

4 Lynn K. Mytelka, 'Fiscal Politics and Regional Redistribution: The Case of the Single Tax System in UDEAC', *Journal of Conflict Resolution.*

5 Calculated from tables presented in the Banque Centrale des Etats de l'Afrique Centrale et du Cameroun, *Etudes et Statistiques*, No. 149 (December, 1969).

6 Mytelka, 'Fiscal Politics'. In a typical case, that of plastic footwear, the Cameroonian product was taxed at 25 per cent of its value when sold in Cameroon and over 30 per cent when sold in the CAR, Congo, Gabon and Chad. The Central African product, in contrast, was taxed at the rate of 18 per cent when sold in Cameroon and the Congo, 15 per cent when sold in Gabon and only 13 per cent when sold in the CAR itself. Even if the costs of production were higher in the CAR, transportation costs and the higher rate of the single tax provided a significant measure of protection for CAR footwear.

7 On the problems of costs and benefits in regional integrative systems see UNCTAD, 'Fiscal compensation and the distribution of benefits in economic groupings of developing countries' in *Current Problems of Economic Integration*, prepared by Peter Robson, UN, New York, 1971 TD/B/322/Rev. 1; UNCTAD, 'The distribution of benefits and costs in integration among developing countries' in *Current Problems of Economic Integration* prepared by Eduardo Lizano, (UN, New York, 1973) TD/B/394; Lynn K. Mytelka, 'The Salience of Gains in Third World Integrative Systems', *World Politics*, xxv, (1973), pp. 236–46 and Andrew Axline, 'Underdevelopment, Dependence and Integration: The Politics of Regionalism in the Third World', *International Organization*, xxi, (1977), pp. 83–105.

8 Although Chad formally withdrew from UDEAC it remained within the Franc Zone and the Banque des Etats de l'Afrique Centrale. It would later also join the Banque de Développement des Etats de l'Afrique Centrale when this was created. Bilateral commission between Chad and its former UDEAC partners was also established and trade relations were largely maintained until the economic devastation wrought by civil war. Negotiations had, in fact, been initiated in the late 1970s with a view to rejoining UDEAC but their successful conclusion was interrupted by the war.

9 Acte No. 8/71 – UDEAC – 1964.

10 This is in keeping with the effort to apportion regional institutions and key posts among the member-states. Thus the UDEAC Secretariat is in Bangui and the Secretary-General is Cameroonian.

11 BDEAC, 'Présentation de la Banque', (Brazzaville, Mimeo, May 1981).

12 BDEAC, *Règles générales de procédure et d'intervention*, (Brazzaville, March 1978), pp. 7–8.

13 *Ibid.*, pp. 4–5.
14 In 1975 beer alone accounted for 22 per cent of the total value of single tax production and it was ranked first among single tax products in intra-regional trade.
15 Calculated from UDEAC, *Bulletin des Statistiques Générales de l'UDEAC*, No 1, (1979).
16 Calculated from data presented in 'L'Industrie Africaine en 1979', Ediafric, Paris, *La Documentation Africaine*, 1980, Vols. 1 & 2.
17 Of some 600 tariff positions, single tax rates differ in approximately 54 per cent of the cases. 'Entreprises soumises au Régime de la Taxe Unique', Appendix C, *Tarif Douanier de l'UDEAC*, (1980).
18 For a more detailed theoretical treatment of this point see Constantine Vaitsos, 'Crisis in Regional Economic Cooperation (Integration) Among Developing Countries: A Survey', *World Development*, vi, (1978), pp. 719–69.
19 The way this has operated in the Andean Common Market is discussed in Lynn K. Mytelka, *Regional Development in a Global Economy: The Multinational Corporation, Technology, and Andean Integration*, Yale University Press, New Haven, 1979, Chapter 5.
20 Calculated from UDEAC, *Bulletin des Statistiques Générales de l'UDEAC*, No. 22 (April 1968) and No. 38 (April 1972).
21 See, Colin Legum, I. William Zartman, Steven Langdon and Lynn K. Mytelka, *Africa in the 1980s: A Continent in Crisis*, McGraw-Hill, New York, 1979, pp. 184–8.
22 The oil refineries case during the 1960s and the pharmaceutical allocation of 1975 are examples of how this worked.

8 The experience of the East African Community: implications for the theory and practice of regional cooperation in Africa

DOMENICO MAZZEO

Introduction

Experimentation and failure are important components of the learning process of individuals and countries. By including the East African Community (EAC) in this book of essays on African regional organizations, we do not intend to provide an historical account of the activities of a defunct Community nor a detailed analysis of the causes and consequences of its collapse.[1] Rather, the East African experience should guide our effort to re-examine the basic tenets of the theory and practice of regional cooperation among developing countries, or at least help us to raise questions and draw conclusions that may be relevant to other African regional groupings. In a world of superpowers and blocs, it seems reasonable to assume that regional cooperation among relatively small or weak countries could be an instrument of accelerated development and an escape from cultural, economic and political domination by major extra-continental or continental powers. On the other hand, the expectations raised by the established theory of regional cooperation have rarely materialized in the case of developing countries. The world economic crisis of the 1970s made the life of regional groupings in the Third World even more precarious. Some of these groupings stagnated, others were dissolved. But the regional trend survived.[2] While the survival of the regional trend justifies a continued interest in the analysis of the promises and constraints of regional cooperation, the generally disappointing results of such cooperation calls for a re-examination of its basic rationale, aims and approaches. This re-examination is particularly appropriate at a time when general development theories and policies are also undergoing a critical reappraisal, partly stimulated by the current world economic crisis.

For the purpose of re-examining the theory and practice of regional cooperation among developing countries, a look at the East African experience could be instructive on several grounds. Firstly, post-independence cooperation between the countries of East Africa was expected to be facilitated by several favourable conditions, namely a common historical experience, cultural affinity, similarity of political institutions, and elite complementarity. The long experience of close association and the broad similarities existing among the East African countries could have generated a search for common solutions to common problems. Secondly, the East African case was one of the best examples of cooperation among developing countries,[3] at least until the early 1970s. At the time of independence, inter-country trade amounted to almost one-quarter of total East African foreign trade. Value added by the East African corporations represented over half the value added by the transport sectors of partner states. The inter-country research budget was estimated at almost two-thirds of the country-based research budgets in East Africa. Even at the time of its collapse, with an employment capacity of about 100 000 people and assets valued at over 500 million Kenyan pounds, the EAC was still an important economic force within the region. The importance of cooperation in East Africa could also be inferred from the negative follow-ups of its demise, notably the closure of the Tanzanian border with Kenya and its paralysing impact on Kenyan trade with Tanzania and Zambia, the Ugandan-Tanzanian war, the danger of a growing arms race within the region, and the implied misallocation of resources for both economic and strategic purposes. Thirdly, cooperation in East Africa went beyond the traditional concern with trade liberalization and harmonization of industrial policies. An impressive set of common services, including joint training and research institutions, put the EAC at the vanguard of similar experiments among developing countries. The EAC already incorporated those aspects of regional cooperation that are increasingly attracting the attention of concerned scholars and politicians, namely joint infrastructural development and cooperation in fields related to science and technology. Which factors, then, prevented the EAC from making further progress or at least preserving past achievements?

Causes of East African disintegration

Students of the EAC generally agree that an adequate explanation of the East African disintegration process must be based on a multi-factor analysis,[4] namely the analysis of a series of inter-related institutional, political and economic factors. Partly because they are easy to identify, institutional weaknesses are often considered a major cause of the failure of inter-country cooperation agreements. But such an explanation would leave unanswered the question of why inadequate policies and mechanisms are adopted in the first place, and why are they not corrected on time. The answer to this question can be found in the national and regional political environment. The political climate determines the degree of partner states' commitment to regional goals at any given point in time as well as the nature of the institutions that embody these goals. Its evolution may favour or impede a restructuring of cooperation. The political environment, on the other hand, affects and is influenced by the nature of member countries' economic development. The root-cause of the success or failure of regional cooperation, therefore, has to be sought in a combination of political and economic factors.

Maldistribution of benefits

Historically, the survival of regional cooperation in East Africa was constantly threatened by the perceived uneven distribution of benefits among member countries, in particular the uneven industrial development. Research aimed at measuring the respective gains and losses of partner states did not produce clearcut results. But researchers generally felt that Kenya benefited more than her partners.[5] Maldistribution of benefits within common markets is usually attributed to the different level of development of partner states, with the more developed reaping the highest benefits. In East Africa, Kenya was considered the more developed, Tanzania the least. If by development one understands both growth and distribution of wealth, this interpretation of the East African situation could be challenged. But in terms of growth, notably of those sectors more directly linked to cooperation, namely infrastructures and manufacturing, Kenya was clearly predominant, at least from the mid-1950s on. This Kenyan predominance was resented by Tanzania and Uganda, who felt that it was mainly the result of advantages derived by Kenya from regional activities, mostly located in or around Nairobi. One could state, with a high degree of confidence, that regional cooperation in East Africa would have survived, if the question of the maldistribution of benefits had been solved satisfactorily. This may have required adequate joint policies and institutions. Starting from the late-1950s, several attempts were made to correct imbalanced development in the region, by a restructuring of inter-country cooperation. The achievement of a more equitable distribution of benefits, notably a more balanced industrial development, was one of the major objectives of the creation of the East African Common Services Organization (EACSO) in 1960, the Kampala-Mbale Agreements of 1964–5, and the 1967 Treaty for East African Cooperation establishing the EAC. The 1967 Treaty was the most comprehensive of these attempts and apparently represented a compromise acceptable to the three partner-states. It took into consideration not only the financial aspects of the distribution of benefits, but also more general socio-economic implications of regional activities, such as employment creation and spill-over effects into other economic sectors of member countries. A more equitable distribution of benefits was expected to result from the implementation of a series of financial, fiscal and administrative measures, regulating the functioning of the Common Market and the Common Services.

In the case of the Common Market, more balanced inter-country trade and industrial development rested upon the combined effect of four measures:

a) the use of transfer tax,[6] which allowed partner states with deficit in inter-country trade of manufactured goods to protect their infant industries and secure additional budgetary revenues;

b) the activities of the East African Development Bank (EADB),[7] expected to invest a greater amount of its resources in the less industrialized member-countries;

c) the working of the industrial licensing system,[8] empowered to control the allocation of certain types of industries with a regional market; and

d) the harmonization of fiscal incentives, aimed at reducing unfair competition in investment policies and eventually directing investments towards the less industrialized members of the EAC.

In practice, the impact of these various measures was quite limited. Harmonization of fiscal incentives never materialized. The industrial licensing system remained mainly concerned with industries already allocated and came to an end in 1973, on expiry of its 25 years duration. The resources of the EADB were too scarce to exert a significant role in the industrial development of the region, and it had little authority to prevent duplication of industries. The transfer tax may have played a role in balancing inter-country trade, but at the expense of a better harmonization of regional industrial development policies. By its very nature, the transfer tax stimulated duplication of industries. Particularly in the case of neighbouring countries with very limited markets, duplication of industries is bound to restrict inter-country trade.

In the case of the Common Services, the Treaty proposed the relocation[9] of some of the services' headquarters and the decentralization of the administration and purchasing policies of the services, notably the corporations. These measures were generally implemented and were expected to facilitate a better distribution of benefits. But the extreme functional approach adopted by the Treaty and the ambiguities of the decentralization policy considerably complicated the task of coordination of infrastructural development in East Africa, particularly in the field of transport. The adoption of a functional approach meant granting greater autonomy not only to the various transport sectors, but also to various branches of the same sector. In the field of civil aviation, for instance, construction of airport was undertaken by national governments, while ground services were provided by the East African Directorate of Civil Aviation and air transport by the East African Airways Corporation. The situation was even worse in the field of land transportation: road transport was a national responsibility and railway transport a Community responsibility. In these circumstances, it was near to impossible to make the best economic choice for the development of road or railway transport, and to harmonize transport rates between road and rail routes. Decentralization of the Common Services was perhaps a desirable and necessary measure. But the lack of clarity as to the final objective of decentralization fomented a power struggle between Community and country headquarters or, more generally, between national and Community bureaucracies, and between public and private interests. When inflation of import prices squeezed foreign exchange earnings of member-countries, the refusal of country headquarters to remit funds in hard currencies to the Community head-quarters was one of the immediate causes of the collapse of the corporations, hence of the entire 60-year-old effort at cooperation in East Africa.

Institutional weaknesses

The Treaty's provisions thus proved inadequate or inappropriate to solve the problem of a more equitable distribution of benefits among the three East African countries. These provisions may have been corrected or improved, had the machineries of the EAC been stronger. But, despite all its complexity, the institutional machinery of the EAC lacked an autonomous body, similar to the Commission of the European Communities or the Junta of the Andean Common Market, with at least power of initiative and supervision. Consequently, the East African regional institutions could hardly play a dynamic and mediatory role in harmonizing partner states' national interest. Also unfortunate was the composition of the supreme decision-making body, the East African Authority, made up of the three countries' presidents. This seems to have increased the danger of transforming personal rivalries into more lasting inter-country conflicts. But it would be misleading to overemphasize institutional weaknesses. Institutions are instruments, whose utility depends on the ability of their makers and users. In many respects, the institutional machinery of the EAC compared favourably with that of other regional groupings, particularly in terms of its financial autonomy[10] and the importance of the East African Legislative Assembly. The fact that the EAC survived for seven years with little guidance from the Authority is in itself an indication of the relevance of previous achievements, the suitability of most of the component parts of the institutional machinery, and the commitment of Community officials, notably the Secretary-General and the East African Ministers. If the institutional machinery proved to be inadequate, this was due mainly to the growing political rivalries between partner states.

Politico-ideological rifts
The development orientations of the three East African countries became increasingly conflictual after independence, owing partly to historical-structural conditions prevailing in the three countries and partly to ideological-personal inclinations of their presidents. The heavier colonial presence in Kenya brought with it a high degree of concentration of wealth, notably land, in the hands of a minority. The temptation was great for the local elite to become the private heirs rather than the public administrators of this wealth in the interest of the nation. Tanzania instead opted for a more egalitarian society, perhaps partly due to the personality of her president. It has become customary to stress the negative impact of the Kenya-Tanzania ideological differences on the process of cooperation in East Africa. Ideology influences the priorities, structure and orientations of national socio-economic systems. In so doing, it affects vital areas of inter-country relations within a regional group. Such areas include the role of the state in the economy, hence the respective role of public and private enterprises, the question of industrial location and trade regulation, and the treatment of direct foreign investments. In the case of the EAC, the widening ideological rift between Kenya and Tanzania considerably undermined the spirit of compromise and tolerance, perhaps the most essential political prerequisite for successful cooperation. Consequently, a revision of the Treaty or at least a more harmonious and dynamic interpretation of its provisions became impossible. Regional industrialization policies and harmonization of fiscal incentives could not even be seriously discussed. The chaos in the transport sector, notably the railroad competition and the controversy over the domestic versus international function of the East African Airways, was aggravated. The growing spirit of acrimony, spreading from the government level to the mass media, created a general atmosphere of immobilism and enmity that did not allow member-countries to take jointly at least the most desperate of all steps: an orderly withering away of the EAC.

The 1971 military coup in Uganda added a second set of conflictual relationships in a community of only three members. It also destroyed the hope of Uganda playing the role of mediator in the growing rift between Kenya and Tanzania. Further, by seriously weakening the national economy, the coup meant that Uganda was no longer an economically significant member of the EAC. By 1974, Ugandan exports to partner-states had practically ceased. Ugandan imports from outside East Africa were also drastically curtailed. This undermined the budget of the Community, as duties on Ugandan imports from outside the region dropped considerably. More specifically, harassment and killings demoralized the Community personnel working in Uganda, most of whom left the country. New appointments of Community officials were delayed. Even worse, the enmity between Amin and Nyerere completely paralysed the Authority, the Community's supreme decision-making body. As we mentioned earlier, if the EAC survived for seven years in the absence of any meeting of the Authority, it was due mainly to its budgetary autonomy and the dedication of some top Community officials.

External dependence
The external dependence of the African continent in general and the member countries of the EAC in particular contributed in several ways to accelerate the process of disintegration in East Africa. The colonial situation in southern Africa indirectly weakened the EAC. As chairman of the 'front-line' states, Nyerere, the only president who in the 1970s could have taken initiatives to save the EAC, was absorbed by the liberation struggle in southern Africa. One may also assume that, as decolonization progressed, Tanzania expected to transform the links established with the liberation movements into more stable inter-state relations with her southern neighbours. She may have been tempted to look southward for new, more rewarding ties, instead of struggling to improve the strained relations with her East African partners.

Ironically, the attempt by member-countries of the EAC to diversify their foreign economic and political relations, a move usually aimed at reducing dependence through a more balanced system of external relations, also complicated the life of the EAC. An uncoordinated diversification of the foreign policies of partner states of a regional group is bound to strain relations among the countries of the region. For different reasons, Tanzania established close links with China,[11] Uganda looked to the Arab and Soviet camps for support, and Kenya remained more attached to her traditional Western connections. As a consequence, East Africa became the theatre of an intensified struggle for zones of influence by extra-continental powers.

Probably more disastrous was the impact of economic dependence, exacerbated by the world economic crisis of the 1970s. The mounting deficit of the balance of payments of Kenya and Tanzania reduced the opportunities for inter-country trade, thus undermining the Common Market.[12] It also disrupted the functioning of the Common Services, by making the transfer of funds in hard currency very difficult, irrespective of the presence or absence of political good will.

Summary

To sum up, regional cooperation in East Africa was undermined by the maldistribution of benefits, institutional weaknesses, inter-country political rifts, and external dependence. These four major sets of factors have a common origin: the low level of development of the partner states of the EAC. The negative impact of the low level of development on inter-country cooperation is pervasive. To begin with, it makes the salience of gains a very sensitive and untractable issue. Differences in the development level of member-countries may be slim, but the low level of development accentuates them, making small inequalities loom large. It also makes imperative a search for immediate results by all member countries, forcing them to take often uncompromising positions. The least developed members of the group find unbearable even a small loss of revenues from trade liberalization, while the relatively more developed members are usually not in a position to offer adequate compensation. Agreement on the location of industries is extremely hard to reach. Within the framework of an underdeveloped economy, the addition of a new factory may have significant favourable implications on the host country's balance of payments, employment creation and government revenues. All members thus strive to host the new industry or factory. Further, as all member countries are inclined to start with simple industrialization, duplication of industries follows and the opportunities for inter-country trade are reduced.

The low level of development is also at the root of most institutional weaknesses and political conflicts within regional groups. The low level of political development, notably the low degree of nation-building, makes the quest for sovereignty and national unity the number one priority of developing countries. This implies that differentiation rather than integration with neighbouring countries is often sought, particularly when the same ethnic populations have to be absorbed into new national cultures. It equally implies an overemphasis on the role of the presidency as symbol of national unity. Personalization of power follows, a phenomenon so common throughout Africa, though not unique to this continent. Ideological differences between African countries are often the reflection of various presidents' different perceptions of national development rather than of popularly established and supported national choices. A low level of economic development reinforces the above trends. A little-diversified economy generally means a lack of societal pluralism. This usually results in greater personalization of power, a rather destabilizing factor in inter-country cooperation.

Finally, the low level of development, almost by definition, strengthens the chains of dependence, making national and regional policies highly vulnerable to the external environment. In fact, if we were looking for a psychologically satisfactory explanation of the chronological origin of 'underdevelopment', we could argue with the proponents of the theories of dependence and imperialism that external dependence, particularly within the capitalist system, is at the root of the present under-development of Third World countries, and consequently at the root of the problems these countries encounter in their cooperation. But, for our purpose, such argumentation would be sterile. We are more concerned with the future than with the past. We want to know why dependence occurs and how it can be broken. For us, dependence is a situation of unequal power, whether mainly of a political, socio-economic, military, scientific and technological nature, or a combination of all these aspects. It can be broken only through determined and concerted action, that is through increased power of the dependents. This calls for appropriate national and regional development policies. Can regional cooperation be an instrument of a more autonomous, self-reliant development of Third World countries? In particular, can regional cooperation assist in the formulation and implementation of more self-reliant national development policies?

Implications for intra-African cooperation

If our analysis of the East African experience is correct, the basic factors responsible for the collapse of the EAC are obviously not specific to East Africa, but common to most regional groups in the Third World, notably in Africa. In fact, as the literature on regional cooperation shows, such groups are beset by problems similar to those encountered by the EAC. On the basis of this, two lines of thought could be pursued: one rejecting the whole idea of regional cooperation as irrelevant to the Third World; the other trying to adapt the theory and practice of regional cooperation to the conditions and aspirations of the developing countries. According to the first viewpoint, regional cooperation is not an instrument of development, but a consequence of development. It remains the privilege of the industrialized countries. The various attempts at regional cooperation in the Third World are likely to fail. They represent the victory of hope over experience. According to the second viewpoint, the relative failure of regional experiments in the Third World may be due to the lack of adaptation of the established theory and practice of regional cooperation to the conditions and aspirations of the developing countries. The basic assumptions, orientations, aims and forms of regional cooperation were heavily influenced by the European experience, that is the experience of industrialized countries. An attempt should be made to re-examine the basic tenets of regional cooperation in the light of the conditions and aspirations of the developing countries. We would like to pursue this second line of thought. To that effect, we will, first, explain why the established theory of regional cooperation may be relevant to the situation of industrialized countries, but is inappropriate to the conditions and aspirations of the developing countries. Then, we will suggest new possible avenues of thought and action concerning regional cooperation among developing countries.

Inadequacy of the established theory

The established theory of regional cooperation, more commonly known as the theory of integration,[13] was elaborated in the aftermath of the Second World War mainly as a response to European aspirations and experience, namely the aspirations and experience of relatively developed and industrialized countries. The major aim of the European countries in fostering cooperation was to secure inter-country and inter-class peace through the speedy reconstruction and restructuring of their war-torn economies, and the quick realization of the welfare state and the consumer society. Within the European context, different approaches to cooperation were adopted, each more consonant with the respective socio-economic system prevailing in the two opposing European camps: the market approach in the West and the planned approach in the East. In practice, the two approaches are often complementary and have in common the most basic features. They take for granted the existence of a relatively high level of political, industrial and infrastructural development of member countries. They also share the anti-nationalist bias as well as the belief in the importance of the economies of scale.

That the established theory of regional cooperation assumed a high degree of development of partner states, or at least some of them, is clearly shown by its very limited concern for the possible negative consequences of the cooperation process on partner-states, while the impact of such consequences on the rest of the world were paid greater attention in theory and practice.[14] Member-countries were expected to benefit from cooperation on the assumption that they shared a relatively equal and high level of development, that is an equal capacity to benefit sustained by their advanced industrial basis, well developed infrastructures and efficient national administrations. Alternatively, theorists envisaged the creation of strong regulatory mechanisms, made possible by the existence of core developed countries within the region with the determination and means to meet the cost of distributive measures, which could convince weaker countries to join the group. But the creation of strong regulatory mechanisms presupposes a high economic capacity of the system as well as a high degree of political commitment of members, hence the existence of well organized political parties and pressure groups with similar ideologies and development orientations.

The anti-nationalist bias of the established theory of regional cooperation can be explained by the circumstances in which the theory was born and grew, namely the experience and aspirations of the European countries following the Second World War. In spite of the different approaches and their largely economic content, the overriding motive for cooperation in Eastern and Western Europe was political: the consolidation of the two opposing blocs and the containment of nationalism, notably that of the defeated countries. After two European-born world wars, nationalism in Europe was considered highly destructive of intra-European political and economic relations. This feeling was shared by wide sections of European elites and masses. Overcoming nationalism was also a common objective of two otherwise conflicting schools of thought on regional cooperation: the federalist and the functionalist. Whether the nation-state would succumb to the frontal assault of the federalists or to the indirect attack of the functionalists, the undoing of the nation-state, as implied in the concept of supranational authority, became a cardinal article of faith of the established theory of regional cooperation. Nevertheless, the peaceful nature of the regional process was always emphasized. Force, a traditional major instrument of economic and political amalgamations, was to be excluded from this process. Participation in it was supposed to be of a totally voluntary nature, based on the satisfaction of the needs of all participants. In that sense, regional cooperation remained a form of permanent multilateral diplomacy or negotiation, and an instrument for the realization of its members' interests. Under specific circumstances, member countries of a regional group may have preferred to disappear as independent political units and submit to a new supranational authority. But one cannot take it for granted that, under all circumstances, a major aim of regional cooperation is to overcome or undo the nation-state. The anti-nationalist bias of the established theory of regional cooperation and its consequent emphasis on supranational authority are unwarranted generalizations of the European situation, if not deformations of the concept of regional cooperation. In any case, if nationalism in post-war Europe was in a decaying stage, this is certainly not the case in developing countries.

Nationalism in the Third World is clearly in the ascendancy. It has only recently been an instrument of political liberation or decolonization. It could become an instrument of greater economic liberation or self-reliance. It remains a major instrument of nation-building. As it has been often remarked, there is hardly anything developing countries consider more sacred than their newly achieved independence and sovereignty. The liberating role of nationalism in the Third World makes any discussion of supranationality unrealistic and counter-productive. Far from undermining cooperation, the respect for the principle of consensus in decision-making could be the best guarantee for facilitating general commitment by partner-states to the goals of cooperation, promoting a spirit of compromise during negotiations on specific issues and securing implementation of decisions. A non-governmental body with power of supervision and initiative will certainly be extremely useful. But final power of decision and implementation must be expected to remain firmly in the hands of national governments. The still dominant concern with nation-building implies, in fact, that cooperation should be seen as an instrument for strengthening, not weakening, the hands of national governments, the major engine of national unification in developing countries.

At the economic level, irrespective of their different approaches to cooperation, the Eastern and Western Europeans were equally strong believers in the importance of the economies of scale, that is the use of capital-intensive technology as an instrument of accelerated economic growth. Development was thus identified with modernization and economic concentration. By widening the market, regional cooperation was expected to create the conditions for a more efficient use of capital-intensive technology, leading to a speedy economic reconstruction, restructuring and specialization, and to the advent of the welfare state and the consumer society. Probably owing to the relative success of the European experiment and the importance of the countries involved, regional cooperation on the European model was widely considered applicable also to the developing countries. In practice, regional groups in the Third World followed more closely the Western European, 'free trade', approach to cooperation. One could argue that if developing countries had adopted the 'planned', Eastern European approach to regional cooperation, results might have been more rewarding. This objection has been partly answered, when we stressed the general similarities of the two approaches in aims and means. Further, a planned approach to cooperation generally puts even greater demands on member countries. In particular, it presupposes a high level of infrastructural development, strong political and ideological commitment, and efficient national administrations. Therefore, a planned approach to regional cooperation among developing countries, following the Eastern European example, might have been more unwieldy than the free trade approach. In brief, regional cooperation in both Eastern and Western Europe was primarily an instrument of economic reconstruction and concentration, not an instrument of basic economic development and diversification, which in Europe had already been achieved. It was a strategy for the creation of the consumer society, not for the satisfaction of basic needs.[15] In the European context, these needs were presumably satisfied. At least, the capacity to satisfy them already existed.

The socio-economic concerns of developing countries are more complex than those of the industrialized countries. They have to do with basic development, that is the creation of previously non-existing conditions and capacities for growth and distribution of wealth. The indiscriminate use of capital-intensive technology may not be the most appropriate way of reaching these objectives. Even at the national level, where central regulatory mechanisms are usually stronger, the indiscriminate use of capital-intensive technology has often been associated with concentration of wealth, growing unemployment, and continued external dependence. These negative effects are easily magnified at the inter-country level, where regulatory mechanisms are generally weaker than at the national level. A reminder of this fact is the burning issue of the uneven distribution of benefits afflicting most regional groups in the Third World. More fundamentally, developing countries are, almost by definition, short of capital and modern skills. Conceived as an instrument of that type of modernization promoted by capital-intensive technology, regional cooperation among developing countries seems to run counter to the basic tenets of even the more traditional economic development theory: the theory of comparative advantage, which calls for a greater use of the more abundant local resources. This underlines the importance of matching local productive activities with local resource endowment, a central point common to more recent and widely accepted strategies for more self-reliant development.

To sum up, the established theory of regional cooperation generally took for granted the validity of the basic assumptions underlying the European model, irrespective of specific conditions, problems and levels of development of partner-states of other regional groups. In fact, the concepts of supranationality and modernization, notably the importance of the economies of scale, have consistently been considered central to all theoretical discussions on regional cooperation. When doubts were expressed on the applicability of the European model to Third World countries, it was usually to dismiss the whole idea of cooperation as irrelevant to developing countries. But it would certainly be more appropriate to recognize that, labouring under different political and economic conditions, developing countries have different concerns calling for different orientations, objectives and methods of regional cooperation. The major concerns of developing countries are still nation-building and satisfaction of basic needs. A relevant approach to regional cooperation among developing countries should meet these major concerns. In other words, regional cooperation among developing countries, to start with, should be an instrument of nation-building and satisfaction of basic needs.

New avenues of thought and action

In the 1970s, the emphasis in development theory has shifted from the concept of modernization and its related growth model towards the basic needs strategy. This implies a more self-reliant approach to development. It recognizes the importance of matching local demand with local needs and local supply. In other words, it calls for greater mass participation in the development effort and consequently emphasizes the importance of the social enlargement of the market within each country. In that perspective, the set of priorities envisaged by the basic needs strategy are development of agriculture, infrastructures, and appropriate or relevant technology. This strategy sees development mainly in national terms, though the regional dimension is not excluded. But, from the point of view of the basic needs strategy, if regional cooperation has to serve as an instrument of development, it must presumably conform to the above set of priorities. This questions the appropriateness of the market approach to regional cooperation, namely the geographical expansion of the market, whether under conditions of 'free' or 'planned' trade. In particular, it questions the appropriateness of capital-intensive industrialization, so far considered as a major justification for regional cooperation. In which direction, then, should the theory and practice of regional cooperation among developing countries move? On the basis of our discussion of the East African experience, the nature of regional cooperation, and the conditions and priorities of developing countries, several guidelines could be established.

First, the anti-nationalist bias of the established theory of regional cooperation should be abandoned. Regional institutions among developing countries should, consequently, be conceived not as centres of supranational authority, a notion that runs counter to the developing countries' basic concern with nation-building, but as forums for consultation and coordination of policies. The principles of consensus in decision-making and voluntary participation in specific programmes and projects should be duly and clearly recognized. In brief, for the time being, a more appropriate form of regional cooperation among developing countries could resemble more closely the Organization for Economic Cooperation and Development, not the European Economic Community.

Secondly, under prevailing circumstances, comprehensive plans of regional cooperation in the form of common markets may be considered premature in the case of developing countries. Such plans usually promote unequal development, because among developing countries the conditions for either preventing or remedying maldistribution of benefits do not yet exist. In other words, unless the social enlargement of the market within each country is relatively advanced, a geographical expansion of the market, based on the economies of scale at the regional level, is more likely to increase inequalities within and between countries. In the Third World, regional cooperation should be conceived mainly as an instrument for improving the formulation and implementation of national policies. More flexible approaches to cooperation could, therefore, be pursued, namely general consultation on broad policy issues, with joint action restricted mainly to voluntary participation in specific programmes or projects, notably with respect to the three above-mentioned priority areas.

Thirdly, as cooperation in specific programmes and projects is concerned, whenever applicable, the joint use rather than the joint ownership of related facilities should be encouraged. The fate of the East African Common Services and its impact on ex-member-countries' relationships should not be forgotten. In practical terms, this means that it may be preferable to promote the establishment of a network of national institutions with a regional vocation, notably in the field of higher technical training and research, and consultancy services, rather than the creation of jointly owned and administered regional institutions. Such an approach would facilitate some form of inter-country specialization, while evading the whole array of problems linked with the question of joint ownership.

Fourthly, if under present conditions an attempt should be made at cooperation in industrial production, the intra-industry approach may prove more acceptable than the inter-industry approach, as the experience of the Council for Mutual Economic Assistance and the Andean Common Market seems to suggest. By allowing member-countries to share in the production of different makes of similar products or parts of the same product, intra-industry specialization seems to better satisfy the developing countries' concern for diversification of their industrial basis. It may also create more compelling commercial ties. On the other hand, one must bear in mind that a successful intra-industry approach presupposes, among other things, a very high level of infrastructural development and administrative efficiency.

Conclusion

This chapter has attempted to determine, in the light of the East African experience and the new development orientations of the basic needs strategy, what should be the major concerns of regional cooperation among developing countries and what should not. In the author's view, such cooperation should be mainly concerned with the creation of flexible frameworks for consultation on general policies and *ad hoc* participation in specific programmes or projects, notably in the fields of agriculture, infrastructures, and the search for appropriate technology. Less attention should instead be paid to matters which were high in the priority list of the established theory of regional cooperation, like the questions of supranational authority and shifting loyalties or the achievement of economies of scale and capital-intensive industrialization. In particular, we have argued against the adoption of comprehensive schemes of regional cooperation among developing countries, notably against the market approach to such cooperation as embodied in free trade areas, customs unions, common markets, and economic communities. The adoption of such schemes overlooks a simple fact: a low level of national development can only sustain a low level of regional cooperation. It is, therefore, unrealistic to expect that comprehensive forms of regional cooperation could work effectively in the absence of national integration, or that inter-country specialization in production could be reached before a substantive degree of diversification of national economies has been achieved. In fact, the market approach to regional cooperation, whether in the form of free or planned trade, assumes a high level of development of member countries. It takes for granted the existence of efficient national infrastructures and substantive diversification of national economies. In other words, it presupposes that the social enlargement of national markets has more or less been achieved. Under these conditions, the geographical expansion of the market, that is inter-country specialization in production or the achievement of economies of scale at the regional level, becomes economically required and beneficial without being socially harmful. Within economic communities of industrialized countries, it is easier to avoid those negative effects associated with the use of capital-intensive technology, namely maldistribution of benefits, constraints on the diversification of skills and monopolistic control of the market. As experience shows, such negative effects are too common and perhaps inevitable in the case of developing countries. If regional cooperation is to have any meaning for these countries, it has to serve, first of all, as an instrument of national development. This leaves little doubt on how the author visualizes the relationship between national and regional interest; between national and regional integration; and between national self-reliance, regional cooperation, and the quest for a New International Economic Order.

On the basis of the predominance of national over regional interest, we have argued why the established theory of regional cooperation cannot meet the aspirations of developing countries. On the same basis, we have suggested how regional cooperation could best satisfy those aspirations, in particular by facilitating the process of nation-building and diversification of national economies oriented toward the supply of the domestic market. In this light, emphasis in regional cooperation among Third World countries may have to shift from the production to the service sector, with the major aim of providing infrastructures for the formulation and implementation of appropriate national development policies.

As to the relationship between national and regional integration, we retain the view that no comprehensive form of regional order can be established before a substantive degree of national integration has been attained. This conclusion stems from the nature of modern regionalism and modern nationalism, based on the concept of equality, a major foundation of social order. By rejecting the use of force, and its connected hegemonic or imperialistic character, modern regionalism defines itself as egalitarian. Since the early 19th century, modern nationalism has generally embodied, in theory and practice, a quest for equality among nations. But, whether within a global or regional context, the extent to which a nation's rights and interest are actually respected, is mainly determined by the degree of national power or the degree of a nation's political integration, administrative efficiency, and economic diversification. Nations will more easily agree, in theory and practice, to the demands of comprehensive schemes of regional cooperation, when they feel politically and economically self-confident. To put it in clearer language, the growth of nationalism or the strengthening of the nation-state is a precondition for the development of regionalism.

The principle of the predominance of national interest also clarifies why the development approaches based on national self-reliance, regional cooperation and the establishment of a New International Economic Order, far from being mutually exclusive, are complementary and convergent development paths. They pursue the same objective, the protection of national interest, through national, regional and global means. Regional cooperation could well serve as an important link between a policy of national self-reliance and the efforts to restructure the international system, by creating opportunities for strengthening the bargaining power of the developing countries both at the national and regional levels. The nature of the international system is, after all, to a good extent determined by the bargaining power of its members. Negotiation and diplomacy remain basic elements of the present international system. One may even ask whether regional cooperation or integration is anything else but a bargaining process. One can also wonder whether it would not be more appropriate to consider the theory of regional integration as part of the power theory, which is basically a theory of bargaining and diplomacy.

Finally, our criticism of the established theory of regional cooperation is not meant to make it geographically specific. It is rather meant to call attention to the fact that regional cooperation should be seen in historical perspective. We do not deny that the European model could be applied in other regions, if and when similar political and economic conditions exist. But we are aware that even in Europe some important conditions for the creation of the Common Market were established during at least a century of less formal harmonization of policies, notably in the field of infrastructural development. Seen in historical perspective, the failure of Third World regional schemes of the type of the EAC may be due more to the complexity of their objectives and structures than to the vagueness of their aims or to institutional weaknesses. This message seems to have been taken into consideration by some recent attempts at regional cooperation among developing countries, including examples in the eastern, central and southern African regions. It becomes increasingly clear not only in theory, but also in practice, that regional cooperation among developing countries should principally aim at strengthening the partners' capacity for national self-reliance. More specifically, it should help members to formulate and implement appropriate national development policies, build efficient national infrastructures, and harmonize their relations with third countries, notably within a North-South context. Stated differently, the first priority of regional cooperation among developing countries should be to create the conditions for more comprehensive forms of cooperation. One may object that such a shift in emphasis represents yet another attempt to escape reality and give hope still another victory over experience. At the same time, one may wonder whether experience cannot teach hope to be more realistic, hence more successful.

NOTES

1 Some elements of the EAC are outlined in notes 3, and 5 to 10.
2 In Latin America, while the Central American Common Market was entering a long period of lethargy, the Andean Common Market was born in 1969. The Latin American Free Trade Area was dissolved in 1980, but, perhaps in anticipation of this, the Latin American Economic System had already been established in 1975.

In Africa, if the EAC came to an end in 1977 and the Customs and Economic Union of Central Africa (UDEAC) has been paralyzed for many years, a potentially ambitious community of 16 members, the Economic Community of West African States (ECOWAS), was launched in 1975. Even in eastern, central and southern Africa new regional groups are emerging, notably the Southern African Development Coordination Conference (SADCC) and the Preferential Trade Area (PTA). SADCC was established in July 1979 and is made up of nine members. PTA is still in the formative stage and should include 18 countries of the region, though the fact that only half of them showed up in Lusaka to sign the agreement, on 21 December 1981, does not augur well for the future of the group.

3 Initiated during the First World War, cooperation in East Africa had evolved, prior to independence, into a *de facto* common market and a valuable set of common services.

The major elements of the common market were a) the relative free movement of the factors of production: labour, capital and goods; b) the industrial licensing system, in existence from 1948 to 1973; and c) a common currency, issued by the East African Currency Board, from 1920 to 1965.

The common services included a) four major autonomous or self-financing corporations: Airways; Harbours; Posts and Telecommunications; and Railways; and b) some 20 general fund services, jointly financed by member countries and comprising i) nine economic and social services, namely the East African Academy, Common Market Tribunal, Common Service Commission, Customs and Excise Department, Development Bank, Directorate of Civil Aviation, Income Tax Department, Literature Bureau, Meteorological Department; and ii) 11 research institutions: the East African Agriculture and Forestry Research Organization, Freshwater Fisheries Research Organization, Marine Fisheries Research Organization, Industrial Research Organization, Institute for Medical Research, Leprosy Research Centre, Trypanosomiasis Research Organization, Institute for Malaria and Vector-borne Diseases, Virus Research Institute, Veterinary Research Organization, and Tropical Pesticides Research Institute.

The institutional landscape of the EAC was quite diversified with a) the Authority as the supreme decision-making body, made up of the three presidents of the member countries; b) a Central Secretariat divided into three main branches: Finance and Administration, Common Market and Economic Affairs, and Communications and Research; c) five ministerial Councils primarily with advisory and coordinating responsibility: the Common Market Council, Communications Council, Finance Council, Economic Consultative and Planning Council, and Research and Social Council; and d) the institution of the three East African Ministers, who in their triple capacity of assistants to the

Authority, heads of the three main branches of the Secretariat, and chairmen of the Councils, were to be the living link between regional concerns and national interests of partner states.

4 This was the almost unanimous view of the participants in a Panel on the collapse of the EAC, at the Annual Convention of the International Studies Association, Toronto, Canada, 20–24 March, 1979. Papers by panelists have been published by Christian P. Potholm and Richard A. Fredland (eds.), *Integration and Disintegration in East Africa*, University Press of America, Lanham, 1980.

5 A summary of this debate is provided in D. Mazzeo, *Foreign Assistance and the East African Common Services*, Weltforum Verlag, Munich, 1975, pp. 30–40.

6 The tax was a duty that a partner state with a deficit in inter-country trade in manufactured goods was allowed to impose on inter-country imports of such goods. The maximum level of the tax was fixed at 50 per cent of the value of the common external tariff on similar goods. The tax could be imposed only if the deficit country was able to manufacture similar goods within three months from the imposition of the tax and if production would either cover at least 15 per cent of domestic consumption or amount to a minimum of £100 000 per annum. The tax had to be terminated whenever the deficit country reached 80 per cent balance in its overall inter-country trade in manufactures. In any case, no single tax could last more than eight years and all transfer taxes should have been abolished 15 years after the coming into operation of the Treaty.

7 The initial capital of the Bank amounted to Shs. 120 million, Shs. 40 m. from each partner state. In 1970 the EADB sold to six foreign banks additional equity shares of Shs. 9 million. In 1972, it received loans amounting to Shs. 109 million from the World Bank and the Swedish International Development Authority. Total funds available early in 1973 were thus 238 million shillings. According to the rules of the EADB, on a five year plan Tanzania and Uganda would receive 38.75 per cent each and Kenya 22.50 per cent of the resources of the Bank, as it has been the case so far. The Bank remained in operation after the break of the EAC.

8 The major aim of the system was to stimulate industrial development and avoid duplication of industrial activities within the region in a certain number of selected industries by giving them access to the East African Market. It began with the cotton textile industry in 1948. A few other industries, such as tobacco, footwear, beer and cement were added through the years. In 1967, it covered cotton and woollen textiles, glass, steel drums, metal doors and windows, and enamel hollow-ware.

9 Up to 1967, most of the Services were located in or around Nairobi. Following the 1967 Treaty, the Secretariat of the EAC was established in Arusha (Tanzania), and the headquarters of the Harbours Corporation in Dar es Salaam. The headquarters of the East African Posts and Telecommunications and the newly created East African Development Bank were located in Kampala. The headquarters of the East African Airways and Railways remained in Nairobi.

10 This was certainly the case of the self-contained or autonomous corporations. But even the General Fund Services were directly financed by EACSO and later the EAC through half of the resources of the Distributable Pool of

Revenues (the other half being used for purposes of financial redistribution). Under EACSO, the Pool was automatically replenished each year by 6 per cent of customs and excise duties, and 40 per cent of the revenue from income tax on manufacturing and finance companies in the three countries. The 1967 Treaty cut these percentages by half.

11 Owing mainly to the construction of the Tanzam (Tazara) Railways. This was conceived to free the Zambian trade from dependence on South Africa and the Portuguese territories. It became a reality through a combination of Chinese generosity and political expediency. The construction of the railway affected negatively not only inter-country transport, but also inter-country trade. *The Weekly Review*, 15 February 1975, p. 9; and 13 December 1976, pp. 4–5.

12 By the mid-1970s, only Uganda was still enjoying a favourable balance of external trade, since the stagnation of its manufacturing sector made unnecessary the purchase of capital goods. Traditionally, Kenya relied on its surplus in inter-country trade to meet between one-third and one-half of its huge deficit in foreign trade. But when, in the early 1970s, the Tanzanian balance of foreign trade turned negative, Tanzania could ill afford to spend hard currencies in Kenya.

13 See Chapter One, footnote 1.

14 Both the principles of Viner's Customs Union Theory and the rules of the General Agreement on Tariff and Trade (GATT) seem to emphasize this point.

15 See Chapter One, footnote 6.

9   ECOWAS, the EEC and the Lomé Convention

S. K. B. ASANTE

Introduction

E. B. Haas, one of the most thoughtful and sophisticated theorists of regional integration, once observed that in international politics, as in other fields, the occurrence of an unprecedented event 'causes apprehension among some and the desire to emulate the event among others'.[1] The growth of the European Economic Community (EEC), in the context of the movement towards regional unification in general, was just such an event. For the early success of the European effort has evoked at least three major reactions in the rest of the world: a) admiration for the successful process of economic integration, b) displeasure over the actual and potential harm to the economies of the non-member states; and c) a mixture of envy and apprehension about the increased prestige and power – economic as well as political – that has accrued to the member states of the Community. Generally, the developing countries would tend to belong to the first category in terms of reaction. For while the initial operation of the EEC caused apprehension in Britain, Sweden and Russia, the developing countries generally saw developments in Western Europe as a model and inspiration as well as a necessary condition for their own economic growth and political stability.

Confronted by intractable economic problems since independence and by their manifest inability to develop separately behind their own national tariff barriers, low per capita incomes, small populations and narrow resource bases, many African states have come to consider economic cooperation as one of the main pillars of development strategy. The post war progress towards integration in Europe has impressed on them the idea of a simple and causal relationship between integration and economic recovery or growth. Their admiration for the operation of the EEC and its potential power has 'triggered a desire for emulation' – both to reap the alleged benefits vouchsafed by larger markets and to seek protection against the EEC's capacity to export and import goods. Thus the experiences of the EEC have demonstrated both the desirability and feasibility of integration among developing African states.

It is against this background of the European experience – coupled with world-wide enthusiasm for economic integration, as reflected in the various resolutions and declarations of the United Nations (UN) and its specialized agencies as well as bodies outside the UN framework[2] that 15 West African countries, already linked to the EEC through the Lomé Convention of February 1975, signed the Treaty establishing the Economic Community of West African States (ECOWAS in English and CEDEAO in French) on 28 May 1975 in Lagos. Cape Verde has since joined as the sixteenth member of the Community. This event represented the culmination of many years of effort by these states a) to increase the economic mass, and therefore the bargaining base, of their economies through a pooling of economic sovereignty; b) to transform their economies so as to improve the living standards of their peoples; and c) to extend the struggle for political decolonization into one of economic decolonization. It is the latest attempt in Africa to apply an 'orthodox regionalist approach' to development, that is, to encourage exchange and industrialization within the periphery. The ECOWAS Treaty became effective in June 1975 when the required minimum of seven member countries had ratified it.

The Community, as reflected in the ECOWAS Treaty containing 65 articles arranged into 14 chapters, has as its central objectives the promotion of 'cooperation and development in virtually all fields of economic activity, particularly in the fields of industry, transport, telecommunication, energy, agriculture, natural resources, commerce, monetary and financial questions and in social and cultural matters, for the purpose of raising the standard of living of its people, of increasing and maintaining economic stability, of fostering closer relations among its members and contributing to the progress and development of the African continent' (Article 2). The Treaty sets specific goals and provisions for realising these declared objectives, notably in the areas of trade, and monetary and industrial cooperation. It is envisaged that the establishment of the customs union would take a transitional period of 15 years after the Treaty has come into force.

While the institutions of ECOWAS are not as elaborate as those of the EEC, the Lagos Treaty recognises the development of adequate institutional machinery as an essential condition for successful coordination of development policies. The highest decision making organ of the Community is the Authority of Heads of State and Government which is charged with administering and directing the integrative movement of the Community. It is assisted by another political body, the Council of Ministers to be made up of two representatives of each member state – who act in an advisory capacity to the Authority, as well as give directions to all subordinate institutions of the Community. The Executive Secretariat of the Community, which is the machinery of execution headed by the Executive Secretary, is the third most important institution of ECOWAS. Apart from the Tribunal to be set up to interpret correctly and apply the provisions of the Treaty and Protocols, there are also four technical and specialised Commissions, namely, the Trade, Customs, Immigration, Monetary and Payment Commission; the Industry, Agriculture and Natural Resources Commission; the Transport, Telecommunications and Energy Commission; and the Social and Cultural Affairs Commission. The Authority of Heads of State and Government at its sixth annual summit meeting held in Freetown, Sierra Leone, in May 1981 approved the establishment of two more institutions – the Defence Council and the Defence Commission.

Briefly, the ECOWAS Treaty represents the aspirations and yearnings of the peoples within the West African sub-region for the promotion of cooperation and development in all fields of economic activity. It also provides the framework within which collective self-reliance and cooperation among member states of the Community could be given concrete expression in line with the New International Economic Order. The recently approved programmes of the Community include, inter alia, industrialization and trade liberalization programmes; monetary and financial harmonization, as well as postal, telecommunications and transport programmes. The protocol relating to the free movement of persons within the Community has been ratified and its first phase – abolition of visa requirements – is currently being implemented throughout the sub-region.

Since the creation of ECOWAS there has not been any comprehensive or systematic attempt at examining the relationship between the fledgling West African Community and the 'maturing' European Community. Sam Olofin's pioneering effort in this area is limited to a brief analysis of whether ECOWAS and the Lomé Convention are indeed an experiment in complementary or conflicting customs union arrangements.[3] For the most part the growing interest in the problems and processes of regional integration is particularly marked in two areas: a) studies centring on regional integration in Western Europe and b) studies focusing attention on this phenomenon in the developing world. On the whole, these efforts have been carried out with minimal reference to each other, despite the similarity of much of the material and the relevance of work in one area for conceptualization and theory-building in the other. In other words, no systematic attempt has been made to explore the extent to which regional groupings in developing areas can profit from the experience of regional integration schemes in industrialized areas. On the other hand, most of the current literature on regional inregration has assessed the prospects and success of regional integration schemes among developing countries from a Eurocentric viewpoint, even though, as Rothchild and Curry have pointed out, such 'Euro-based intellectual concepts and integration schemes', when strictly applied, have not proved to be adequate bases on which to construct integration in the non-European world.[4]

This Eurocentric research is also limited in the theoretical foundations on which the recent drive towards economic integration has been based. Unable to 'provide for separate theories' designed to fit conditions in developing countries, the literature on economic integration has stressed that these countries do not satisfy the criteria of neo-classical customs union theory. Consequently, it is contended that developing countries will not reap the traditional welfare gains from integration.[5] Then, too, although scholars like Green and Krishna have not hesitated to argue – and rightly so, of course – that the European experience can provide 'some obvious guidelines' for cooperation in Africa,[6] they are conspicuously silent as to the extent to which the EEC can also constitute a bottleneck to the realisation of the objectives of regional groupings in Africa.

It is in the light of these observations that this chapter attempts to focus attention on three principal themes. First, to examine the theoretical bases for regional economic integration with a view to justifying the need for its establishment in developing areas. Second, to explore the extent to which the European experience can be of relevance to the operation of ECOWAS. While it may be argued that the European experience has only marginal relevance to the developing countries of West Africa, it can hardly be disputed that the European approach to cooperation, as well as the detailed institutional pattern that has been evolved over the years, will leave an imprint on the current attempt at integration in West Africa. This much has been recognised by the Executive Secretary of ECOWAS, Diaby Aboubakar Ouattara, when he recently stated that ECOWAS 'is intentionally emulating the European Economic Community, as the most successful regional economic community so far in operation'.[7] The third purpose of this study is to examine the extent to which the EEC may also constitute an impediment to the realisation of ECOWAS' objective of regional self-reliance.

Theoretical bases for economic integration

Although most cases of regional economic integration are to be found among Third World countries, research in this field has been dominated by theory based on the European experience. The EEC has thus become, in the words of Joseph Frankel, 'a living laboratory for the integration theory'.[8] Not surprisingly, the literature on economic integration and development has pointed out that developing countries do not satisfy the criteria of neo-classical customs union theory and that they will not reap the traditional welfare gains from integration. Hence some economists, such as Jacob Viner and R. G. Lipsey deny that integration schemes will benefit developing countries.[9] Their argument is based upon the concept of trade creation and trade diversion. Viner defines trade creation as a shift in trade from a high-cost to a low-cost source of supply within the integration area, and trade diversion as a shift from a low cost source of supply outside the integration area to a high cost producer within it. In Viner's view, if there is more trade diversion than trade creation within a customs union, then the net effect on world welfare and the welfare of the members will be negative. Since trade diversion (at least in the short-run) will obviously prevail over trade creation in a Third World customs union as the members shift from low cost producers in the developed world to high cost producers among their neighbours, Viner and Lipsey are opposed to the creation of customs unions among developing countries.

On such a theoretical basis, therefore, there might appear to be little to justify economic integration in the developing countries. Hence in the context of the developing countries, the relevance of orthodox customs union theory is severely limited. As recently emphasized by Brewster and Thomas, the restricted treatment of the theory of integration, especially that based on the Vinerian neo-classical postulates, does not pose any serious problems when applied to 'mature' economies in the EEC. When however this 'theoretical framework and construct ideas' are applied uncritically to the analysis of problems of economic integration among economically 'immature' economies, it provides cause for profound concern.[10] For Viner's approach relies heavily on neo-classical assumptions of full employment, perfect competition, constant returns to scale, perfect internal mobility of factors of production and equality of private and social costs. It also evaluates the desirability of a customs union from the viewpoint of global welfare considerations only.

However, in recent years, there has been a growing criticism of applying Viner's criteria and Lipsey's general conclusions to the possible effects of customs unions among developing countries. Specifically, most writers concerned with the problems of Third World countries have rejected neo-classical trade theory and neo-classical customs union theory and argued that the problems of economic integration among peripheral countries should be analysed within the context of development economies rather than as a branch of tariff theory.

This argument is based on the fact that conditions in the developing countries are strikingly different from those which exist in the developed world on which the established theoretical framework for economic integration has been based. The critical factors on which the Viner criteria and Lipsey's conclusions were based are among the ones the developing countries, like those in West Africa, are desirous of changing through economic integration. In effect, remarked the renowned Nigerian economist, H. M. A. Onitiri, 'the underdeveloped areas are involved in a huge effort to alter the structure of their economy and to integrate their foreign trade more closely with it than before'.[11] In other words, these countries aim at changing the structure of production and trade, and then at evolving a new trade mechanism based on regional specialization. These changes are not marginal but structural.

Thus, in evaluating the desirability of economic integration among developing countries, the emphasis should be placed on dynamic rather than static effects. More specifically, we should be concerned with the dynamics of economic growth and stress positive effects in the creation of regional markets on the developmental pace of member countries. Dynamic effects refer to the several possible ways in which integration affects the rate of growth in the GNP of participating countries. They include, for example, the economies of scale brought about by the enlargement of the size of the market for firms producing below optimum capacity prior to integration; the effect on the volume and location of investment; and, also, the effect on economic efficiency and smoothness of trade transactions due to change in the degree of competition and change in uncertainty and unilaterality of trade policies of individual countries.[12] Indeed, as Gerald Meier has noted, the dynamic effects that are derivable through new investment are very important to any group of developing countries that wants to establish a customs union:

Where the objective is accelerated development for members of the region, the dynamic gains over the longer run may prove more important than the short-period welfare gains through reallocation of a given amount of resources. The case for a customs union rests ultimately on a belief that these dynamic gains will be realised and will more than offset any possible welfare loss through trade diversion.[13]

These considerations seem to be of overriding importance in the decision to integrate the economies of such developing countries as the West

African states. For while there could not be sufficient justifications on a 'purely static analysis basis' for the creation of a West African customs union, the contrary is the case on dynamic grounds.[14] It can be seen, therefore, that the theoretical bases for regional economic integration in developed and industrialized Europe and in developing and non-industrialized Africa are significantly different.

Indeed, on the whole, regional economic integration in a developing area such as West Africa is in many respects a very different phenomenon from that in an economically developed area such as Western Europe. Granted many features are the same; but many other features – important ones – are different. First, for example, we may readily point to important differences in infrastructure, market mechanisms, external dependence, administrative resources, political group structure, interdependence of social sectors, national consciousness, and ideology. Amitai Etzioni has thus argued that limited horizons, lack of administrative and political skills, and preoccupation with problems of domestic modernization all present major barriers to successful integration efforts in the developing world.[15]

Second, West European nations could afford to treat economic integration as a 'matter of welfare politics' without foreclosing their 'high-politics option' because each started from a relatively industrialized base. The case is quite different in the developing regions of the world.[16] As Joseph Nye has pointed out, integration involving developing countries seems to produce not 'gradual politicization' but 'over-politicization'. Such premature politicization of economic issues greatly reduces the scope for bureaucratic initiatives and quietly arranged package deals. Nye cites, for example, the Arab countries where economic activity has a high political content.[17] Thus conditions that may be termed requisite for successful economic integration in the developed areas cannot reasonably be applied to the developing areas. The same criteria for judging the success or failure of an integrative process cannot be applied to efforts in both the developed and developing areas. Besides, to some extent, the integrative process itself is different in developed and developing areas.

More significantly, the objectives of economic integration in developing areas are different from those in developed areas. In the latter the overall or general objective of regional economic integration is to maintain and enhance an already existing sustained economic growth. Hence the principal economic goal is to aid the development of already established industries in highly industrialized countries through trade expansion and increased competition.

In the case of developing countries, we would venture to redefine the goal of economic integration. Here, the ultimate purpose of economic integration is a) either to achieve an acceleration of economic growth in the partner countries, given the limited amount of scarce resources available or b) alternatively, to maintain the same rate of growth as before integration, but at lower cost in terms of the use of scarce resources. Put differently, regional economic integration in developing countries is seen primarily as a means of contributing to economic development. The consequences of integration are thus evaluated for their contribution to development and not necessarily to greater efficiency. Hence some economists, like Ismail S. Abdalla, would prefer to substitute the concept of collective self-reliance for that of economic integration, because the latter, it is contended, is 'imprecise, static and irrelevant' to the development issue.[18] To this extent, therefore, regional economic integration in developing countries may more properly be called 'developmental regionalism',[19] or an instrument of collective betterment, because it is designed not only to expand trade but also to encourage new industries, to help diversify national economies and to increase the region's bargaining power with the developed nations.

Up to this point in my analysis, it has become quite obvious that there is an important distinction between regional integration in developing West Africa and that in industrialized Western Europe. Thus, in looking at the undertaking of the West African sub-region one is not looking at a replica of the European one. This, however, should not lead one to conclude that ECOWAS at its present stage of development has little or nothing to learn from the experience of the EEC. For while the European experience can only be judged against the 'peculiar conditions' prevailing there in the post war period, the whole philosophy of European union and the multiplicity of institutions 'have provided some obvious guidelines' for cooperation in Africa. Thus, while recognizing the fundamental differences between Europe and Africa, our next section attempts to examine the extent to which the European experience can be a useful guide for West African cooperation.

EEC: an 'objective model' for ECOWAS?

Generally, the process of integration necessitates the creation of suitable institutions to deal with the complex problem of linking the economic destinies of several nations. Green and Krishna attribute much of the success of EEC to the wide range of institutions which have 'been instrumental in translating its programmes and policies into action'.[20] Under the Treaty of Rome clear provisions were made not only for setting up the organs of the Community, but also for a gradual transfer of initiative from member states 'to these supranational entities'. A significant result of these built-in provisions is that integration among the member states of the Community 'has become a continuous process, whose scope is expanding along a previously determined time-path'.[21]

The institutional pattern

While the Lagos Treaty which created ECOWAS recognizes the development of adequate institutional machinery as an essential condition for successful coordination of development policies, the formulation of its institutional pattern is a reflection of the peculiar conditions in Africa. It is worth noting, therefore, that in contrast to the EEC where the locus of supranational authority is found in the European Commission, in ECOWAS, that power rests with the Authority of Heads of State and Government. This direct involvement of political leaders in ECOWAS integration reflects what Mutharika has stressed; namely that it is difficult in Africa 'to consider economic development problems without considering the political realities'. This political element is particularly important because economic policies must get the blessing of the politicians before they can be implemented, and where political considerations clash with economic considerations the former usually prevail.[22]

It is pertinent to point out, however, that although the Treaty of Rome did not create any institutional forum for heads of government of the EEC countries, recent institutional innovation reflecting the political evolution of the Community, is gradually moving towards this process. This is the introduction of summit meetings by the heads of government which were formalised in 1974 under the name of the European Council. This evolution suggests that in the next stage of the Community, 'broad political initiative may rest with national political leaders rather than with the Commission', whose dynamic role as the initiator forcing the pace of European integration, as originally prophesied by neo-functional theorists like Haas, has been, at least temporarily, superseded.[23] Such regular summit meetings are likely to limit the formal supra-national character of the European Community. To this extent, it may be said that it is the EEC which is 'learning' from the practice of regional groups in Africa.

On the other hand, while the ECOWAS countries do recognize the prospects and benefits that can be derived from integration, they are nevertheless extremely cautious in negotiating binding commitments. Thus while the decisions and directions of the Authority of Heads of State and Government 'shall be binding on all institutions' of the Community, they cannot be binding immediately on member states themselves. This situation is creating difficulties in the current process of implementing some

ECOWAS Treaty provisions. A characteristic case in point is Liberia's declaration at the sixth summit of ECOWAS Heads of State and Government held in Freetown, in June 1981, not to implement the first phase of the Community's protocol relating to free movement of persons approved at the Dakar summit in May 1979.[24]

In contrast, strange as it still appears to British legal doctrine, the legislation of the EEC takes precedence over national laws and is automatically binding upon the member states. The directives of the European Assembly and Council of Ministers do not require national legislation – as is the case in ECOWAS – to become effective in the member states. It is an agreed practice in the EEC that national laws cannot override EEC laws.

The significance of this provision for the growth and development of a regional grouping like ECOWAS cannot be over-emphasized. A moment's reflection will show that this is a necessary precondition for a regional grouping to work at all, for it will be impossible otherwise to create the single economic unit, to establish the necessary confidence between the members about the environment in which they operate, or to handle external economic relations. Indeed, the success of the EEC is based on the inherent confidence of member states in their ability to meet the challenge of integration.

Interest groups

One other aspect of the EEC institutional pattern from which ECOWAS must take a cue is related to the extent to which the Treaty of Rome provides for a forum for an exchange of views with the interest groups or the private sector in Europe. Theoretically, the importance of the role of interest groups in promoting integration has been stressed almost ad nauseam by the neo-functionalist scholars like Haas and Lindberg.[25] According to neo-functional theorists, by participating in the policy-making process, interest groups are likely to develop 'a stake in promoting further integration' in order to acquire 'economic payoffs and additional benefits' from maintaining and stimulating the organization through which certain demands can be articulated and goals attained.[26] This implies that in the integration process interest groups can play an instrumental role in the maintenance of the integrative system. Through their involvement in the policy-making process of an integrating community, these groups will 'learn' about the rewards of such involvement and undergo attitudinal changes inclining them favourably towards the system. The result of this process is quite significant for the growth of an integrating community. For while the interest groups would be interested in working steadily towards the perpetuation of the system, the decision-makers would in turn develop an interest in being responsive to the demands of these groups. Through this process, the supportive clientele of the integrating community, which is of paramount importance for its growth and operation, would be wide and considerable. Thus the interest groups can enhance the position of responsive institutions.

Given the importance which neo-functionalists attach to the role of interest groups in promoting integration, it is not surprising that discussions leading up to the establishment of the EEC considered the formal involvement of economic and social groups in the policy-making process. Hence within the EEC channels have been developed through which economic and social interests participate in discussions, although it is not clear what influence they can exert on outcomes. The main formal channel provided under the Treaty of Rome is the Economic and Social Committee (ESC) set up under Articles 193–198. According to Article 193 the ESC shall consist of representatives of the various categories of economic and social life, in particular, representatives of producers, agriculturalists, transport operators, workers, merchants, artisans, liberal professions, and of the general interest. In practice about one-third of the members are trade unionists. It was thought that this body would provide a stimulus to interest groups to participate directly in Community discussions, from which support for policy proposals would flow. That the ESC has not developed as an institutional resource for mobilizing opinion at the supranational level to respond to interest group demands, has led recent commentators like Lodge and Herman to assign minimal weight to its role in the EEC decision-making process.[27] However, this does not entirely diminish the significance of its existence as a forum for the articulation of interest group positions. It is worth noting that neo-functionalist premises have been realized for the EEC outside the ESC, that is, through channels other than the ESC. Interest groups have 'pressurized' supranational policy and decision-makers through alternative mechanisms which have been found to be more effective than the ESC. By 1965 there were 231 regional offices of business and trade associations and 117 regional agricultural associations with offices in Brussels.[28]

This experience of the EEC is not reflected in the institutional structure of ECOWAS. Yet there are various interest groups in West Africa which will be directly affected by the gains and losses from integration; and these have some access, however limited, to the political process at the national or regional level. These may include the local private business sector, both commercial and industrial (represented by chambers of commerce), employers' associations or manufacturers' associations, and labour, both industrial and agricultural (possibly represented by individual trade unions and confederations of unions and sometimes closely aligned with political parties). Indeed, ECOWAS can rightly be criticized for not having any popular roots and because the personalities and institutions controlling it have little contact or involvement with the man in the street. The whole institutional structure can be described as a 'brain child' of the elite, and there is no organ through which interest groups can bridge, as neo-functionalists suggest, the elite-mass gap. Being inter-governmental in nature, key ECOWAS decision-makers are generally top level political elites and bureaucrats. Participation in decision-making processes by even the staff of the executive secretariat is minimal while the various parliamentary bodies play, if at all, only a very peripheral role. The bulk of the people is virtually excluded from effective participation in the regional economy as both producers and consumers. This low economic mobilisation of the broad masses means that 'they are unlikely to be involved in regional integration efforts based on functionalist strategies'.[29] Although the Federation of Chambers of Commerce in West Africa meaningfully participated in the negotiations leading to the creation of ECOWAS, to date only observer status has been accorded it by the Community.[30]

It must be pointed out, however, that interest groups need not necessarily be in favour of integration. In general, many of these groups remain a weak force, as Werner Feld has concluded in his study of European interest groups.[31] In many cases the types of interests that are aggregated at the regional level tend to be very general with more specific interests and structures remaining at the national level. For instance, as Nye has emphasized, despite the existence of regional trade union secretariats in Brussels, the idea of collective bargaining at the European level in response to the creation of a European market has not taken hold. In part this is because of divisions in the labour movement, in part it is also because of the importance of national governmental power in collective bargaining.[32]

Besides, many interest groups are opposed to integration. A character-istic case in point was the opposition mounted by the Venezuelan private sector against the country's entry into the Andean Common Market. The private sector was effective in turning its interests into government policy. Specifically, Federacion de Cameras (Federation of Chambers), the best organized pressure group in Latin America, representing 168 Venezuelan trade associations and federations, stoutly opposed its country's member-ship in the Andean Group. Consequently, although the Andean Pact was signed in 1969, Venezuela did not join the common market until 1973.[33]

In spite of these observations, the argument favouring the importance of interest groups or the private sector as relevant actors in promoting integration remains valid. Although these groups lack authoritative decision-making capacity, they should not be considered unimportant. They may prove to be very significant. By building in the involvement and collaboration of the private sector, these groups may well play a vital role, as they have done in the case of the EEC. In his examination of the place of trade unions as an interest group in the EEC, Colin Beever has come to the conclusion that as far as general community policy is concerned the unions in the EEC countries, with the exception of the World Federation of Trade Unions (WFTU), 'have almost unreservedly supported the principles of European integration and the Common Market itself and have . . . pressed for more progress and a greater degree of supranational power to be given to the community institutions'. They claim that they are the true defenders of the principles of the Treaty of Rome and they have never wavered in this belief.[34] Similarly, in the 1969 crisis of the Central American Common Market, it was the Federation of Chambers of Commerce and Industry of Central America which issued statements defending the common market. Furthermore, in addition to representing a shift of political activity toward the regional level and a potential source of regional pressure on national governments these non-governmental groupings themselves are subject to and encourage elite socialization effects.[35]

In this regard, the failure to involve the private sector in the ECOWAS decision-making process appears to be more serious than may usually be appreciated. For in the final analysis cooperation among West African countries is not or rather should not be just the concern of governments. If the political will to cooperate or to pool sovereignty is the 'subsoil in which we must nurture the tree of collective self-reliance', then the intellectual inputs in terms of ideas and especially the sustained pressure of the working population and organized opinion on their governments to push ahead is the water which must continually nurture the growth of that tree.[36]

Social welfare
Not only does the EEC provide for a forum for exchange of views with interest groups; it has also established an extensive social policy to cater for the social welfare of the labouring population, including migrant workers. And perhaps there is no area in which ECOWAS can learn more from the experience of the European integration than in the area of social policy.

EEC social policy focuses attention on problems of employment, industrial health, wages and the social cost of industry, labour mobility and the role of social spending in economic management (Articles 117–28). Its objectives include an accelerated raising of the standard of living, the free movement of people and a social fund to help employment problems. The social policy section of the Treaty of Rome is placed within a recognition by members of the need to improve living and working conditions and of their expectation that policies will gradually align under the impact of the new system. The Treaty was of the view that economic expansion was not an end in itself: social considerations were also important. Disparities in living conditions should be reduced and this should be achieved with the participation of all social partners. The quality of life as well as the standard of living should be improved, particular attention being given to 'intangible values and to the protection of the environment'. All this was intended to give the EEC, to quote Dennis Swann, 'a human face'.[37]

By contrast, while the ECOWAS accord provides for a progressive movement towards free mobility of goods and citizens within the Community (Art. 27), it is almost completely silent over the 'social welfare' aspects of this provision which could make this particular provision both effective and attractive in its implementation. Besides, the free movement of persons is accorded only a fragmentary freedom, at least as far as the implementation of the present phase (Articles 3 & 4) of the protocol relating to this subject is concerned. For whereas the free movement of persons provision in the EEC Treaty confers rights upon individuals justifiable before national courts irrespective of nationality,[38] the ECOWAS protocol confers no such rights. In the circumstances, a Community citizen who is faced with a deportation order in an ECOWAS member state has no implied legal right to any hearing. Although the Lagos Treaty provides for a setting up of a tribunal to adjudicate in matters regarding the interpretation or application of the treaty provisions,[39] its jurisdiction is clearly limited to disputes between member states. Individuals cannot initiate action before such a tribunal. Briefly stated, then, the doctrine of the 'primacy' of Community law has not been acceptable to the national courts of the ECOWAS member states. The absence of such regulations of the EEC type in the ECOWAS Treaty is one of the fundamental differences between the legal structure of ECOWAS and EEC. It identifies ECOWAS as less of a supranational organization.

Perhaps in order to make the ECOWAS free movement protocol effective, a cue should be taken from the EEC, which has shown the political will to make it possible for its free movement provisions to be implemented a full 18 months ahead of the Treaty requirements.[40] This is particularly important when it is recognized that the freeing of the labour movement within the West African sub-region could create as many problems as it solves if certain other complementary measures and social cushioning measures are not introduced as well, such as the right of free establishment for the self-employed, social security for migrants, social services and housing for migrants, and possibly vocational training provisions.

In West Africa, as in the EEC, the exchange of labour among the various national markets cannot rely exclusively on the blind forces of supply and demand, for this could lead to results that would be prejudicial to the regional economy and to the migrants themselves – particularly so if there were a lack of knowledge about prevailing conditions in the countries of destination.[41] In this respect, inter-governmental agreements and legislation ought to lend themselves to organizing systematic forms of more permanent cooperation among national employment services in order to make adequate provisions for maintaining a balance between labour supply and demand, based on a standard classification of skills and jobs. In this regard, ECOWAS can take a leaf from the experience of the European Co-ordinating Office (European Office for the Co-ordination and Balancing of Employment Supply and Demand) and could establish an agency like an 'ECOWAS citizens' bureau' to act as an intra-regional labour clearing-house capable of meeting effectively the needs of industry, agriculture, and public services. It could also be capable of serving the interests and aspirations of the working classes by preventing any migration that would result in unemployment in the country receiving immigrants and a shortage of labour in the country from which they migrate.

One other serious barrier to the free movement of population with which the West African governments will have to deal, and about which the EEC experience can be a useful guide, is the fact that the migrant, while losing the social security rights he has already acquired or is in the process of acquiring in the country where he has been residing, cannot easily obtain similar protection in his adopted country. In other words, lack of provision for social security for migrant workers or insufficient arrangements which mean that rights acquired in different member countries are lost will tend to reduce intra-union labour mobility. If also the purchasing power of social security contributions differs from country to country, perverse movements may be generated.

To avoid undesirable repercussions on both the strength and the direction of labour movements, it would be necessary for ECOWAS to establish social security rights based upon the example of their application within the EEC. In such a case discrimination towards migrants on grounds of nationality, and any difficulty stemming from the existence of territorial principle and the loss of rights acquired are automatically removed. In other words, in determining the right to benefits and the calculation of them, all insurance periods valid in the law of the various member states should be added together. An agency similar to the EEC's Administrative Commission for the Social Security of Migrant Workers could be set up to specify the ways of assessing compensation between social security institutions of different member countries of ECOWAS and to administer and interpret regulations governing this exercise.

Briefly stated, then, there seems to be no doubt that so far as the institutional framework of the European integration scheme and its social policy provisions are concerned, there are many ways in which ECOWAS could benefit from the experience of the EEC. It may be argued, however, that at its present stage of development, ECOWAS as an institution is not sufficiently equipped in terms of resources and power to take full advantage of the European experience. Such other laudable aspects of the EEC social policy as the establishment of vocational training institutions for training migrant community workers, or the setting up of a social fund like the European Social Fund designed to complement the free movement of labour provision, may well seem at the moment to lie beyond the capability and resources of the infant ECOWAS. All this, however, is relevant for the future.

But while there is much to be learned from European integration, it would be 'both misleading and dangerous', as Green and Krishna have correctly warned, to transfer all 'its concepts and institutions' – and especially the entire arsenal of instruments that are used to give effect to the integration policy – to a context which by its nature is quite different.[42] There is therefore the need for ECOWAS to be selective in its intention to emulate the experience of the EEC. Moreover, while the EEC provides some useful guidelines worthy of emulation by the West African grouping, it can hardly be disputed that at the same time its foreign policy, notably as embodied in the Lomé Convention, constitutes an impediment to the development of ECOWAS as an autonomous integrated grouping. In the next section of this chapter, therefore, I attempt to explore the extent to which the EEC tends to perpetuate the dependency and under-development of the ECOWAS countries.

The Lomé Convention and the ECOWAS strategy of self-reliance

The extent to which colonialism, imperialism and continued incorporation into the world capitalist system has structured the political economy of ECOWAS countries has been analysed in recent studies[43] and therefore should not detain us here. Suffice it to say that the political economies of these countries, like those of other developing countries, are a product of several centuries of contact with the capitalist, industrial countries of Europe and, more recently, of North America. This long period of contact has shaped the political economies of ECOWAS and other African countries in such a way as to serve the needs of the metropoles.[44] The attainment of formal political independence by these countries over two decades ago has not qualitatively altered this pattern of structural imbalance and dependence on former metropolitan powers. Rather political independence has in some ways made for more effective external penetration while altering some of the most obvious structural features internal to the colonial economy.

The direct consequences of 'centuries of extroverted development' for the peripheral African countries include a fundamental lack of congruence between what Brewster and Thomas have described as 'the structure and pattern of domestic output',[45] continued uneven development, income inequality, regional disequilibria, low integration amongst economic sectors and a segmentation of the society such that certain social classes and fractions of classes in the periphery are closely tied through transnational networks to classes in the centre countries.[46] The result is:

a lack of capacity to manipulate the operative elements of an economic system . . . an absence of interdependence between the economic functions of a system. This lack of interdependence implies that the system has no internal dynamic which could enable it to function as an independent autonomous entity.[47]

The central objective of ECOWAS as an institution is substantially to alter this pattern of (under)development. The aim is to enhance the economic opportunity of the West African states so as to enable them to reduce this pattern of external dependence and to break free from the historical conditions in which they find themselves. Hence Article 32 of the Lagos Treaty calls upon the Council of Ministers to 'take steps to reduce gradually the Community's economic dependence on the outside world'.

The major objectives of the ECOWAS strategy of self-reliance – a logical prescription of Latin American dependency writers – are therefore to avoid dependence and to promote development. This strategy involves a partial disengagement of the West African countries from existing patterns of dominant economic and political relationships which prevail in the international system. This disengagement process is to induce or accompany a restructuring of basic international and domestic relations. An important aspect of this restructuring is to increase both the frequency and magnitude of economic exchanges among ECOWAS member states, including increased trade, improved communication links, tariff reductions, industrial planning, technological acquisition, expansion of educational and technical exchanges, and the exploitation of natural resources on a regional basis.

Against this background, the relationship of ECOWAS countries to the EEC through trade agreements or through development programmes since February 1975 raises some fundamental questions. For example, to what extent does this relationship facilitate the realization of the objectives of the ECOWAS strategy of self-reliance or its goal to function as an independent autonomous unit? How does the EEC-ECOWAS relationship tend to perpetuate (or de-emphasize) the client status of the West African countries as a consequence of their age-old integration into the international economic system? Or can it be said that the genuine transformation of ECOWAS would not be constrained in the long run by the logic of its continued dependent relationship with the EEC?

Together with other African states, the ECOWAS countries negotiated with the EEC in the hope of achieving a superior rate of development, or at least of reducing the level of underdevelopment. The aim was to seek 'enhanced opportunity and equity to meet basic human needs'. In general Africa's main interest was first to 'guarantee the traditional markets in Europe' and, second, to 'restructure its exports' to include more processed and manufactured goods.[48] On the other hand, the main interest of Europe in negotiating the Lomé system was to ensure 'a reliable flow of cheap primary products' and to retain her already established markets in Africa for manufactured and capital goods.[49]

The Lomé Convention thus represents essentially an agreement between producers of industrial raw materials on the one hand (ACP countries) and of industrial products (EEC countries) on the other hand. It is a scheme 'to maintain the status quo' whereby the supplies of badly needed raw materials to the EEC countries would be guaranteed and the African countries, who through specialization would remain primary producers, would also be able to 'provide ready markets for the manufactured products of the industrialised EEC countries'.[50] I thus agree with Mytelka and Dolan that the Lomé agreement is at one and the same time 'a means to preserve certain elements of the old international division of labour' and a device to encourage those structural changes most in 'keeping with the changing global distribution of manufacturing production'.[51] To this end, Lomé is not only neo-colonial in tone but it also perpetuates the client status of Africa.

Thus the interests of the EEC are basically incompatible with the major objectives of the ECOWAS strategy of self-reliance. More specifically,

EEC interests would seem to constitute an impediment to West African efforts to industrialize and achieve the needed diversification of their economies. This is most readily apparent from an analysis of the key provisions of the Lomé Convention, namely the Stabex scheme aimed at 'stabilizing' ACP export-earnings from traditional products, regulation of access of ACP processed and manufactured goods to the EEC markets, and measures to increase direct EEC investment in ACP countries. As an analysis of these key provisions has already received adequate attention in recent years,[52] I intend to confine myself to a very brief review of the extent to which the Lomé provisions may constitute a bottleneck to the realization of ECOWAS objectives.

To start with, the Stabex scheme is not only inadequate because of the arbitrary content of trade and listed commodities between EEC and ECOWAS countries; it also constitutes a disincentive to further forms of processing of raw materials since it applies primarily to raw materials.[53] Specifically, the scheme applies by and large to primary commodities released for home use in the EEC or brought under the inward processing arrangements of the EEC in order to be processed. ECOWAS countries are being encouraged to engage in the production of products with a declining return in earnings. This is a disincentive to industrialization. There is thus a large measure of truth in Lynn Mytelka's assertion that the Stabex scheme is at one and the same time 'an incentive to maintain present levels of production' in the specified commodites covered by the scheme and 'a disincentive to diversify commercial agricultural production, process raw materials locally or develop domestic food production – all activities which would promote domestic linkages and bring the structures of demand and production more into line'.[54]

It is obvious, therefore, that Stabex is not intended to facilitate implementation of ECOWAS's objective of regional self-reliance, particularly since it is geared towards the perpetuation of inherited one-sided market structures. It is a scheme for short-term compensation rather than necessary long-term change and diversification. It does not interfere with the functioning of the international market mechanism governing trade in the products in question. Moreover, the scheme is a deterrent to ECOWAS's participation in producer associations – with regard to products covered by it – that may interrupt supply to the EEC. In general, the spirit of the Lomé Convention goes against the current strategy of most of the developing countries to strengthen the actions of producer organizations like the Organization of Petroleum Exporting Countries (OPEC), including joint marketing arrangements, orderly commodity trading, and improvement in export income of developing countries and in terms of trade.[55]

Stabex, therefore, cannot be expected to deal effectively with the problems of growing inequalities, unemployment and structural change which ECOWAS is designed to tackle. It is, to be precise, opposed to any actions that may lead to ECOWAS implementation of its strategy of self-reliance. Thus the scheme, to quote Daniel Mloka's succinct phrase, looks like 'stabilising poverty'.[56]

The problem posed by Stabex in relation to the realization of ECOWAS objectives is compounded by the failure of the Lomé Convention explicitly to recognize or sufficiently encourage the full permanent sovereignty of ECOWAS and other African countries over their own economic activities and natural resources, a subject which has received a great deal of attention in the recent UN deliberations on the New International Economic Order (NIEO). Instead, the principle of non-discrimination is used with regard to the arrangements that may be applied in matters of establishment and provision of services (Article 62) and to measures related to foreign transactions linked with investments and current payments (Article 66). In accordance with the non-discriminatory clause, the governments of ECOWAS members should not refuse the establishment of a company from a particular EEC country and leave companies from other EEC countries free. By these uniform arrangements, argue Coppens, Faber, and Lof, 'the scope for national development policy may be narrowed in certain fields' such as investments or social policy.[57] Indeed, in view of the continuing severe economic imbalance in relations between the EEC and ECOWAS countries, the fact that the Lomé scheme stresses the principle of non-discrimination would create a restrictive atmosphere with regard to the exercise of sovereignty by the appropriate ECOWAS authorities.

One other obvious point worth noting is the fact that the Lomé system does not attempt to regulate and supervise the activities of European multinational corporations by taking specific measures in the interest of the national economies of the African countries where such corporations operate. Specifically, the EEC has no 'binding code of conduct for corporations' in order either to prevent interference in the internal affairs of ECOWAS countries or to regulate their activities.[58] As stipulated in Title V, chapter 2 of the Lomé Convention, for example, European corporations operating in ECOWAS and other African countries are allowed to repatriate their profits, while the governments of these countries are prevented from making any attempt to 'regulate direct foreign investment and technology transfer'. Thus as a regional grouping ECOWAS cannot take a leaf from the experience of the Andean Common Market,[59] and initiate regional policies that regulate external linkages in the interest of domestic development.

Moreover, the willingness of the ECOWAS countries to plan and their ability to control the regional economy in the interests of autonomously generated development have both been vitiated by the close ties that have been fostered between the European multinational sector and the section of the petite bourgeoisie in control of the state. The Lomé Convention seems to stimulate primarily an EEC-ECOWAS elite relationship with elite benefits. As a result of solid material benefits, the local elite may get a vested interest in continued elite-elite relations. Consequently, first, ECOWAS-EEC relations would not substantially benefit the masses who form a large part of the West African population. And second, since multinational companies seek to shape the integration process to suit their own needs and interests, transnational linkage would exacerbate the 'tendency toward nationalistic competition, thus thwarting efforts at integrated planning'. This tendency would result in the shifting of the 'distribution of gains in favour of international capital'[60] and reduce the positive role of the ECOWAS integration strategies in the development process.

All this would seem to constitute a limitation upon the justified and necessary striving for self-reliance by ECOWAS members. Thus, although greater economic self-reliance is a necessity for ECOWAS as a regional economic integration scheme, since it enables it to escape from the historic dependency on the industrial centres and facilitates its development, the successful implementation of this strategy within the framework of the Lomé Convention remains problematic.

Conclusion

I have attempted in this chapter to see the ECOWAS-EEC relationship from two distinct viewpoints. First, the EEC could be seen as a 'potential workable model' for ECOWAS. It is, of course, recognized that the experience of European integration may 'not offer a valid basis' for teaching the developing West African states the methods by which the various kinds of specialization can be brought about while maintaining a proper balance between efficiency and equity, which is the supreme difficulty that such a cooperation scheme must eventually resolve. There is, nevertheless, much that ECOWAS as an economic integration scheme can learn from Europe, particularly in the areas of institutional patterns and social policy. The European experience has also highlighted some problems which inevitably arise as the area of cooperation is widened and moves are made to lift cooperation to more complex levels and forms. Second, considered from the viewpoint of the objectives of ECOWAS' strategy of self-reliance, its links with the EEC may constitute an obstacle to the transformation of the West African economies from a dependent structure responsive to the external demands of the world market to an integrated economy responsive to domestic needs and resources. Given the degree and nature of dependence on Western Europe arising from the structures of trade and technological relations inherited from the pre-emptive colonial intrusion into the West African body politic, it is not surprising that the EEC-ECOWAS linkage would tend to delay and prevent indigenous industrialization and perpetuate unequal exchange. More seriously, the ECOWAS countries find themselves restricted by their relationship with the EEC through the Lomé Convention in making autonomous decisions. For the Lomé system has a tendency to encourage a sharing of part of the political and economic decision-making of ECOWAS with EEC countries and/or companies, and to maintain the existing separation between elites and masses. Thus instead of the ECOWAS countries moving towards greater autonomy, towards national and collective self-reliance and towards orienting economic decisions around their national and regional political constituencies, the locus of decision-making of these countries tends to gravitate towards the private and public sector of the EEC. Briefly, then, the Lomé Convention can be perceived as a 'threat to development' in West Africa, because it enables Europe to 'exert more neo-colonial pressure' on the sub-region.

NOTES

1 E. B. Haas, 'Foreword' to Stuart I. Fagan, *Central American Economic Integration: The Politics of Unequal Benefits*, Research Series No. 15, Institute of International Studies, University of California, Berkeley, 1970, p. v.
2 See for example, *Proceedings of the UNCTAD I: Final Act and Report*, UN, New York, 1964, p. 11; United Nations: Resolution Adopted by the General Assembly on the Declaration of the Establishment of a New International Economic Order. A/RES/320, (S – VI), 9 May 1974.
3 Sam Olofin, 'ECOWAS and the Lomé Convention: An Experiment in Complementary or Conflicting Customs Union Arrangements?', *Journal of Common Market Studies*, September, 1977, pp. 53–72.
4 D. Rothchild and R. L. Curry, Jr., *Scarcity, Choice, and Public Policy in Middle Africa*, University of California Press, Berkeley & Los Angeles, 1978, p. 199.
5 W. Andrew Axline, 'Underdevelopment, Dependence, and Integration: the Politics of Regionalism in the Third World', *International Organization*, xxxi, (1977), p. 83.
6 R. H. Green and K. G. V. Krishna, *Economic Cooperation in Africa: Retrospect and Prospect*, Nairobi, Oxford University Press, 1967, p. 2.
7 *West Africa*, 11 May, 1981.

8 Joseph Frankel, *Contemporary International Relations Theory and the Behaviour of States*, Oxford, Oxford University Press, 1973, p. 48.

9 Jacob Viner, *The Customs Union Issue*, Stevens and Sons, London, 1950; R. G. Lipsey, 'The Theory of Customs Union: A General Survey', *Economic Journal*, lxx, (1960), pp. 496–513.

10 H. Brewster and Clive Thomas, 'Aspects of the Theory of Economic Integration', *Journal of Common Market Studies*, viii, (1969), p. 110.

11 H. M. A. Onitiri, 'Towards a West African Economic Community', *Nigerian Journal of Economic and Social Studies*, v, (1963) p. 33.

12 For further details, see Uka Ezenwe, 'The Theory of Integration: A further reassessment with particular reference to LDCs', Paper presented at the international conference on ECOWAS, Lagos, August, 1976.

13 Gerald M. Meier, *The International Economics of Development*, Harper & Row, New York, 1968, p. 210.

14 Olofin, 'ECOWAS and the Lomé Convention', p. 60.

15 Amitai Etzioni, *Political Unification: A Comparative Analysis of Leaders and Forces*, New York, 1964, pp. 318–21.

16 Roger D. Hansen, 'Regional Integration: Reflections on a Decade of Theoretical Efforts', *World Politics*, xxi, (1969), p. 261.

17 J. S. Nye, 'Comparing Common Markets: A Revised Neo-Functionalist Model', *International Organization*, xxiv, (1970), pp. 831–2.

18 Ismail Sabri Abdalla, preface to 'Economic Integration and Third World Collective Self-Reliance', *Third World Forum*, Occasional Paper, No. 4, 1979, p. 10.

19 John W. Sloan, 'The Strategy of Developmental Regionalism: Benefits, Distribution, Obstacles and Capabilities', *Journal of Common Market Studies*, x, 2 (1971), p. 142.

20 Green and Krishna, *Economic Cooperation in Africa*, p. 44.

21 *Ibid.*

22 Bingu Mutharika, *Toward Multinational Economic Cooperation in Africa*, Praeger, New York, 1972, p. 15.

23 C. D. C. Collins, 'History and Institutions of the EEC' in A. M. El-Agraa (ed.), *The Economics of the European Community*, Philip Allan, London, 1980, p. 36.

24 *National Concord* (Nigeria), 30 May 1981. For details of the protocol relating to free movement of persons see (A/P/1/5/79), ECOWAS *Official Journal*, i, June 1979, pp. 3–6.

25 Ernst B. Haas, *The Uniting of Europe: Political, Social and Economic Forces 1950–57*, Stanford University Press, Stanford, 1968; L. N. Lindberg, *The Political Dynamics of European Economic Integration*, Stanford University Press, Stanford, 1963.

26 J. Lodge and V. Herman, 'The Economic and Social Committee in EEC Decision-Making', *International Organization*, xxxiv, 1980, p. 265.

27 *Ibid.*, pp. 266–84.

28 Stephen Holt, *The Common Market*, Hamish Hamilton, London, 1967, p. 60.

29 Abdul A. Jalloh, 'Regional Integration in Africa: Lessons from the Past and Prospects for the Future', *Africa Development*, i, (1976), pp. 48 and 53.

30 C/DEC 1/5/79, ECOWAS *Official Journal*, ii, (June 1980), p. 11. For a detailed discussion of the role of Federation of Chambers of Commerce in

West Africa in the creation of ECOWAS, see chapter 3 of S. K. B. Asante, *ECOWAS: A Case Study in Economic Integration Among Developing Countries* (forthcoming).
31 Werner Feld, 'National Economic Interest Groups and Policy Formation in the EEC', *Political Science Quarterly*, lxxxi, 3 (1966), pp. 392–411.
32 Nye, 'Comparing Common Markets', p. 809.
33 For details, see Roger W. Fontaine, *The Andean Pact: A Political Analysis* (The Washington Papers, Volume V: Sage Publications Ltd., London, 1977), pp. 33–4. See also William P. Avery, 'Oil Politics, and Economic Decision Making: Venezuela and the Andean Common Market', *International Organization*, xxx, (1976), pp. 541–71.
34 R. Colin Beever, *Trade Unions and Free Labour Movement in the EEC*, Chatham House; PEP, London, 1969, pp. 18–19.
35 Nye, 'Comparing Common Markets', p. 809.
36 Adebayo Adedeji, 'Collective Self-Reliance in Developing Africa: Scope, Prospects and Problems', Paper presented at the International Conference on ECOWAS, Lagos, 23–27 August 1976.
37 Dennis Swann, *The Economics of the Common Market*, Penguin, Harmondsworth, 1975, p. 195.
38 See for example, Rutili v. Minister for the Interior (1975) ECR 1219 a case in which a French born Italian invoked the EEC provisions on free movement before French Courts.
39 See Art. 56 of the Lagos Treaty.
40 Beever, *Trade Unions and Free Labour Movement*, p. 29.
41 For a detailed examination of this subject, see S. K. B. Asante, 'ECOWAS and Freedom of Movement', *West Africa*, 3 July 1978.
42 Green and Krishna, *Economic Cooperation in Africa*, p. 44.
43 For a more extended discussion see my 'ECOWAS: Towards Autonomy or Neocolonialism?', in Timothy Shaw and Ralph Onwuka, (eds), *Africa and World Politics*, George Allen and Unwin, London, 1982. The literature on this subject in respect of developing countries as a whole is vast. It includes, for example, Rita Cruise O'Brien, 'Factors of Dependence: Senegal and Kenya' in W. Morris-Jones and Georges Fischer (eds), *Decolonisation and Africa: The British and French Experience*, Frank Cass, London, 1980, pp. 283–309; B. Campbell, 'Social Changes and Class Formation in a French West African State, (Ivory Coast)', *Canadian Journal of African Studies*, viii, (1974), pp. 295–306.
44 Lynn Mytelka, 'The Lomé Convention and a New International Division of Labour', *Journal of European Integration*, i, (1977), p. 72.
45 Brewster and Thomas, 'Aspects of the Theory of Economic Integration', p. 117.
46 Mytelka 'The Lomé Convention', p. 72.
47 H. Brewster, 'Economic Dependence: A Quantitative Interpretation', *Social and Economic Studies*, xxii, (March 1973), p. 91.
48 Timothy Shaw, 'EEC-ACP Interactions and Images as Redefinitions of Eurafrica: Exemplary, Exclusive and/or Exploitative?', *Journal of Common Market Studies*, xviii, (1979), p. 142.
49 *Ibid.*
50 Olofin, 'ECOWAS and the Lomé Convention', p. 67.

51 Lynn Mytelka and Michael Dolan, 'The EEC and the ACP Countries', in Dudley Seers and Constatine Vaitsos (eds), *Integration and Unequal Development: The Experience of the EEC*, Macmillan, London, 1980, p. 237.
52 See for example, Frank Long (ed.), *The Political Economy of EEC Relations with African, Caribbean and Pacific States: Contributions to the Understanding of the Lomé Convention on North-South Relations*, Pergamon Press, Oxford, 1980; Ellen Frey-Wouters, *The European Community and the Third World: The Lomé Convention and Its Impact*, Praeger, N.Y., 1980; Steven Langdon and Lynn Mytelka, 'Africa in the Changing World Economy', in C. Legum et al. (eds), *Africa in the 1980s: A Continent in Crisis*, McGraw-Hill Book Company, New York, 1980, pp. 123–211.
53 For a brief discussion of the Stabex scheme, see S. K. B. Asante, 'Lóme II: Another Machinery for Updating Dependency?', *Development and Cooperation*, iii, (May-June 1981), p. 18; S. K. B. Asante, 'The Lomé Convention: towards Perpetuation of Dependence or Promotion of Interdependence?', *Third World Quarterly*, iii, (1981), pp. 658–72.
54 Mytelka, 'The Lomé Convention', p. 74.
55 Frey-Wouters, *The European Community and the Third World*, p. 153.
56 Daniel Mloka 'Development without Dependence', *The Courier*, No. 44, July-August, 1977, pp. 57–81.
57 H. Coppens, G. Faber and Ed Lof, in Frans Alting Von Geusau (ed), *The Lomé Convention and the New International Economic Order*, A. W. Sijthoff, Leyden, 1977, p. 181.
58 Frey-Wouters, *The European Community and the Third World*, p. 153.
59 A detailed analysis of the experience of the Andean Common Market with multinational corporations is discussed in Lynn Mytelka, *Regional Development in a Global Economy: The Multinational Corporation, Technology, and Andean Integration*, Yale University Press, New Haven, 1979.
60 Langdon and Mytelka, 'Africa in the Changing World Economy', p. 188. Also see B. W. T. Mutharika, 'Multinational Corporations in Regional Integration: The African Experience', *African Review*, v, (1975), pp. 365–90.

10 The Southern African Development Coordination Conference (SADCC) and regional cooperation in southern Africa

PETER MEYNS

Introduction

One of the most recent initiatives towards regional cooperation in Africa is the Southern African Development Coordination Conference (SADCC), which was initiated in 1979 by the 'front-line' states and established with its initial membership of nine independent African states at the 1st SADCC Summit Meeting in Lusaka on 1 April 1980. The nine countries which came together in Lusaka were Angola, Botswana, Lesotho, Malawi, Mozambique, Swaziland, Tanzania, Zambia and Zimbabwe, the latter represented by the then Prime Minister designate Robert Mugabe.

SADCC grew out of the political struggle for the liberation of southern Africa and the support of the liberation struggle in Zimbabwe, Namibia and Azania/South Africa by the OAU and, in particular, the 'front-line' states. SADCC's own focus is on economic cooperation, based on the understanding that liberation in southern Africa, given the regional hegemony of South Africa, of necessity has an economic dimension, too. The 'front-line' states retain their separate identity and task of continuing support for the national liberation struggles in Namibia and Azania distinct from, and not institutionally linked to SADCC. This chapter looks at SADCC – the political and economic conditions of its emergence, its distinctive features compared to other African regional organizations and the prospects for its success.

South Africa in southern Africa

Economic cooperation among independent African states in southern Africa is specifically motivated by their opposition to the apartheid regime in South Africa. Their initiatives have to confront the dominating role

196

which South Africa occupies in the political economy of southern Africa. Indeed, this role is a necessary point of departure when analysing SADCC. It is not the purpose of this chapter to discuss South Africa's dominating economic role in, and its policy towards southern Africa in detail, but given its importance as a conditioning factor with regard to the aims of SADCC it must be dealt with briefly.

South Africa's outreach

South Africa's dominating role in southern Africa is based on the unequal development in the region initiated by the establishment of colonial rule and precipitated by capitalist penetration since the late-19th century when the mines were opened in South Africa. The relationship which developed between the mining industry and the neighbouring African colonies was based on migrant labour. This feature has come to characterize the economies of southern Africa to such an extent that they have been called 'labour reserve economies'.[1] The main suppliers of migrant labour to South Africa from outside are all among the SADCC countries. In 1976/77 there were close to 400 000 foreign migrant workers in South Africa. Of these, 200 000 came from Lesotho; 65 000 from Botswana; 50 000 from Zimbabwe, then still under white settler rule; 40 000 from Mozambique; 20 000 from Swaziland; and 17 000 from Malawi.[2]

Until 1975, when it gained independence, Mozambique had been a still more important source of migrant labour, supplying an average of over 100 000 per year. After it achieved independence in 1980 Zimbabwe announced its intention of stopping migrant labour to South Africa. Migrant labour is of greater significance to the economies of Botswana, Lesotho and Swaziland (the BLS states). Lesotho is the most clear-cut case of a labour reserve economy. Its migrant labourers represent one-third of its estimated total labour force, and more than six times the number of people, 32 000, in wage employment within its boundaries. The earnings the 200 000 migrant labourers bring or send home constitute 41 per cent of Lesotho's GNP.

While the economies of the colonial countries were being distorted in their own path of development, the South African mining industry was thriving. As new raw material reserves were discovered in southern Africa exploitation was controlled to a large extent by the same mining trusts, increasingly geared to expansion. South African companies like Anglo American and De Beers, together with international companies like American Metal Climax (AMAX) and Rio Tinto Zinc operating from a base in South Africa, were spreading the tentacles of their economic empire across southern Africa:[3] in the diamond mines in Angola's Luanda

Province, Botswana's copper/nickel and diamond mines, the copper mines in Zambia, the Wankie coal mines in Zimbabwe, the Mwadui diamond fields in Tanzania.

This incorporation of large parts of southern Africa into the sphere of influence of the South African economy led to the concomitant establishment of infrastructural networks in transport and communications and other areas in accordance with the requirements of the latter, thereby rendering the independent development of the other southern African countries more difficult still. Given the unequal development in southern Africa and the rapid growth of the South African economy, South Africa was obviously the first choice for many capitalist enterprises seeking lucrative markets in the region. The amount of investment by international capital in South Africa alone is higher than the amount invested in the rest of sub-Saharan Africa (where again the few countries with rich mineral resources take the lion's share).

As a result considerable production capacities have been established with the help of which South Africa has become an important supplier of agricultural products, consumer goods and industrial inputs to southern African states. Even the most ardent opponents of racism in South Africa, such as Tanzania, have taken resort to supplies of maize from South Africa in times of dire need. Table 10.1 shows the extent of the import and export trade which SADCC members conducted with South Africa in 1976. The virtual monopolization of the BLS countries' markets by South Africa is particularly striking. All these factors together constitute the economic power of South Africa in the region from which the independent southern African states want to liberate themselves.

The carrot: aid and co-operation
As South Africa has expanded and institutionalized its system of racial discrimination since 1948, international condemnation of apartheid has become more concerted. Spurred on by the anti-colonial struggles in Africa and such examples of racially-biased political oppression as the Sharpeville massacre in 1960 and the response to the Soweto uprising in 1976, opposition against apartheid spread so that South Africa can hardly find any open supporters in the international arena today. Its economic ties with international capital, however, continue to provide it with strong support. In the face of the advance of the anti-colonial struggles in southern Africa, leading to the independence of Mozambique, Angola and Zimbabwe with Namibia next on the list, South Africa has adopted a policy of 'the carrot and the stick' in order to secure its own position.

On the basis of its economic power it has endeavoured to present itself

Table 10.1. *SADCC countries' exports to, and imports from, South Africa in 1976, as percentage of their total foreign trade (million US dollars)*

	Exports		Imports	
	Total	South Africa % of total	Total	South Africa % of total
Angola[1]	1 202.4	—	614.3	9.9
Botswana	176.2	15.1	208.4	81.4
Lesotho	16.9	90	206.5	94
Malawi	160	5.5	206	29
Mozambique	149.8	7.7	300	15
Swaziland	193.7	20	146	87
Tanzania	490.1	—	638.8	—
Zambia	910.8	—	714.1	—
Zimbabwe[2]	685	16	460	38

[1] Figures refer to 1974.
[2] Figures refer to 1977.
Source: Amon J. Nsekela (ed.), *Southern Africa: Toward Economic Liberation*, Rex Collings, London, 1981, pp. 261–3.

as a suitable partner, familiar with African problems, for its northern neighbours. With the aim of gaining respectability as an African country it has projected itself as a 'regional power', similar to Nigeria, the Ivory Coast or Kenya, whose economic growth is supposed to (but rarely does) trickle down to its poorer neighbours.[4] For the past 20 years South Africa has put forward a variety of proposals for regional cooperation in southern Africa with itself as the regional power invariably serving as the patron.[5]

Significantly, when Verwoerd advanced his notion of a 'commonwealth' in 1969 it was related to his policy of separate development within South Africa, i.e. the establishment of African 'homelands' eventually to be granted 'independence'. Once they were 'independent' they were to be absorbed into Verwoerd's commonwealth. This aim of gaining recognition for its apartheid policy through regional cooperation is a constant theme in South Africa's propsals, right up to Botha's 'constellation of southern African states'.

Outside South Africa, Verwoerd's commonwealth and his related plan of establishing a common market in the region was directed principally at the BLS countries. Even as British colonies, Botswana, Lesotho and Swaziland had been tied to South Africa in a Customs Agreement since 1910. Though South Africa did not achieve its aim of incorporating the three territories as homelands, a new agreement, constituting the Southern

African Customs Union (SACU), was signed in 1969 after they had been granted independence by Britain. These three states remain very strongly dependent on South Africa economically.[6]

In 1967 Vorster, who had followed Verwoerd as Prime Minister, initiated his policy of 'dialogue' and later 'détente' with independent African states, not only in southern Africa. Informal contacts with a number of countries ensued. The détente exercise initiated by Vorster together with Zambia's President Kaunda in 1974 to defuse the liberation struggle in Zimbabwe temporarily stalled that country's advance to independence. Finally, however, only one country, Malawi, really swallowed Vorster's bait, accepting South African aid and advisers. Malawi is still the only independent African state to maintain diplomatic relations with South Africa.

In 1979, Botha, who took over from Vorster after the Muldergate debacle, called for a Constellation of Southern African States (CONSAS) in a speech to government officials and South African businessmen. Again, his proposal reflects South Africa's desire to buy allies and thereby prolong its own apartheid rule with the help of the superior economic resources it has at its disposal.[7] However, when CONSAS was formally constituted in July 1980 South Africa was alone as a member, together with its internationally ostracized, 'independent' homelands: Transkei, Bophuthatswana and Venda. Whatever South Africa may have hoped for CONSAS is, as one South African observer put it, 'to all intents and purposes an institutionalised formula to reshape relations on the economic, political and military/security levels between the Republic of South Africa and its former homelands', with much stress being put on the economic level in 'an attempt to redress the economic inadequacies of separate development'.[8] This predictable outcome shows the limitations of South Africa's economic leverage in southern Africa.

The stick: open and covert military action

The other side of South Africa's policy in southern Africa is geared towards strengthening its military power, with the help of its Western allies, and using it to attack other countries in the region from which it feels threatened, in a desperate attempt to change the tide of events. Such military action is conducted behind the flag of a crusade against communism. The irony of history is that it is South Africa itself through its incursions onto the national territory of other countries which provides the Soviet Union with the best cover to pursue its own hegemonic ambitions. Events before and after Angola's independence are the most obvious, but not the only example of this in the region.

South Africa's most drastic military action is presently directed at and around Namibia in order to thwart the South West Africa People's Organization (SWAPO)-led armed struggles and to maintain a balance of power favourable to its forces as the United Nations and the Western contact group continue their search for a negotiated independence settlement. South African incursions into southern Angola, allegedly on anti-SWAPO hot pursuit operations, have become a practically daily occurrence. Similarly, the districts of Senanga and Sesheke in south-western Zambia bordering on the Namibian Caprivi strip appear to be under constant South African surveillance.

It is clearly part of South Africa's military policy in southern Africa to destabilize the governments in those countries most sympathetic to the liberation struggle by supporting opposition groups. The União Nacional de Independência Total de Angola (UNITA) in Angola, a movement founded in 1966 with some support in the central plateau and which has opposed the Movimento Popular de Libertação de Angola (MPLA) government and Soviet/Cuban presence in the country since independence and the Mozambique National Resistance Movement (MNR) in Mozambique, a post-independence creation, are two cases in point. Both continue to engage in military actions in parts of Angola and Mozambique respectively. But the Zimbabwean government has also criticized South Africa several times already for harbouring remnants of the Rhodesian security and Bishop Muzorewa's military forces, known as 'auxiliaries', and training them for future military adventures.

It has been suggested that a link between South Africa's offers of cooperation to its northern neighbours and its destabilization policy can be seen in the fact that by disrupting transport through Angola and Mozambique it strengthens other countries' dependence on 'the southern routes.[9] The incidence of sabotage against the Benguela railway and, in particular, the Salisbury-Beira rail link and Beira harbour by UNITA and MNR respectively since the foundation of SADCC lends credibility to this hypothesis. Certainly, South Africa can be expected to use all means at its disposal to prevent closer unity of independent states in southern Africa. To be realistic, therefore, the strength of the South African position in the region, with its combined economic and military power, should not be underestimated.

The Southern African Development Coordination Conference (SADCC)

Origin and aims

When the 'front-line' states, Angola, Botswana, Mozambique, Tanzania and Zambia met in Arusha in July 1979 their discussion focused on the possibility of economic cooperation in southern Africa to supplement what has and continues to be their objective, the political liberation of the people in the white minority, colonial-ruled countries in the region. As President Seretse Khama of Botswana said in April 1980, 'whilst in pursuit of this objective, we realised the urgent need to extend the struggle from the political to the economic sphere.'[10]

This 'urgent need' imposed itself upon the 'front-line' states because, as they had been intensifying their support of the struggle for political liberation in Zimbabwe since the Smith regime's unilateral declaration of independence in 1965, their economies had become increasingly dependent on South Africa. For instance, when Zambia applied sanctions and cut its trade links with the Smith regime in 1973 its dependence on trade relations with South Africa increased. And when in 1978 it decided to reopen its border with Zimbabwe to let rail traffic from South Africa pass, its vulnerability to pressure from the South African government increased further.[11] Similarly, when Mozambique applied sanctions against the Smith regime in 1976, thereby forfeiting considerable income from Rhodesian use of its railways and harbours, its dependence on South Africa for such entrepôt trade traffic increased. To quote Seretse Khama again: 'We may be proud of our political independence; but before we achieve some degree of economic independence, our task is not complete.'[10] In southern Africa this implies to a large extent economic independence from South African regional hegemony.

The strategy which the 'front-line' states put forward to advance their aim was intensified economic cooperation among themselves and other 'majority-ruled states of southern Africa'. The political breakthrough in Zimbabwe which led to that country's independence in April 1980 was particularly significant in getting the SADCC initiative off the ground. Not only is Zimbabwe geographically centrally located in the region and represents an enormous economic potential, but it had also occupied a major place in South Africa's attempt to launch its own CONSAS. Once the South African-backed bid for power by Bishop Muzorewa had failed, CONSAS as an attempt to expand South Africa's political influence into southern Africa was doomed to failure.

It was under the impact of the resounding election victory of ZANU-PF in Zimbabwe that representatives from nine southern African countries met in Lusaka on 1 April 1980. In addition to the 'front-line' states, Lesotho, Malawi, Swaziland and Zimbabwe attended. With the political independence of Zimbabwe achieved, it was a most suitable moment to focus more strongly on economic development. The governments present at the Lusaka Summit Meeting adopted a declaration entitled *Southern Africa: Toward Economic Liberation*, which has become the blueprint for

SADCC. The development objectives to be pursued by the coordinated action of the SADCC member countries are defined as follows:–

1 the reduction of economic dependence, particularly, but not only, on the Republic of South Africa;
2 the forging of links to create a genuine and equitable regional integration;
3 the mobilisation of resources to promote the implementation of national, inter-state and regional policies;
4 concerted action to secure international co-operation within the framework of our strategy for economic liberation.[12]

It was agreed at Lusaka that SADCC would not engage in elaborate institution building, but would concentrate on practical efforts to implement projects beneficial to regional development. To this effect, areas of common interest were identified and individual member-countries were given the mandate to prepare draft programmes and propose projects for consideration by SADCC.

The area of transport and communications has been given highest priority by SADCC. It was recognized that the improvement of such links is fundamental to the implementation of projects in other important areas, such as food security, industrial production and trade. As the sectoral paper prepared by a group of consultants for the Arusha conference argued: 'No serious degree of economic integration can be achieved within the region as a whole until it becomes significantly easier, faster and cheaper to move messages, persons and goods than it is today.'[13]

Moreover, six SADCC members, the BLS states, Malawi, Zambia and Zimbabwe, are landlocked and, with the exception of Malawi, all are heavily dependent on transit routes through South Africa for their overseas trade.[14] This makes especially the 'front-line' states among them vulnerable to pressure from South Africa. Indeed, South Africa has on several occasions already used the reduction of trade passage to Zambia and Zimbabwe to show them its muscle. As all SADCC countries have economies strongly dependent on foreign trade, this dependency is a serious potential constraint on their development. Angola, Mozambique and Tanzania do provide outlets to the sea, but for various reasons, civil war, repercussions of support for the liberation struggles in Namibia and Zimbabwe, lack of skilled personnel and mismanagement, or low capacity, their rail links are at present unable adequately to cater for the region's overseas trade.

Transport and communications development, therefore, is the area in which SADCC countries started identifying projects immediately after the Arusha conference. The areas of cooperation (and their coordinators)

agreed upon in the programme of action formally adopted in Lusaka are as follows:–
– the creation of a Southern African Transport and Communications Commission (SATCC) based in Maputo (Mozambique);
– regional food security (Zimbabwe);
– coordinated control of foot-and-mouth disease in cattle on a regional basis (Botswana);
– establishment of a regional sub-centre of the International Crops Research Institute for the Semi-Arid Tropics (Botswana);
– regional industrial development (Tanzania);
– formulation of a regional energy conservation policy (Angola);
– sharing of national training facilities and assessment of need and opportunities for cooperation in manpower training (Swaziland);
– establishment of a Southern African Development Fund (Zambia).[15]
Subsequent SADCC conferences held in 1981 identified additional areas of cooperation to be incorporated into the programme of action:–
– forestry, fisheries and wildlife (Malawi);
– regional mining development (Zambia);
– soil conservation and land utilization (Lesotho, Zimbabwe).

Programmes and pledges
The four-point SADCC strategy cited above explicitly refers to 'concerted action to secure international cooperation', as SADCC members realized that they would not be able to finance their projects without international credits and aid. Annual meetings between SADCC and its international development cooperation partners have, therefore, become a specific feature of SADCC's mode of operation. The initial conference in Arusha was the first such meeting. Its topic was the formulation of a viable framework for regional cooperation in southern Africa, and the SADCC strategy adopted in 1980 was drafted there.[16]

The Maputo Conference in November 1980 was quite different in nature. It was a pledging conference with the purpose of securing financial and technical support for the projects of regional cooperation which SADCC had agreed upon. Apart from the SADCC members, 30 governments and 19 international organizations attended.

In accordance with the priority given to transport and communications the main focus was on this area. SADCC members had agreed on a detailed programme of 97 projects prepared by the Maputo-based Southern African Transport and Communications Commission, 26 of which were road projects; 25, railways; eight, ports and water transport; 12, airports and air transport; 25, telecommunications; and one was multi-modal, covering technical assistance for SATCC itself.[17] The total estimated cost for this programme was US$1912 million. To guide implementation SADCC established four priority classes. Top priority was given to the 43 projects involving the rehabilitation or upgrading of existing facilities. Next in order of priority were the 21 new telecommunications projects, followed by 13 new transport projects and, fourthly, studies. The rehabilitation and upgrading projects did, however, require the bulk of the estimated finance, a total of US$1533 million.

The SADCC transport and communications programme argued that 'in the short run it seems that rehabilitation or up-grading of existing railway and port facilities will create sufficient capacity to take care of the transport demand, even if it increased by additional mining activity.'[18] This explains the stress put on such projects. Close to half the funds earmarked for this top priority class will be spent in Mozambique. With three large harbours, Maputo, Beira and Nacala, all of which need rehabilitating and/or upgrading, Mozambique is the main regional trade outlet for Malawi, Swaziland and Zimbabwe as well as an important potential outlet for Botswana, Zambia and even Zaire. Investments are also needed to improve railway links between Mozambique and the other landlocked countries of the region. The other two regional railway outlets, the Benguela railway through Angola and the Tanzania-Zambia-Railway (TAZARA) are also to be rehabilitated, US$60 million and US$50 million respectively being earmarked for that purpose. TAZARA was allocated an additional US$43 million for various projects under priority class 3.

The total amount pledged at the Maputo Conference was over US$650 million. The bulk of these funds will go towards financing the transport and communications projects. Unless otherwise specified the amounts pledged were for the budget periods 1980/81 and 1981/82. It is likely, therefore, that these countries will make more funds available in the following years. Similarly, unspecified pledges will materialize as projects are submitted for approval by donors. As Table 10.2 shows, apart from the African Development Bank with by far the largest single pledge and UNDP, all other pledges came from Western capitalist countries. Though a number of Eastern bloc countries, Bulgaria, Czechoslovakia, GDR, Hungary and Romania, attended and Comecon sent an observer, only the GDR made an unspecified pledge. This confirms the general pattern that Third World countries must rely essentially on Western and oil funds for the external funding of their development efforts.

In the case of SADCC this is an interesting observation as two of its members, Angola and Mozambique, are closely allied to the Eastern bloc.

Table 10.2. *SADCC Maputo Conference, November 1980: pledges of support (million US dollars)*

Country/Organization		Amount pledged	Comments
Sweden	(11 + 11)	22	
Netherlands	(16 + 16)	32	
Norway		6	
Finland		6	
Denmark		10	
USA	(25 + 25)	50	
Italy		15	
Fed. Rep. of Germany		2	
Australia		1	
Belgium		8.50	
African Development Bank		384	1982–1986
EEC		100	spread over 5 years
UNDP		20	over 5 years
Total		656.50	

Unspecified pledges were made by GDR, UK, Switzerland, Canada, Austria, Yugoslavia, Brazil, France, Venezuela, Kuwait Fund, OPEC Fund, BADEA, World Bank
Source: SADCC, Record of the Ministerial Meeting held in Maputo, Mozambique on 26 Nov. 1980 and reconvened on the afternoon of 28 Nov. 1980. Annex VI

This was a controversial issue at the Maputo Conference in a different context, namely with regard to the European Economic Community (EEC) pledge. It will be made available to member countries of the Lomé Convention only, i.e. to SADCC members with the exception of Angola and Mozambique. This is in line with EEC policy to favour development in the ACP-states associated with the EEC, but obviously runs counter to SADCC's aims of regional cooperation. It appears that West Germany is reluctant to extend the EEC funds for SADCC to Angola and Mozambique as both so far refuse to accept the so-called 'Berlin clause', which incorporates West Berlin into agreements like the Lomé Convention of which West Germany is a signatory. This problem shows the difficulties of regional cooperation among countries with different international relations. On the other hand, the loose institutional structure SADCC has opted for will make it fairly easy to accommodate such specific policies of partner countries or institutions, as pledges are made for given projects. As Table 10.2 shows, a number of EEC member states made separate pledges. Some of these are for projects in Angola and particularly Mozambique.

It has been argued that the pledges made at the Maputo Conference do not constitute really new funds, that the US$100 million pledged by the EEC, for instance, would have been available to the signatories of the Lomé Convention in the region anyway. This may be so. The significance of the Maputo Conference, however, is that pledges were made within the framework of a programme drawn up by SADCC, thereby allowing international credits and aid to be channelled into development priorities as perceived by the countries of the region themselves. In this respect the Maputo Conference was an important step forward in the fulfilment of the SADCC strategy.

By mid-1981 it was reported that of the 97 projects tabled at the Maputo Conference 22 were being implemented, 29 had been prepared and submitted to agencies which had pledged support, 43 were in the process of detailed proposal preparation before submission to prospective donors, and three projects had been withdrawn.[19]

The only other area of cooperation for which a programme was submitted to the Maputo Conference was 'regional food security'. The serious food shortages several SADCC members have suffered during the past years, notably Angola, Mozambique, Tanzania and Zambia, and the fact that they have had to rely on South Africa to supply part of the shortfall make this an important programme in the context of SADCC's aims. Though Zimbabwe had a considerable surplus of maize at the end of the 1980/81 crop season there were bottlenecks in the transport network to the other SADCC countries as well as shortfalls in storage facilities. These are the problems a programme in this sector has to tackle.[20] Zimbabwe prepared the report on 'Regional Food Security' tabled at Maputo.

The report proposes initial projects to establish the basic infrastructure of agricultural cooperation, namely the formation of an agrarian coordination body for regional interaction on all agrarian issues; the elaboration of a regional and national early warning system for regional food security;[21] the establishment of a regional data bank for basic agricultural information; and the compilation of an inventory of regionally or nationally available or potential agricultural resources. Other projects, such as a regional food reserve system; improved storage techniques and facilities; development of food processing technology; an improved marketing system; and coordination of regional food imports if required, can then build up on the available infrastructure. Only a small part of the sum pledged during the Maputo Conference went into the regional food security programme. Even in future, it is likely to be much less costly than the transport programme.

As the pledges made at Maputo covered several years, some up to 1986, the third SADCC conference with its international partners, held in

Blantyre in November 1981, had an essentially consultative nature with regard to areas of cooperation for which programmes had already been tabled. Nevertheless some new pledges were made and others confirmed. The 19 countries and 11 international organizations which attended the Blantyre Conference reflected the composition of SADCC's international partners already apparent in Maputo the year before, comprising African organizations, oil funds, UN agencies and Western countries.[22] SADCC had cleared documents in two further areas of cooperation for presentation to the Blantyre Conference, on manpower and industrial development prepared by Swaziland and Tanzania respectively. The four areas of cooperation, transport and communications, food and agriculture, manpower, and industry, were considered in separate working groups to allow consultations to concentrate on the specific issues involved in each case.[23] The Blantyre Conference, therefore, saw a further expansion of the scope of SADCC's links with its international development cooperation partners.

Institutionalization

Just as SADCC's principal focus on transport and communications projects makes it a novel initiative in regional cooperation among Third World countries, so too does its approach to its own institutionalization. However, the way it is shaping its institutions does bear considerable resemblance to the non-aligned movement. The idea behind this approach is to establish as loose an organizational set-up as possible, allowing for maximum independence and sovereignty of individual member states, and as structured a set-up as is necessary to implement the objectives agreed upon. It implies, in other words, that the establishment of institutions beyond what is needed to achieve the organization's aims is avoided, and that decisions are taken essentially at the political level rather than by technocrats appointed at the administrative level. At the political level, given the basic agreement on common interests which led to the formation of, or adherence to the organization in the first place, decisions can be based on the principle of consensus.

In accordance with this approach, which can perhaps be called the non-aligned approach to the institutionalization of cooperation agreements, SADCC's most important bodies are the Summit Meeting and the Council of Ministers. The institutions necessary to ensure the technical functions of SADCC are the Commissions for sectoral areas, and the Secretariat. The second Summit Meeting, held in Salisbury in July 1981, two years after SADCC's inception, formally adopted a 'Memorandum of Understanding on the Institutionalisation of the Southern African Development Co-ordination Conference (SADCC)', on the basis of earlier draft proposals prepared by Botswana. The Final Communiqué issued after the Salisbury Summit said: 'SADCC has eschewed the creation of a large and unwieldy bureaucracy in favour of a system which places responsibility for the implementation of its programme on the Governments of Member States.'[24] The only new institution to be agreed upon at Salisbury was the SADCC Secretariat. It was decided that the Secretariat would be based in Gaborone, that it would be established as from 1 July 1982 and that Zimbabwe would nominate its first officer-in-charge, the Executive Secretary.

The supreme body of SADCC is the Summit Meeting. It is 'responsible for the general direction and control of the performance of the functions of SADCC and the achievement of its objectives.'[25] It meets at least once a year. The body charged with the overall execution of SADCC policies is the Council of Ministers, which also meets at least once a year. It is responsible 'for the overall policy of the SADCC, its general co-ordination, the supervision of its institutions and the supervision of the execution of its programmes.'[26] Commissions for sectoral areas and the Executive Secretary, while established or appointed by the Summit Meeting, report to the Council. The Council of Ministers may, if the need arises, appoint ad hoc Committees of Ministers for particular programme areas. The Council has a Standing Committee of Officials to assist it in its business, and may appoint Sub-Committees of officials for particular programme areas, if the need arises. The Council also convenes the annual consultative conference with SADCC's international development coordination partners. Decisions taken by the Council of Ministers are subject to the approval of the Summit Meeting. The chairmanship of the Summit Meeting and the Council of Ministers has, during the initial years of SADCC from 1979 and into 1982, been held by Botswana, but in future it will rotate among members.

The main technical bodies of SADCC are the Commissions for sectoral areas. By the end of 1981 only one such commission, the Southern African Transport and Communications Commission (SATCC), based in Maputo, had been established. Not every area of cooperation SADCC has embarked upon may need such a commission. The Summit Meeting will decide, according to practical requirements, on the establishment of further commissions. SADCC Commissions are governed by separate Conventions approved by the SADCC Council of Ministers and ratified by member countries.[27] The supreme body of SATCC is the Council of Ministers, its executive body is the Coordinating Committee supported by a Technical Unit.[28] SATCC's objectives are to contribute to the fulfilment of SADCC's four-point strategy by promoting rational and integrated utilization of the transport and communications systems existing in the region; by promoting new development programmes and projects, and the modernization of existing systems; and by seeking participation of the independent states in the region.

The SADCC Secretariat is a purely administrative body established 'for the general servicing of the SADCC and for liaison with its specialized institutions.'[29] As SADCC activities expand to cover more specific areas of cooperation, the Secretariat can ensure the smooth functioning of the organization by providing the Council of Ministers with administrative support.

SADCC is conceived as being fairly open. Like the non-aligned movement, it is geared to incorporating other like-minded members. The Lusaka Declaration explicitly states that the nine signatories 'do not envisage this regional economic co-ordination as exclusive. The initiative toward economic liberation has flowed from our experience of joint action for political liberation. We envisage regional co-ordination as open to all genuinely independent Southern African States,'[30] i.e. those recognized by the OAU. What is actually seen to belong to the southern African region has not been defined, but can be assumed to be flexible. Tanzania, for instance, is geographically East African, but by virtue of its support for the liberation struggles in southern Africa and its chairmanship of the 'front-line' states it has politically become part of southern Africa and a founder member of SADCC. Namibia and Azania/South Africa are, of course, part of the region. SWAPO was invited to attend the Lusaka Summit Meeting of SADCC, and Namibia under SWAPO leadership is confidently expected to become SADCC's tenth member once independence is achieved, though South Africa has still not given up its own designs for Namibia's future.[31] The SATCC Convention explicitly accords all liberation movements of southern Africa recognized by the OAU, i.e. SWAPO for Namibia, and ANC and PAC for Azania/South Africa, observer status on its Council of Ministers and Co-ordinating Committee. Further north, Zaire attended the Maputo Conference as an observer because of its interest in the regional transport system, particularly the Benguela railway, and might consider joining SADCC in the future.

Members are free to maintain other ties of cooperation outside the framework of SADCC, such as the BLS states' membership in the Southern African Customs Union (SACU) with South Africa. Members are also not obliged to participate in areas of cooperation within SADCC from which they do not expect to reap any benefits. This flexibility built into SADCC's institutional framework in numerous respects ensures that members' national independence and sovereignty remain uppermost and that they can participate in joint regional activities in line with their national interests as they perceive them.

SADCC: problems and prospects

Having looked at the aims and activities of SADCC and its member states we now turn to a discussion of its prospects. Numerous arguments can, have and will continue to be brought forward to argue why SADCC is bound to fail or, at best, will only achieve very limited results. None of these arguments is without foundation. Therefore, they warrant closer consideration.

The nine SADCC members – a mixed group

A look at the nine signatories of the Lusaka Declaration quickly reveals the diversity among them with regard to political systems, level of development, socio-economic structures and basic demographic features. Angola and Mozambique profess scientific socialism; Tanzania and Zimbabwe, while also in favour of socialism, stress the indigenous character of their development path more strongly; Zambia with its own humanist philosophy sees socialism as a transitional phase on the way to humanism; Malawi, an autocratic regime, is the only African state to maintain diplomatic relations with South Africa; Botswana, Lesotho and Swaziland are tied to South Africa through a Customs Union agreement, all three have moderate, if not conservative governments. Again, some of the nine, notably Angola, Botswana, Zambia and Zimbabwe, have rich mineral resources, while others, like Tanzania, Malawi and Mozambique, are principally producers of agricultural products. The extent of dependence on South Africa differs substantially among them (see Table 10.1). Angola and Tanzania have very few economic ties with South Africa, while the BLS states are most dependent on it. The list of differences could be continued. (see also Table 10.3).[32]

What does the undisputed existence of such differences mean in relation to cooperation among the countries concerned? Asked how cooperation among the nine would affect Mozambique's aim of socialist development Samora Machel answered:

we look at cooperation as based on relations of equality, mutual benefit and non-interference. (. . .) The conference on regional cooperation that took place in Lusaka has very concrete objectives, common to the 9 countries involved. What unites us is very much stronger and much more important than the fact that we have different political options. What unites us is the common desire to intensify our relations, to exchange our experiences, to cooperate in projects of regional development, to free ourselves gradually from economic dependence on South Africa in which the history of imperialist domination has placed our countries.

Table 10.3. *Selected demographic and economic indicators: 1979*

	Area ('000 km²)	Population Mill.	Population Density per km²	GDP (US $m.)	GNP per capita	Main exports
Angola	1 247	7.2	5.8	2 490	440	Oil, coffee, diamonds, sisal
Botswana	582	0.8	1.3	460[1]	620[1]	Copper/nickel, diamonds, livestock
Lesotho	30	1.3	43	240	340	Cattle, diamonds, sheep
Malawi	119	6	50.6	1 220	200	Tobacco, tea, sugar, groundnuts
Mozambique	783	11.7	15	2 360	250	Cashew nuts, sugar, cotton, tea
Swaziland	17	0.6	34.6	310[1]	590[1]	Sugar, wood, iron ore, asbestos
Tanzania	945	18.6	19.7	4 130	260	Coffee, cotton, cashew nuts, sisal
Zambia	753	5.7	7.6	3 240	500	Copper, cobalt, zinc, lead
Zimbabwe	389	7.1	18.3	3 640	470	Tobacco, gold, asbestos, maize
Total/Average	4 865	59	12.1	18 090	—	
South Africa	1 224	29.2	23.9	52 920	1 720	Gold, diamonds, coal, maize

[1] Figures are for 1978.
Sources: Amon J. Nsekela (ed.), *Southern Africa: Toward Economic Liberation,* Rex Collings, London, 1981, pp. 248–9. World Bank, *World Development Report 1981,* Annex, Tables 1, 3.

Not one of the 9 present at the Lusaka conference manifested the preoccupation that the type of cooperation we wish for may condition us politically.

On the other hand, by subscribing to the declaration proposed by the ministerial meeting in Arusha, all of us reaffirmed the idea that by promoting cooperation we would all be freer from the sub-imperialism of South Africa and, therefore each one of us could more freely promote the projects for our national development.[33]

Differences exist, but common interests are also there. If the latter are seen as being more important then cooperation is possible, though contradictions which result from the continuing differences can always disrupt the process of cooperation. It is this fragile nature of mutual ties in specific areas of cooperation which has given sceptics their ammunition. However, continuing efforts by developing countries to establish such ties would appear to indicate that the awareness of the importance of cooperation among themselves to promote their own respective national development efforts is increasing, notwithstanding setbacks and disappointments. The recognition of common interests the pursuance of which provides each participant with tangible benefits is certainly the only basis on which cooperation can thrive. This principle has become the basis of cooperation among Third World countries generally. It has been developed essentially through the non-aligned movement in its endeavours to strengthen the position of the poor countries in international relations. Speaking to the Conference of the 'Group of 77' in Arusha in 1979 Julius Nyerere argued the point forcefully that unity was needed to achieve the aims of the Third World given its countries' external dependencies and that to achieve unity the focus must be on the agreed areas of joint action and all other issues left aside. He said:

The immediate reason for each nation joining the Group of 77 depended on the point at which it had experienced the economic frustrations of power external to itself. (. . .)
I stress the fact that it was our nationalism which has forced us together. (. . .)
. . . our diversity exists in the context of one common and over-riding experience. What we have in common is that we are all, in relation to the developed world, dependent. (. . .)
We may have to co-operate functionally with governments which we intensely dislike and disapprove of. For the object is to complete the liberation of the Third World countries from external domination. That is the basic meaning of the New International Economic Order. And unity is our instrument – our only instrument – of liberation.[34]

Competition or complementarity?

Can and do developing countries complement each other, or are they rather in competition with each other? This is obviously an important issue when embarking on regional cooperation. Again, a straightforward answer is not possible.

Certainly, given the inherited orientation of their economies towards the world market the competitive relationship is very marked. Developing countries are in competition for markets to sell their raw materials, be they coffee, copper or cotton. Furthermore, as raw material producers and exporters their demand for manufactured goods can usually only be satisfied by importing from the industrialized countries. This strengthens their competition for export markets needed to earn foreign exchange to pay for their imports.

Competition also exists for international aid to finance development projects. This again reflects the dependent and underdeveloped structure of Third World economies, as a result of which internal sources of accumulation are inadequate or inadequately exploited. Competition between developing countries will also persist when they embark upon nationalist policies of development aimed at creating an integrated national economy. For instance, Mozambique, Tanzania as well as Zambia, each having recognized the importance of basic industries for national development, have all declared their intention to establish an iron and steel industry, though market capacity is below 500 000 tons a year for each of them.[35]

Such competition is a reality, and it limits the scope for cooperation. It is strengthened by the orientation of Third World countries' production and trade towards world market requirements. This makes it difficult to develop relations of exchange between each other. Trade among SADCC members is still negligible and represents only a fraction of their total external trade,[36] not to mention the inadequacy of transport and communications links which SADCC members have made their initial priority area of cooperation.

Even given their present economic structure, however, SADCC countries are not only in competition with each other. As Table 10.3 shows, they do not all export the same raw materials. Also, all have some production of manufactured goods though admittedly it does often cover the same range of consumer-oriented, import substituting industries.[37] But complementarities do exist. In their bilateral relations Mozambique and Tanzania, for instance, have begun using them for their mutual benefit. Mozambique, with an excess capacity in its cement industry, provides Tanzania with cement to meet its internal shortfall, while Tanzania provides Mozambique with commodities in short supply there, e.g. printed cotton materials, in exchange.

As a regional group SADCC has a resource endowment which would allow it to establish industries basic to economic development from its own resource base. The region has sizeable quantities of coal, iron ore, diamonds, gold, uranium, bauxite, chrome, copper ore, lead, nickel, zinc, asbestos, substantial potential for the generation of hydroelectric power – and still vast areas of unexplored subsoils. The very diversity often cited as a stumbling block for Third World cooperation is, as far as economic resources are concerned, a strong point of departure for cooperation. Agricultural resources can also be incorporated into this picture of complementarity or, at least, potential complementarity. The case of Zimbabwe's surplus production of maize has already been mentioned. As long as Tanzania, Zambia or Mozambique have not achieved national self-sufficiency in basic food crops, Zimbabwe can meet their shortfalls. What is needed to develop such complementarities in the region is joint action to eliminate impediments to their realization, be it in the area of transport and communications, manpower training or availability of suitable technology.[38]

In short, diversification as an important element of national self-reliant development strategy can strengthen collective self-reliance by increasing complementarities between developing countries.[39] As competition between developing countries is largely determined by their dependence on the world economic system, reducing dependence by diversification will also reduce such competition.

The extent of cooperation

The SADCC countries have opted for a low level of organization and obligation in their cooperation. This approach contrasts with the forms of cooperation usually referred to in discussions on economic integration or the establishment of a common market. Both economic integration and the common market involve a higher level of organization and a greater extent of cooperation. This very fact, however, has in practice frequently led to problems in the relations between the member states. A greater extent of cooperation requires a more profound agreement on political and socio-economic policy options to be successful. If such agreement is not achieved cooperation undergoes severe strains. In the case of the East African Community this was one of the main reasons for the demise of this common market in 1977.[40]

To some extent cooperation between several countries will always involve forfeiting part of one's own independence for the benefit of mutually advantageous terms of cooperation. However, depending on the concrete power relations within an established group of countries a member state might find itself obliged to forfeit a greater amount of its independence than it would really wish to. Such a country may find it extremely difficult to break away from such a tightly-knit and highly organized group of countries. Its relations within such a structure can only be described as relations of dependence, though in fact a greater extent of economic cooperation and integration of production patterns will have been achieved. Relations within the Eastern bloc 'Council of Mutual Economic Aid' (Comecon) have been described in these terms.

The SADCC countries place principal stress on their national independence.[41] For them national development efforts are basic; regional cooperation is geared to supplement and coordinate national efforts. The conscious limitation of the extent of cooperation and institutionalization SADCC has opted for draws the lessons from experiences of cooperation based on textbook theories of economic integration which proved unsuitable in reality. What is more important, their form of regional cooperation is concretely related to the conditions in southern Africa, i.e. the overall aim of reducing dependence on South Africa and the need to establish a broad common denominator so that even those southern African states presently most dependent on South Africa and even linked to it by cooperation agreements can participate in this initiative and benefit from it. In this sense it would seem that SADCC can claim to be making a novel contribution to economic cooperation in Africa, and the specific organizational structure it has adopted may prove to be an important element of its progress.

Who will benefit?

Even though SADCC has established regional cooperation at a fairly low level of organization and obligation, the question still arises whether all member states will benefit equally.

Two areas of concern can be identified here. Firstly, there is the possibility that some member states will benefit more than others, that one, say Zimbabwe, will establish itself in a position of regional supremacy. Given the distinctly unequal development of the SADCC member-countries the economically better off might well strengthen their position further. SADCC can only play a secondary role in reducing regional inequalities, secondary to each country's own efforts. To succeed in its objective of creating an 'equitable regional integration', however, it must consciously attempt to avoid an unequal distribution of benefits which would enhance already existing inequalities. This will be important if SADCC reaches a stage where the formation of industrial enterprises to cater for the region is considered so as to reap economies of scale. The location of such industries then becomes an issue. The case of the BLS states which, as members of the Southern African Customs Union, are swamped by South African goods is a negative example.[42]

With regard to the present situation in the region, it should be noted that the form of organization SADCC has adopted is well-suited to avoid unequal distribution of benefits from regional cooperation. It does not establish a common market area with free or privileged flow of goods across the borders. No trade tariff reductions are involved at all so that there is nothing to prevent member-countries from maintaining protective tariffs or introducing new ones. Free trade areas of various kinds are the forms of organization of economic cooperation which tend to enhance unequal development within a region,[43] and, as a result strain the partnership.

With regard to potential benefits, the relations within SADCC ultimately also have to be analysed in the context of the present situation in the whole of southern Africa. It is precisely to counter the attempts by South Africa to strengthen and expand its regional supremacy that SADCC was initiated. Its prime aim, therefore, is clearly defined, and if progress is made towards that aim all member states will benefit.

This aim also has a longer-term implication. On the assumption that a future government of Azania under African majority rule would maintain the country's present wealth, it would inherit a situation of regional predominance. If progress towards greater independence of SADCC members from South Africa has been made by then, cooperation with Azania could take place on a slightly less unequal footing than would be the case today.

The second area of concern is that regional cooperation in southern Africa will not benefit the SADCC member-countries as much as the multinational corporations. The international finance being sought by SADCC to develop transport and communications, and the economic potential of the region generally will, it is argued, only enhance penetration by the multinational corporations and allow them to strengthen their already existing network of links in southern Africa. This is undoubtedly a real danger, all the more so as some multinational corporations, take for instance Lonrho,[44] already have established links in some SADCC member countries, in particular Zimbabwe. This concern ties up with the first one in that the multinational corporations' investment pattern favours, in terms of location, the infrastructurally more developed industrial centres in countries with a favourable investment climate. In southern Africa this has led to most of them setting up their base in South Africa. Given their sense of economic advantage and the realization that it will be very difficult for SADCC countries to cut their trade links with South Africa, multinational corporations' reaction to SADCC will not necessarily be negative. Indeed, as one South African writer put it, 'it is perhaps not surprising that some South African businessmen tend to welcome SADCC's plans: by improving the black states' infrastructures, trade penetration could be facilitated.'[45]

SADCC's aims do not, in principle, run counter to cooperation with multinational corporations. Having opted against a free trade model, however, again shows its importance here in that those members who for reasons related to their own political and economic systems aim to curb or prevent multinational corporation activities in their countries – Tanzania, for instance, took over all Lonrho assets in 1978 – can pursue their policies unhindered. With regard to trade links among themselves, which might benefit multinational corporations as well, SADCC's approach is to plan them carefully. Talking about preferential trade arrangements within SADCC, the late Seretse Khama said: '... they should be planned ones so as to flow from and serve the needs of coordinated national and regional development. Our trade arrangements should not be at the mercy of free market forces or foreign companies.'[46]

In sum, the political strength and clarity of orientation of SADCC member-states will be crucial in deciding whether economic cooperation between them enhances their independence, or increases their dependence within the capitalist world system on multinational corporations and their agencies within the region.

Prospects

How far can SADCC go in reducing the region's dependence on South Africa? As has been shown SADCC's aims and objectives are to achieve economic liberation to complement the political struggle for liberation in Namibia and South Africa. That struggle can only be successfully conducted by the people in those countries themselves; here outside forces can at best play a supportive role. In political terms SADCC's objectives can be described as enhancing the 'front-line' states' capability to support the liberation struggle by reducing economic dependence on South Africa.

Even the more limited aim of greater economic independence in the region is no mean task. Its achievement is conditioned by two factors. The first is the dominating role of South Africa in the economic structure of the region and the concomitant dependent relations which tie most SADCC member states to South Africa in some way. This fact alone makes it unlikely that dependence on South Africa can be eliminated in a short- or even middle-term perspective if the political regime there remains unchanged.

The second factor refers to the ruling classes in the SADCC member states who have their own entrenched interests to defend, interests which do in most cases (with the exception of Angola and Tanzania) incorporate benefits, such as the supply of basic foodstuffs or consumer goods and the employment of migrant labour, based on relations with South Africa.

Of course, economic cooperation between the SADCC member states is aimed precisely at providing alternatives to such dependence on South Africa. But taking the two factors mentioned above together, the realistic middle-term expectation is that SADCC, by developing closer ties among its members, could succeed in strengthening their bargaining power in relation to South Africa, so they may deal with that country on better terms. Attracting more international finance to the SADCC countries thereby increasing their importance as a focal point of investment in the region fits in well with such an aim. By determining the areas of priority for international finance themselves the SADCC countries can ensure that it is in line with their overall strategy.

The prospects for the viability of SADCC within the framework of what it can realistically hope to achieve do seem to be quite good. This view is supported by a look at other regional endeavours which are trying to get off the ground, notably the UN-ECA sponsored eastern, central and southern African 'Preferential Trade Agreement' (PTA), which covers 18 states in the region reaching from Ethiopia to Lesotho and including the nine SADCC members. In December 1981 a Summit Meeting was convened in Lusaka to sign the treaty, which had been drafted in four years of hard negotiations, but only nine countries signed. Some obviously feared that lowering regional trade barriers would not benefit them. Tanzania, learning from the experience of the East African Community and the still unsolved problems of its dissolution, was a case in point. On the other hand, the failure of the PTA to get off the ground was seen as a blow to the 'export drive to the south' of a country like Kenya which did sign the treaty.[47] The flexibility of the PTA is limited by the lengthy treaty which, once signed and ratified, binds the member countries. SADCC with its loose contractual framework, based on the Lusaka Declaration and decisions of its Summit Meetings, is much more flexible. The consensus of its members can always be redefined. Membership in other groupings can also be accommodated more easily. If Zambia and Malawi, the two SADCC members who did sign the PTA treaty in December 1981, allow goods from other PTA signatories to enter their markets at reduced customs rates, this does not have to worry other SADCC members. The prospects for maintaining the cohesion of the grouping in the face of changing conditions of development in the region are, therefore, more favourable in the case of SADCC than they are for more tightly-knit regional groupings like the PTA.

Regional cooperation and collective self-reliance:
the wider context of non-alignment

All SADCC member states are also members of the movement of non-aligned countries. In a number of ways the initiatives embarked upon by SADCC to develop regional cooperation in southern Africa reflect the principles adopted by the non-aligned countries and contribute to their implementation.

The focus of SADCC on practical action is in line with an increasing concern of non-aligned countries generally with the promotion of collective self-reliance.[48] After many resolutions have been adopted and many hours and days spent negotiating for changes in international relations with the developed countries, mostly with meagre results, cooperation among Third

World countries is increasingly recognized as being an important way of solving some of the developing countries' problems. This is also what SADCC hopes to achieve. As President Khama of Botswana put it in April 1980:

We seek to overcome the fragmentation of our economies and, by co-ordinating our national development efforts, to strengthen them. The basis of our cooperation, built on concrete projects and specific programmes rather than on grandiose schemes and massive bureaucratic institutions, must be the assured mutual advantage of all participating states.[49]

More generally, SADCC is said to have put forward 'a new development strategy for Southern Africa'.[50] The strategy of collective self-reliance has been described in similar terms.[51] The specific aims of the SADCC strategy have been discussed at length in this chapter. They are to enhance economic development and the material well-being of the people in the region, to reduce the member-countries' dependence on South Africa and the concomitant vulnerability of their national sovereignty. But the SADCC strategy does also reflect a strategy of collective self-reliance in a more comprehensive sense, defined as follows:

a strategy of collective self-reliance embodies the potential for joint action by developing countries that will strengthen their capacity to negotiate with developed countries and reduce their dependency on them, and (. . .) intensifying trade and economic linkages among developing countries is part of the structural change needed for a more rational international division of labour, leading to a more efficient use of world resources.[52]

It is implied that, as the strategy for collective self-reliance is a Third World strategy for development, initiatives to implement it should come from the developing countries themselves. It is a strategy based on the developing countries' self-conscious definition of their own interests and their attempt to negotiate agreements of international cooperation on that basis. Collective self-reliance encompasses the national and international dimension. National development and regional cooperation are fundamental. SADCC is based, to use Zimbabwe Prime Minister Robert Mugabe's words, on a recognition 'of our individual responsibilities as nation states and of our collective responsibility as a group of friendly neighbouring majority-ruled African countries.'[53] But international cooperation is an important part of the strategy, too, though regional cooperation should not be made dependent on it. The Lusaka Declaration is quite explicit on this point:–

We are committed to a strategy of economic liberation. It is a strategy which we believe both needs and deserves international support. Southern African regional development must be designed and implemented by Southern Africans. It will, however, be achieved more rapidly and will be more effective if development takes place within the context of global cooperation. (. . .)

However, as with the struggle for political liberation, the fight for economic liberation is neither a mere slogan to prompt external assistance nor a course of action from which we can be deflected by external indifference. The dignity and welfare of the peoples of Southern Africa demand economic liberation and we will struggle toward that goal.[54]

Collective self-reliance is a strategy to enhance economic development in Third World countries and to exert pressure in favour of the restructuration of the existing international economic order. The same can be said of SADCC within the context of southern Africa.

NOTES

1 S. Amin, 'Underdevelopment and Dependence in Black Africa: their Historical Origins and Contemporary Forms', *Journal of Modern African Studies*, x, (1972).

2 Amon J. Nsekela (ed.), *Southern Africa: Toward Economic Liberation*, Rex Collings, London, 1981, p. 255. For a historical analysis of migrant labour in South Africa, see F. Wilson, *Labour in the South African Gold Mines 1911–1969*, Cambridge University Press, Cambridge, 1972.

3 Ann Seidman and Neva Seidman Makgetla, *Outposts of Monopoly Capitalism*, Zed Press, London, 1980, pp. 93–118.

4 G. M. E. Leistner, 'Can Southern Africa get together?', *South African Journal of African Affairs*, ix, (1979), p. 84.

5 For a South African overview of these proposals, see D. Geldenhuys and D. Venter, 'Regional Co-operation in Southern Africa: a Constellation of States?', *International Affairs Bulletin*, iii, (1979).

6 F. Baffoe, 'Some Aspects of the Political Economy of Economic Cooperation and Integration in Southern Africa: The Case of South Africa and the Countries of Botswana, Lesotho and Swaziland (BLS)', *Journal of Southern African Affairs*, iii, (1978).

7 Centro de Estudos Africanos (Maputo), 'The Constellation of Southern African States: A New Strategic Offensive by South Africa in the Region', Analysis No. 2, 1980.

8 Deon Geldenhuys, *The Constellation of Southern African States and the Southern African Development Co-ordination Council: Towards a New Regional Stalemate?*, South African Institute of International Affairs, Braamfontein, 1981, pp. 15, 34.

9 F. A. Kornegay, Jr. and V. A. Vockerodt, 'Lusaka and Regional Cooperation in Southern Africa, Part II: The South African Dilemma', *SADEX* (Washington), ii, (1980).

10 Seretse Khama, President of Botswana, Opening Statement to the Summit Meeting on Southern African Development Coordination, Lusaka, 1–2 April, 1980. Zambia Information Services, Background No. 10/1980.

11 Contingency Planning Secretariat, Cabinet Office, Why Zambia Re-opened the Southern Railway Route. Lusaka, n.d.
12 Southern Africa: Toward Economic Liberation. A Declaration by the Governments of Independent States of Southern Africa, made at Lusaka on 1 April 1980.
13 'Transport and Communications', in Nsekela (ed.), *Southern Africa*, p. 71.
14 Guy Arnold and Ruth Weiss, *Strategic Highways of Africa*, Julian Friedman, London, 1977.
15 Southern African Development Coordination Conference. Communiqué. Zambia Information Services, Press Release No. 4/1980.
16 The collected 'sectoral papers' submitted to the Arusha Conference have been published on behalf of SADCC, see Nsekela (ed.), *Southern Africa*.
17 This information is drawn from the official conference paper: Transport and Communications Projects. In: Aloysius Kgarebe (ed.), *SADCC 2 – Maputo. The Proceedings of the Second Southern African Development Co-ordination Conference, held in Maputo, People's Republic of Mozambique on 27/28 November 1980*, SADCC Liaison Committee, London, 1981, pp. 169–219.
18 *Ibid.*, p. 172.
19 'SADCC, Progress Report on Lusaka Programme of Action (submitted to the Summit Meeting in Salisbury, July 1981)', *SADEX* (Washington), iii, (1981), p. 4.
20 In an article in the *New African*, May 1980, Richard Carver points to the fact that the bulk of Zimbabwe's commercial agriculture is in the hands of white farmers, whose interests might, he suggests, run counter to SADCC aims.
21 R. Laishley, 'Food Monitor paying off, *Times of Zambia*, 18 January 1982.
22 The delegations present at the Maputo Conference were:–
Countries:– Algeria, Australia, Austria, Belgium, Brazil, Bulgaria, Canada, Czechoslovakia, Denmark, Finland, GDR, FRG, Hungary, India (observer), Iraq, Ireland, Italy, Japan, Luxemburg, Netherlands, Norway, Romania, Sweden, Switzerland, UK, USA, Venezuela, Yugoslavia, Zaire (observer);
International organizations:– African Development Bank, Arab Bank for Economic Development in Africa (BADEA), Comecon (observer), Commonwealth Secretariat, ECA, EEC – European Investment Bank, FAO, IFAD, Kuwait Development Fund, International Communications Union, Nordic Investment Bank, OAU, OPEC, SIDA, UN – Office of the Secretary General, UNCTAD, UNDP, World Bank.
The delegations present at the Blantyre Conference were:–
Countries:– Australia, Belgium, Brazil, Canada, Denmark, Finland, FRG, France, India, Ireland, Italy, Japan, Netherlands, Norway, Portugal, Sweden, Switzerland, UK, USA;
International organizations:– African Development Bank, BADEA, EEC – European Investment Bank, ECA, FAO, ILO, UNCTAD, UNDP, UNFPA, World Bank.
23 *Tempo* (Maputo), No. 582, 6 December 1981, pp. 48–50.
24 'SADCC, Summit Meeting, Salisbury, July 20, 1981, Final Communiqué', *SADEX* (Washington), iii, (1981), p. 1.
25 Memorandum of Understanding on the Institutionalisation of the Southern African Development Co-ordination Conference (SADCC), n.p., n.d.
26 *Ibid.*

27 The SATCC Convention was ratified by July 1981.
28 The Convention on the Establishment of the Southern African Transport and Communications Commission. n.p., n.d.
29 Memorandum of Understanding on the Institutionalisation of the Southern African Development Co-ordination Conference (SADCC), n.p., n.d.
30 Nsekela (ed.), *Southern Africa*.
31 For a discussion of some of Namibia's options from an economic perspective, see W. Zehender, 'Außenwirtschaftspolitische Perspektiven für ein unabhängiges Namibia', *Afrika Spectrum*, xv, (1980), pp. 135–144.
32 'First Steps Toward Economic Inegration', in Nsekela (ed.), *Southern Africa*, pp. 15–17.
33 Interview with Samora Machel, President of Mozambique. In: *Africa*, No. 107, July 1980.
34 J. K. Nyerere, *Unity for a New Order*, Arusha, 1979.
35 Zambia announced in 1980 that it would abandon its 'Tika' iron and steel project, but not as a result of regional considerations. Internal reasons were given for the decision one of which was that the project was not economically viable.
36 Nsekela (ed.), *Southern Africa*, p. 236.
37 International trade figures show that trade among developing countries represents a small percentage of total world trade, 7 per cent in 1980 according to the World Bank, *World Development Report 1981*.
38 'Economic Dependence and Regional Co-operation' in Nsekela (ed.), *Southern Africa*, pp. 45–9.
39 S. S. Mushi, 'Tanzania Foreign Relations, and the Policies of Non-Alignment, Socialism and Self-Reliance', in K. Mathews and S. S. Mushi (eds.), *The Foreign Policy of Tanzania*, Nairobi, (forthcoming).
40 Ngila Mwase, *The East African Community: a Study of Regional Disintegration*, The University of Dar es Salaam, ERB Paper 77. 10, Dar es Salaam, 1977.
41 R. H. Green, 'Southern African Development Coordination: Toward a Functioning Dynamic?', *IDS Bulletin* xi, (1980).
42 James H. Cobbe, 'Integration among Unequals: The Southern African Customs Union and Development', *World Development*, viii, (1980), pp. 329–36.
43 The East African Community as well as the Southern African Customs Union are examples of this in practice.
44 S. Cronjé, M. Ling and G. Cronjé, *Lonrho – Portrait of a Multinational*, Penguin, Harmondsworth, 1976.
45 Deon Geldenhuys, *The Constellation of Southern African States*, p. 43.
46 Sir Seretse Khama, 'Introduction', in: Nsekela (ed.), *Southern Africa*, p. xii.
47 *Daily Nation* (Nairobi), 22 and 23 December 1981.
48 M. Barratt Brown (ed.), *The Anatomy of Underdevelopment. Documents on Economic Policy in the Third World*, Spokesman Books, Nottingham, 1974. See also K. M. Khan and V. Matthies (eds.), *Collective Self-Reliance: Programme und Perspektiven der Dritten Welt*, Einführung and Dokumente, München, 1978.
49 Seretse Khama, Opening Statement to the Lusaka Summit.
50 *SADCC 2. A Perspective*, Maputo, Nov. 1980.
51 E. Oteiza and F. Sercovich, 'Collective Self-reliance: selected issues', *International Social Science Journal*, xxviii, (1976).

52 UNCTAD V, Arusha Programme for Collective Self-Reliance and Framework for Negotiations. TD/236, 28 February 1979, pp. 7–8.
53 Robert Mugabe, Prime Minister of Zimbabwe, Address of welcome to the SADCC Ministerial Meeting, held in Salisbury, Zimbabwe, on 11 September 1980.
54 Nsekela (ed.), *Southern Africa.*

11 Conclusion: problems and prospects of intra-African cooperation

DOMENICO MAZZEO

Contributions by regional cooperation to the development of the Third World during the past 20 years may have been meagre. Scholars may have lost confidence in regionalism as an instrument of development and focused their attention on other development approaches. Yet, regional experiments have continued unabated, particularly in Africa. This is a clear indication of the strongly felt need for such cooperation and the persistent belief of African policy-makers in the usefulness of regionalism as an instrument of greater political and economic independence of the African continent. This faith has been solemnly reaffirmed in the recent Lagos Plan of Action, the child of the two more authoritative institutions with continental African membership, the OAU and ECA. Apparently, nowhere else in the world could a call for a higher degree of collective self-reliance be more justified.

Africa is a relatively balkanized continent. With only ten per cent of the world population, Africa numbers one-third of the countries of the world. While struggling to consolidate their recently won independence, most African countries still feel militarily, politically and economically exposed to the vagary of extracontinental forces. The level of all forms of power is generally lower and more diffused in Africa than in other continents. Despite the presence of some potential great powers like Nigeria and South Africa, no African country has the actual power to counterbalance extracontinental encroachments in Africa or to promote African interest at the global level. It would therefore seem that mainly through collective efforts and common institutions could Africa have a voice in world affairs and transform its rich natural resources into diversified production. With an average of five to fifteen million people, most African national markets are generally considered inadequate to meet the requirements of modern economic development. But problems of regional cooperation remain as stubborn as are needs and expectations. These problems have been sufficiently debated in previous chapters not to need detailed recollection. One may simply stress here that the solution of problems or harmonization of conflicting interests is a major function of politics in general and regional cooperation in particular. The solution of problems depends however on increased capabilities and their relevance to the objectives sought. To assess more accurately the prospects of regional cooperation in Africa, one has therefore to understand both the evolving environment and the proper nature of such cooperation.

The environment of regional cooperation

Regional cooperation being part of the foreign policy process, the main purpose of this section is to look into the implications for regional cooperation of the global, intra-African and domestic conditioning factors of the foreign policy of African states likely to prevail until the turn of this century. Will these factors be more favourable to regional cooperation for the next 20 years than they were for the past two decades? Or, can one expect a substantive increase in the capabilities needed to solve the problems that afflicted intra-African cooperation in the past?

Global environment

The global politico-strategic and economic conditions do not look promising. The difficulties in East-West détente and the world economic crisis are likely to continue well into the 1980s and beyond. The recrudescence of East-West competition, notably the reactivated superpower rivalry, will probably affect Africa more than any other major region of the world. The rules of the East-West game in Europe are quite clear and generally respected. The growing importance of Brazil, Mexico, the Andean Group, and a possible recovery of Argentina could loosen the United States hold on Latin-America without necessarily making room for other extra-continental powers to play a major role in that part of the world. The emergence of China, India and Japan, together with the Association of South East Asian Nations, could successfully challenge superpower influence in Asia. Should the Iran-Iraqi war be contained and the Palestinian issue solved, even in the Middle East such an influence could be checked, eventually by a revived Arab League and the newly born Gulf Cooperation Council. By contrast Africa remains highly exposed to superpower interference. And Africa is too important to be left alone, particularly at a time when other continents are acquiring greater capacity to contain the influence of the superpowers. The influence of ex-colonial powers in Africa has probably declined, but superpower presence has been consolidated throughout the continent, particularly since the mid-1970s. Curtailing superpower influence may prove more difficult than breaking links with the declining colonial powers. United States and Soviet rivalry over Africa would be a lasting phenomenon. The Reagan administration has hardened the cold war terminology, but has not added new policy elements to the East-West competition in Africa, the Middle East and the Indian Ocean. It is basically implementing the policy of Reagan's predecessor. Such a policy is likely to be followed also by Reagan's successor. One of the most visible elements of this policy is the creation of the Rapid Deployment Force, admittedly intended for situations arising in the Middle East, notably the Arabian Peninsula. However, the actual partial deployment of the Force and related facilities are sought mainly in North and eastern Africa, apart from some islands of the Indian Ocean itself. An increased military connection of African countries with superpowers could become a new bone of contention in intra-African relations or even a destabilizing factor in the domestic policy of those countries. Awareness of these trends and dangers may eventually also generate within the continent greater determination to forestall further superpower penetration in Africa. But it seems more realistic to assume that, at least for the next decade or so, the global politico-strategic environment will continue to pose major threats for intra-African solidarity. Will the world economic conditions be more favourable to intra-African cooperation?

The international economic system is moving toward a higher degree of pluralism and competition, partly as a result of the persistent economic crisis. It may be an oversimplification to say that the world or at least the Northern Hemisphere has entered the post-growth, post-Bretton Wood and post-industrial era. But despite numerous channels of consultation, the painful restructuring of economic systems required to solve the persistent crisis and readjust to the new era will most probably stiffen competition not only between planned and market economy countries, but also among the latter and even the developing countries. Hardened East-West, West-West and South-South economic competition creates opportunities and challenges for the Third World, notably Africa.

Increased economic competition among industrialized countries may strengthen the general bargaining power of developing countries and widen their choice of more advantageous sources of assistance, imports and investments. Of special significance here is the extent to which heightened competition may facilitate governmental control of transnational corporations. We have dealt with this issue elsewhere.[1] In our view, the growing determination of the state to control the transnational corporations is assisted by two major developments, both of which reinforce competition among transnational corporations, namely: the proliferation of transnational corporations from market economy, planned economy and even developing countries; and the strategy of diversification of production adopted by the transnational corporation to reduce risks. However, the major factors and mechanisms for the control of transnational corporations, that is efficient public administrations, labour unions and consumer associations, are weak in developing countries, notably in Africa. Control of transnational corporations is thus an area where African governments and local producers could strengthen their position through common regimes and joint actions similar to those adopted by the Andean Group.

But increased competition among industrialized countries, particularly in a situation of high domestic unemployment, will also retard if not prevent the realization of international measures still valued by many developing countries. Agreement on the North-South Dialogue and implementation of eventually agreed guidelines would become more difficult and remote. Export-oriented industrialization aimed at finding markets in the industrialized countries would have a lower chance of success. The restrictive clauses of the General Scheme of Preferences and the Lomé Convention may be invoked more often. In any case, even if the market of the industrialized countries remained open to the manufactured exports of the Third World, the major beneficiaries would be the more advanced developing countries of Asia and Latin America.

The South-South gap is, in fact, likely to become wider as a result of the protracted world economic crisis. The more advanced developing countries are in a stronger position to overcome the crisis, while the economies of the least developed countries may almost be paralysed. The cohesiveness of the Group of 77 and the Non-aligned Movement could be further undermined. As Asia and Latin America move closer to self-sustained growth, Africa will feel increasingly isolated in its struggle against underdevelopment and may finally adopt a more decisively inward looking development strategy.

As far as Africa is concerned, the long-term consequences of the increasingly hostile global environment thus need not be necessarily negative. Better ways of taking advantage of the limited opportunities offered by the Lomé Convention could be explored or hopefully a genuine search for more self-reliant development policies generated. This search for self-reliance will take a purely national or also a regional orientation, depending on the evolution of the intra-African and domestic environments.

Intra-African environment

Weak infrastructural links, persistent border and ideological disputes, and growing inequalities among African countries are some of the major obstacles to intra-African cooperation.

The overall capacity for interaction between African countries is clearly on the increase. National administrations have generally been consolidated and communications become easier. But transactions are still hampered by the structure of African economies and by poor road and rail links. Improvement of intra-African infrastructures has been a major concern of ECA, culminating in the United Nations Transport and Communications Decade for Africa (1978–88). Particularly significant and encouraging in this respect are the systematic and concrete efforts of sub-continental groups like SADCC. Improvement of intra-African infrastructures remains a major preoccupation and challenge to African governments and organizations.

Border conflicts in Africa have been and still are mainly confined to the Horn of Africa and North-West Africa. Morocco and Somalia, who opposed the acceptance of colonial frontiers at the founding Conference of the OAU, continue to press their territorial claims through military means. However localized, these territorial conflicts have serious continental and global repercussions, as the Somali-Ethiopian and Western Sahara wars clearly show. Since all frontiers are by necessity arbitrary and divide people of the same ethnic groups or cultures, regional cooperation apparently offers an ideal solution to border disputes by simply diluting the strategic, economic and cultural thickness of frontiers, as in the case of France and Germany within the EEC. But such an apparently simple solution hardly works among newly independent countries. Looking at the history of other continents, one can only hope that border conflicts in Africa will not become more widespread. One can also hope that guidelines will be elaborated and mechanisms established for the solution of such conflicts, eventually within the framework of the OAU.

The disruptive impact of ideological differences on intra-African cooperation has been evidenced by the history of the OAU and the recent demise of the EAC. Such differences also provide a fertile soil for the growth of superpower rivalry on the continent. To at least partially neutralize the persistent danger of ideological differences, one could envisage either a situation of increased mutual tolerance or, in the case of subcontinental groups, the development of compact ideological regions. The second solution does not seem to be feasible within the African context in the near future. Increased mutual tolerance thus becomes the only viable alternative at both the continental and subcontinental level. Confronted with similar severe development problems, African countries may be prepared to play down the role of ideology in intra-African relations. But if tolerance must not be stretched to the breaking point, the type of cooperation pursued is of crucial importance, as suggested by the collapse of the EAC and the creation of SADCC.

More pervasive, lasting and intriguing is the role of growing inter-country inequalities in intra-African cooperation, as the South-South gap spreads throughout the continent. The power of South Africa under majority rule may become more dominant over its neighbours, as the racial dam collapses. This preoccupation must have surfaced in the minds of the founding fathers of SADCC. Within the West African sub-region, Nigeria is and will increasingly find itself in a similar dominant position. The pathetic continuous degradation of Ghana's political and economic system contrasts sharply with the still prevailing relatively prosperous situation in the Ivory Coast for instance. As inequalities grow in Africa, concerned scholars and policy makers must assess their significance carefully.

The general implications of severe inter-country inequalities in a competitive continental environment can be appreciated by simply recalling the history of intra-European colonialism during the last four centuries or intra-American neocolonialism for the past 150 years. In this respect, Africa may be more fortunate. African countries attained independence roughly at the same time. Power in Africa remains quite diffused, despite the presence of Nigeria and South Africa.[2] Guidelines and frameworks for the regulation of intra-African relations were practically born at the time of independence.

But growing inequalities are bound to affect in several ways intra-African cooperation and organizations. One may expect a loosening of African solidarity on North-South economic issues, even within the framework of the UN or the Lomé Convention. The danger of maldistribution of benefits within regional groups will increase. On the other hand, as more African countries reach the level of self-sustained development and are eventually able to assist their neighbours, more continental and extra-continental financial resources could be released to stimulate economic growth in the least developed countries, promote regional projects or at least alleviate the consequences of uneven distribution of benefits from regional cooperation.

In brief, growing inequalities are likely to become an increasingly dominant factor in intra-African relations. But, for the next decade at least, border and ideological conflicts will continue to play a major role. On this account, the chances of success of regional cooperation in northern and eastern Africa look slimmer than in western or southern Africa. Paradoxically, North Africa is the best endowed African sub-region in terms of the classical preconditions for successful cooperation: a long common political and economic history, common culture, language and religion. It lacks however the most basic of all political prerequisites: tolerance. Such situation arises from the still unresolved conflict between the individual nationalisms of Arab-speaking countries and pan-Arab nationalism, that is the appeal of strong historical and cultural bonds. This suggests that the most crucial elements in inter-country cooperation are the domestic environment of member-states and a proper understanding of the nature of regional cooperation itself.

Domestic environment

Our discussion here shall be confined to the implications of one basic factor, nationalism, often made the scapegoat for the failure of regional cooperation, notably in the Third World. Regional cooperation is said to be undermined by a lack of political will, due to governments' preoccupation with narrow national interests. The nationalist fever is running higher in the developing countries, because of their recently won independence. One could refer to Morocco manoeuvring to split the OAU on the question of Western Sahara or to the members of UDEAC fragmenting the regional market.

To put it bluntly, we are more worried by the weakness than the strength of nationalism in the Third World. What we find disturbing is not so much the economic nationalism of the members of UDEAC, but their unsound national economic policies, of which the transnational corporations may reap the benefits without having necessarily contributed to engineering them. In any case, what really matters is to understand the root-causes of the so called nationalist fever in developing countries and draw the relevant implications for the theory and practice of regional cooperation in the Third World, notably in Africa.

In the light of the precolonial and colonial history of Africa, the government of any newly independent African country must perform two urgent functions: nation-building and diversification of the national economy. As a consequence, the country's energies are almost wholly absorbed by domestic considerations. Foreign policy is assigned a secondary role in the struggle for national survival. Mechanisms for the formulation and implementation of foreign policy remain weak. While this weakness favours the joint use of other continental and global instrumentalities of foreign policy, it cannot meet the heavy demands of subcontinental cooperation, notably of a comprehensive nature. The overwhelming concern with nation-building in the absence of societal pluralism, usually associated with economic diversification, also breeds unchecked personaliz-ation of power, a phenomenon even more dominant in foreign than in domestic policy. As the experience of the EAC proves, personalization of power easily undermines two important elements required to sustain a complex regional effort: a sufficient degree of stability in inter-country relations and the appreciation of long-term national interests. Finally, a low level of economic diversification or a heavy external dependence makes the foreign policy of developing countries more oriented towards countries from outside the continent than towards their neighbours. In brief, a weak, personalized and extra-continentally oriented foreign policy puts serious constraints on intra-African cooperation. To what extent can the domestic environment of the foreign policy of African countries be expected to improve substantially in the next two decades?

Nation-building and diversification of national economies will undoub-tedly make considerable strides in Africa during the next 20 years. But the realization of these objectives will remain the major concern of most African countries during this period. Though this national concern and regional cooperation both aim at alleviating the twin evils of underdevelop-ment and external dependence, the above concern seems to militate against regional cooperation. One is apparently caught in a vicious circle: regional cooperation is impeded by the same evils that it is supposed to cure. The reason for this lies mainly in the divergent regional and national approaches to the solution of these problems. A way out of the dilemma could be a redefinition of major concepts of regional cooperation and a reorientation of both the theory and practice of regionalism. Possibilities must be explored of better matching national and regional development approaches, with regional efforts fully assuming the national concerns of member-countries. To be more exact, we want to know whether regional cooperation could be put squarely at the service of national development.

The nature of regionalism

Fully aware of the structural differences underlying the process of regional cooperation among industrialized countries and in the Third World, the contributors to this book have generally stressed the need to revise the theory and practice of regionalism among developing countries. Yet, views seem to differ on the extent and nature of this revision. Should one advocate an adaptation of the classical production approach to regional cooperation and still retain the validity of the concepts of integration and economies of scale at the production level? Or should one concentrate on the service sector and emphasize the mainly national capacity-building role of regional cooperation? The different conception of the nature and scope of regionalism in the Third World is clearly reflected in the different terminologies used to characterize this phenomenon. The debate on regionalism is several decades old. But the reader of this book may be amazed, if not confused, by the lack of a common terminology in this respect. The terms integration, cooperation, developmental regionalism or collective self-reliance have been used to define the process of closer interaction between the countries of a region. Reference has even been made to the similarity between this process and the strategy of non-alignment. At the root of the terminological maze is a problem of conceptualization or, more precisely, the conflict between the theory and practice of regionalism. As practice diverges from theory, it becomes imperative to search for different terms and concepts more reflective of practice. We do not intend to undertake here an elaborated discussion of this issue, but shall make a few general remarks that may help in clarifying the debate. In particular, we wish to challenge the validity of the concept of integration and its major economic justification, the concept of economies of scale.

Terms and concepts: integration or cooperation?

The phenomenon of regionalism may be better understood, if the term and concept of integration be abandoned. This concept is based on misguided assumptions and raises false expectations. It assumes that the era of the nation-state is close to an end. Consequently, it envisages at the culmination of the process some kind of supra-national body. The creation, at some point in time, of elaborated regional institutions with supranational authority and the shifting of loyalties of the citizens of member states toward the new authority thus become basic features of the regional process. This presupposes the willingness of states to surrender at least part of their sovereignty, that is their autonomous power of decision-making, and the need for citizens to reorient their loyalties, eventually under the convincing impact of modern technology. Particularly in its functionalist version, the concept of integration therefore takes for granted the predominant role of economics over politics and of class over state in international relations. Such assumptions and expectations misread the realities of contemporary interstate relations and grossly exaggerate the impact of modern technology on the international behaviour of states and citizens. Practice even among socialist countries clearly shows that the state remains dominant. The impact of technological development on the international system is certainly not unidimensional: in some respects it strengthens interdependence, in others it reinforces the autonomy of the units. Notably in the Third World, the nation-state will undoubtedly remain for many generations a valid framework for the satisfaction of practically all needs of its citizens either independently or through the widened scope of diplomatic interaction. Expectations of the integration theory have in fact proved increasingly unrealistic not only among developing but also among industrialized countries, as the practice of Comecon and the EEC reveals. The experience of the past 30 years suggests that, irrespective of the founders' original intentions or of Charter provisions, intergovernmental global and regional organizations are simply instrumentalities of the nation-state and their decisions are subject to the voluntary compliance of members. In other words, these organizations are basically forms of *institutionalized multilateral diplomacy*. The difference between global and regional organizations is eventually a question of various degrees of intensity and pervasiveness of such diplomatic interaction.

For the above reasons we have avoided during the past ten years the term integration when discussing the regional process, preferring the less ambitious term cooperation, which may range from consultation on general policies to joint participation in specific programmes and projects. But developmental regionalism and collective self-reliance are to us equally appropriate characterizations of the process of closer interaction among countries of a region. We wish to emphasize that this applies in the case of developed and developing countries as well. After all, what is the EEC if not a relatively successful attempt at collective self-reliance among industrialized countries? Development being a relative concept, EEC member-countries are obviously concerned not only with consolidating but also with promoting their development through structural readjustments, if necessary. To reduce external dependence is also a major concern of industrialized countries: by increasing their degree of collective autonomy, the EEC member-countries expect to be in a stronger position to face jointly the challenge of the two superpowers and, in the long-run, that of the emerging Third World. Therefore, we cannot agree with those scholars attempting to differentiate the regional process among developing countries from that among industrialized countries on the basis of these general objectives. Development, structural changes and loosening of external dependence are aims common to all regional groups, irrespective of the level of development of their members. We could agree even less with the more classical formulation of this issue, based on the customs union theory, namely that regional cooperation among developed countries is facilitated by the complementarity of their economies and exploits mainly the static effects of trade liberalization, while regional cooperation among developing countries is impeded by the competitiveness of national economies and can only benefit from dynamic effects by eventually creating economic complementarities. As economic restructuring implies, industrialized countries are also interested in the dynamic effects of regional cooperation. A simple look at the EEC will reveal that the economies of member-countries are more competitive than complementary. A differentiation of the regional process among industrialized countries and in the Third World based on the above arguments looks to us more confusing than illuminating. In our view, the source of such differentiation must be sought in the simple fact of the respective level of development or, to be more specific, the respective degree of diversification of the economies of member-countries. The specific aims, policies and forms of regional cooperation as well as the type of restructuring needed or dependence to be broken will presumably differ, depending on whether member-countries are at the pre-industrial, advanced industrialized or post-industrial stage of their development. A low level of development, that is a low level of national autonomy, can hardly generate sufficient self-confidence, hence that famous political goodwill, to enter into comprehensive forms of cooperation. Indeed, it makes such forms of cooperation unnecessary, if not harmful. This suggests that national autonomy is a precondition for healthy interdependence. Regional cooperation among developing countries should therefore aim, first of all, at corroborating rather than debilitating national autonomy or self-reliance.

If strengthening of national autonomy becomes the key objective of regional cooperation in the Third World, the implications for the theory and practice of such cooperation may be far-reaching. The whole debate on the subject may have to be seen in a different light, including the discussion of conditioning factors, consequences and models of cooperation. In particular, increased transactions and strong institutions as indicators of cooperation will lose most of their significance. We do not intend to elaborate here on all major implications, as this may require a completely new paper. We shall however indicate briefly how a redefinition of the regional process affects what we consider the most fundamental element in the whole debate: the justification or rationale of regional cooperation.

Economic justification: economies of scale or appropriate technology?

The established theory of regional cooperation is mainly concerned with the production sector either indirectly by favouring trade liberalization or directly by advocating regional allocation of industries. The rationale for this production approach has to be found in the concept of economies of scale. But is this concept valid in the context of developing countries and can it be considered the foundation of regional cooperation also in the Third World? Our answer is rather negative for several reasons.

Firstly, the economies of scale call for the widespread use of modern capital-intensive technology. This militates against the factor endowment of developing countries, where labour is generally more abundant than capital.

Secondly, by promoting regional industrial specialization, the search for regional economies of scale may prevent diversification of national economies. By definition, the economies of developing countries are little diversified. Diversification of national economies is an essential dimension of national development strategies. It obviously means duplication of productive facilities within the region. Duplication of industries in an underdeveloped market is said to breed production overcapacity, hence a waste of capital. But can the effects of duplication be evaluated independently from the type of technology used in the production process? There may be nothing wrong with duplication of economic activities, if appropriate technologies are adopted. From this perspective, cooperation for the transfer and development of more appropriate technologies could be a good starting point for regional cooperation among developing countries, following the example of the Andean Group. In any case, our general contention is that, at the level of simple industrialization for the satisfaction of basic human needs, there is little room for regional economies of scale and consequently for increased regional transactions. Food, textile and construction related industries may well prosper within national borders even in a relatively small national market. But, as the experience of the EAC and UDEAC proves, it is mainly in these fields that attempts were made at regional industrial specialization. No wonder that results have been disappointing, irrespective of the question of ownership of those industries. The use of more appropriate technologies could, however, also reduce the need for foreign investments and prevent the monopolistic control of the market by local or foreign producers, including transnational corporations.

Thirdly, the use of capital-intensive technology tends to reinforce the concentration of development within the already more advanced countries of the region, as the history of economic regionalism in the Third World has made abundantly clear. At least in the case of a market approach to cooperation, maldistribution of benefits becomes intolerable and regional efforts collapse or are paralysed.

Finally, while allowing the elites to reap the benefits of the geographical enlargement of the market across frontiers, the use of capital-intensive technology may delay the social enlargement of national markets, as pointed out by the dependency theorists. Under these circumstances, regional cooperation resembles an elites' alliance aimed at getting the best of both worlds: perpetuation of their foreign-oriented consumption patterns through local production.

If our remarks are relevant, at least at the present level of development of most African countries, one may wonder whether a production approach to regional cooperation, including a policy of industrial specialization, is a development or an anti-development strategy! An answer to this question must take into account three elements: the level of development of the countries concerned, the type of industries subject to specialization and the approach chosen. The need for specialization in simple industries hardly exists. In advanced industries, such as chemical or mechanical industries, regional specialization certainly makes more sense. If a policy of industrial specialization is adopted, judging from experience in Eastern Europe and Latin America, a more acceptable form of specialization is the intra-industry approach. Its main advantages over the inter-industry approach consist in the promotion of diversification of national economies while allowing a healthy measure of intra-regional competition, as in the case of the automobile industry within the Andean Group.

Generally speaking, however, the chances of success of the production approach to regional cooperation in Africa may remain extremely low for several decades to come. But this does not mean that, under prevailing circumstances, regional cooperation has no role to play in African development. On the contrary, innumerable opportunities for fruitful intra-African cooperation exist in what we may call the service sector. The term services shall be interpreted in the widest possible sense as covering all abilities and infrastructures needed to support the national development effort. In many respects, it is the equivalent of national capacity-building. Cooperation in the service sector could thus include the creation of an awareness of development problems and their possible solutions, that is a better understanding of the development process and policies; the elaboration of appropriate legal, financial and social frameworks or policy instruments; and the coordination of physical infrastructures. In particular, it may be concerned with the development of diversified expertise, eventually through joint training and research activities; the adoption of common positions and mechanisms for the control of foreign investments; or the solution of the complex issue of the transfer, adaptation and development of technology.

Cooperation in the service sector may be politically more acceptable, since it is basically oriented towards national capacity-building. Even the realization of regional economies of scale in the service sector appears to work more equitably than at the production level. While economies of scale at the production level rather limit the range of diversification of economic activities of individual member countries, economies of scale in the service sector seem to increase the range of national abilities for all members, thus creating for each country more opportunities than constraints.

In many respects, the reorientation of regional cooperation we have been talking about, including the shift in emphasis from the production to the service sector, is already a fact of life. Practice usually feeds theory. But it is vital for theory not to remain too far behind practice and to possibly help, if not in guiding, at least in understanding new developments.

Trends and implications

A comparative look at the evolution of regional cooperation in various parts of the world, notably during the past decade, reveals at least two clear trends: a growing politicization of the regional process and a search for more selective approaches to cooperation. The first trend affects also the EEC, following the formalization of the periodical Summit Meetings of Heads of State and Governments. A more intensive politicization of the regional process is particularly evident in Latin America, where the experts or *tecnicos* had traditionally been accorded a wider role in inter-country cooperation. Apart from attendance at founding conferences or other occasional meetings, presidents did not generally play a prominent role in the Latin American regional process. Top regional decision-making bodies were usually made up of ministers or government representatives. In recent years, the presidential role has become more pervasive and institutionalized. This tendency seems to weaken the autonomy, if not the importance, of regional institutions and is a clear reassertion of the predominance of national interest. From this point of view, Latin America and Europe are moving closer to the prevailing practice in Africa, where the control of the regional process has always remained firmly in the hands of presidents and heads of government. We have serious reservations about any form of unchecked personalization of power at any level, but we do not see anything wrong with greater politicization of the regional process. A stronger defence of national interests today may be the best way of preventing the death of regional efforts tomorrow.

Disenchantment with comprehensive forms of regional cooperation of a common market type and the search for more selective approaches to such cooperation are also widespread, the major exception being the EEC. The evolution of the regional process in Latin America could have special significance for Africa. One may reflect on the long paralysis of the Central American Common Market, once the more complete implementation of a classical attempt at regional cooperation in Latin America. By contrast, one could analyse the performance of the Andean Group, where the establishment of the customs union has been considerably delayed, while more satisfactory progress has been reported in the implementation of the more specific programmes of intra-industry specialization, the common regime on foreign investments, and cooperation in science and technology. But even more important is to consider the fate of the Latin American Free Trade Area (LAFTA) created in 1960 and abolished in 1980. After twenty years of assiduous efforts at establishing a pan-Latin American free trade area and eventually a common market, the Latin American countries decided to abandon this idea altogether, mainly because of the negative impact of their different levels of economic development on the distribution of benefits among them. The banner of intra-Latin American cooperation passed to a looser organization: the Latin American Economic System (SELA, in Spanish), born in 1975 probably in anticipation of the dissolution of LAFTA and in commemoration of the 150th anniversary of the Panama Congress, the first unsuccessful bid at pan-Latin American cooperation on the eve of independence. One of the fundamental principles of SELA is respect for different types of political and socio-economic national systems. Its major aims are consultation on general development policies, harmonization of foreign economic policies, and implementation of specific programmes or projects through *ad hoc* action committees, on the basis of voluntary participation of those concerned.

Regional experiences in Africa certainly move in the same direction. Suffice it to compare the still active Entente Council with the short-lived Ghana-Guinea Union and Mali Federation or the defunct EAC and paralysed UDEAC. But most African countries seem still reluctant to draw the full implications from the Latin American or their own experience. The myth of African unity and the promised land of some kind of pan-African political kingdom or common market still haunts the minds of scholars and policy-makers. It is true that since the early 1960s the only major new regional experiment of a classical type in Africa was the launching of ECOWAS in 1975. But comprehensive forms of cooperation still have a strong appeal in Africa. Ambiguities on the role of regionalism persist. In this respect, we find it disturbing that in 1980, the year of the dissolution of LAFTA, the African countries issued in Lagos the most solemn and action-oriented declaration yet of their support for the establishment of a pan-African common market by the year 2000. During 1978–81, 18 eastern and southern African countries negotiated the Treaty creating the

Preferential Trade Area (PTA), though the poor show at the signing ceremony in Lusaka, on 23 December 1981, was an ominous warning on the low chances of the Treaty being implemented or even ratified.

But parallel to this persistent interest in comprehensive forms of cooperation, a strong current favouring more specific forms of cooperation is permeating the African continent. We refer not only to regional arrangements of the type of SADCC or the Kagera River Basin, but also to the emerging network of continental and subcontinental centres of excellence, professional associations and intergovernmental bodies dealing with infrastructural coordination or cooperation in science and technology. We have already embarked on a major research project on cooperation in science and technology in Africa and hope to unveil considerable evidence of this growing African concern for greater collective self-reliance in such a basic field. The intensity of this concern could however be grasped by noting that some 40 new institutions and programmes for scientific and technological cooperation in Africa were launched during the 1970s, 12 of which began in 1978 alone, as against only seven in the previous decade.

To recapitulate or restate our position, several implications of theoretical and practical relevance in the prevailing African context can be drawn from the above trends and arguments.

a) Regional cooperation should *aim* more at reinforcing the autonomy of the national productive capacities rather than at inter-country interdependence at the productive level. As we have argued earlier and contrary to widely held assumptions on the subject, greater national economic autonomy is not only politically but also economically viable and desirable, at least at the present level of development of most African countries, if more appropriate technologies are adopted in the production process.

b) The *scope* of regional cooperation should focus on selective rather than comprehensive programmes and on the service rather than the production sector. Stated differently, regional cooperation should help in creating and strengthening the instruments of greater national self-reliance. The approach to regional cooperation based on trade liberalization and systematic industrial specialization may have to be abandoned.

c) A service-oriented approach to regional cooperation facilitates the exploitation of *complementarities* between global, continental and subcontinental organizations or levels of cooperation. We are aware of the potentially disruptive effects of institutional rivalries and the intrusion into Africa by the international system, including the UN and the EEC. Such disruptive effects can be magnified by the heavy external dependence of most African countries. But the global system and extra-continental links also provide opportunities. Through joint positions, the unwarranted intrusion by extra-continental forces could more easily be contained and some favourable outputs of the international system, notably in terms of information, training, research and financial resources, better utilized. Joint African positions and actions could also exert a more convincing impact on the transformation of the international system. Harmonization of foreign, in particular economic, policies could thus be a major concern of regional cooperation.

d) Regional *institutions* should emphasize voluntary over compulsory participation in programmes and projects, consensus formation over majority voting procedures, and national over regional control of implementation of decisions. Generally, this calls for a downgrading rather than an upgrading of the regional institutional apparatus.

e) Finally, if search for *models* is justified, one has to look at frameworks and organizations other than the EEC. One could benefit from the institutional and policy experiences of the OECD, notably its action-oriented analysis of member countries' economies and common problems; or from Comecon's programmes of intra-industry specialization and cooperation in science and technology; or from SELA's concern with the harmonization of foreign economic policies and the role of its action committees; or from the Andean Group's Common Regime on foreign investments and its technology-related policies, in particular the unpackaging of imported technologies. If fascination with Western European experience persists, one may wish to study more Europe of the 19th century Public Unions, that is Europe of the harmonization of modern infrastructural development, than Europe of the Common Market.

The significance of these conclusions is to recognize the need for stronger, not weaker, political and economic nationalism in Third World countries. In our view, the whole debate on regionalism has been vitiated from the start by an overwhelming concern with peace, nationalism being considered the trouble-maker. This also applies to the functionalist school, despite its apparent interest in welfare. But peace and order are often the paramount concern of those who control the system. As for the others, even in the nuclear age, peace probably remains a means for the achievement of other goals such as welfare. In any case, it may well be that a better way of insuring peace is by a higher degree of satisfaction of national interests rather than by a higher degree of interdependence between nations. In given circumstances, national interest could be better served by greater interdependence, but this cannot always be taken for granted.

To conclude, we hope that the remarks made in this chapter and the analysis carried over by the various authors of previous chapters will provide some useful guidelines for both the theory and practice of regional cooperation. We intend to pursue investigation in this field. Other scholars may also wish to deal in greater depth with some of the questions raised here. Analysis of case-studies may also shift from the more classical to less ambitious, but perhaps equally significant, forms of cooperation. The policy-maker may also discern guidelines for action or at least for a better evaluation of the maze of regional institutions, programmes and projects proliferating in Africa. However, the book provides few, if any, specific solutions to the many problems of intra-African cooperation. Concrete solutions can only be arrived at by the policy-makers and their experts through the old and perhaps boring art of day-to-day negotiation or diplomacy.

NOTES

1 D. Mazzeo, 'The State and the Transnational Corporation: an International Perspective', *Journal of Eastern African Research and Development* (Nairobi), x, (1980).
2 In the long-run, the future of continental African politics may well depend, to a good extent, on the intensity of rivalry or cooperation between Nigeria and South Africa under majority rule.

Bibliography

BOOKS

ADAMS, F. G. and GLICKMAN, N., *Modeling the Multiregional Economic System: Perspectives for the Eighties* (Wharton Econometric ser.), Lexington Books, New York, 1980.

AIBONI, S. A., *Protection of Refugees in Africa*, Swedish Institute of International Law, Uppsala, 1978.

AJALA, A., *Pan-Africanism: Evolution, Progress and Prospects*, André Deutsch, London, 1973.

AKE, C., *A Theory of Political Integration*, Odyssey Press, New York, 1967.

AKE, C., *A Political Economy of Africa*, Longman, London, 1981.

AKINTAN, S. A., *The Law of International Economic Institutions in Africa*,- Sijthoff, Leiden, 1977.

ALTING von GEUSAU, F. A. M. (ed.), *The Lomé Convention and a New International Economic Order*, Sijthoff, Leyden, 1977.

ALUKO, O. (ed.), *The Foreign Policy of African States*, Humanities Press, Atlantic Highlands (NJ), 1977.

AMIN, S., *The Maghreb in the Modern World: Algeria, Tunisia, Morocco*, Penguin, Harmondsworth, 1970.

ANDEMICAEL, B., *The OAU and the UN*, Africana Publishing Co., New York, 1976.

ANDEMICAEL, B., *Regionalism and the United Nations*, Oceana Publications, Dobbs Ferry, 1979.

ANDIC, F. et al., *Theory of Economic Integration for Developing Countries*, University of York Studies in Economics, Toronto, 1971.

ANDREIS, M., *L'Africa e la Comunitá Economica Europea*, Einaudi, Torino, 1967.

BALASSA, B. A., *The Theory of Economic Integration*, Irwin, Homewood, 1961.

BAYLISS, B., *The European Communities and the Associated (ACP) States*, Gower, London, 1981.

BOUC, A. et al., *Problêmes de Développement en Afrique de l'Ouest*, African Institute for Economic Development and Planning, Dakar, 1966.

BOURRINET, J., *La Cooperation Économique Euro-Africaine*, Presses Universitaire de France, Paris, 1976.

BOUTROS-GHALI, B., *L'Organization de l'Unité Africaine*, Colin, Paris, 1969.

CANTORI, L. and SPIEGEL, S. L., *The International Politics of Regions: a Comparative Approach*, Prentice-Hall, Englewood Cliffs, 1970.

ČERVENKA, Z., *The Organization of African Unity and its Charter*, C. Hurst, London, 2nd edn, 1969.

ČERVENKA, Z., *The Unfinished Quest for Unity*, Julian Friedman, London, 1977.

CHIME, C. S., *Integration and Politics among African States: Limitations and Horizons of Midterm Theorizing*, Scandinavian Institute of African Studies, Uppsala, 1977.

COHEN, D. L. and DANIEL, J. (eds), *Political Economy of Africa*, Longman, London, 1981.

COLLOQUIM, A. R. C., *Toward a New Strategy for Development*, Pergamon Press, Oxford, 1979.

COSGROVE-TWITCHETT, C., *Europe and Africa: from Association to Partnership*, Gower, London, 1978.

DECRAENE, P., *Le Panafricanisme*, Presses Universitaire de France, Paris, 1970.

DIEJOMAOH, V. P. and IYODA, M. A. (eds), *Industrialization in the Economic Community of West African States (ECOWAS)*, Heinemann Educational Books, Ibadan, 1980.

DOIMI DI DELUPIS, I., *The East African Community and Common Market*, Longman, London, 1969.

DREUX-BRÉZÉ, *Le Problème du Regroupement en Afrique Equatoriale*, R. Pichon, et R. Durand Auzias, Paris, 1968.

EL-AGRAA, A. M. and JONES, A. J., *Theory of Customs Unions*, St. Martin's Press, New York, 1981.

EL-AYOUTY, Y. and BROOKS, H. G. (eds), *Africa and International Organization*, Martinus Nijhoff, The Hague, 1974.

EZE, O. C., *The Legal Status of Foreign Investments in the East African Common Market*, A. W. Sijthoff, Leiden, 1975.

FALK, R. A. and MENDLOVITZ, S. H., *Regional Politics and World Order*, W. H. Freeman, and Co., San Francisco, 1973.

FAUNDEZ, J. and PICCIOTTO, S., *The Nationalization of Multinationals in Peripheral Economies*, Macmillan, London, 1979.

FELD, W. Y. and BOYD, G. (eds), *Comparative Regional Systems: West and East Europe, North America, the Middle East and Developing Countries*, Praeger, New York, 1979.

FOLTZ, W. J., *From French West Africa to the Mali Federation*, Yale University Press, New Haven, 1965.

FRANK, T. M., *East African Unity through Law*, Yale University Press, New Haven, 1964.

FREY-WOUTERS, E., *The European Community and the Third World: the Lomé Convention and its Impact*, Praeger, New York, 1980.

FRIEDRICH, C. J., *Trends of Federalism in Theory and Practice*, Praeger, New York, 1968.

GEISS, I., *The Pan-African Movement*, Methuen, London, 1974.

GREEN, R. H. and KRISHNA, K. G. V., *Economic Cooperation in Africa: Retrospect and Prospect*, Oxford University Press, Nairobi, 1967.

GREEN, R. H. and SEIDMAN, A., *Unity or Poverty? The Economics of Pan-Africanism*, Penguin, Harmondsworth, 1968.

GRUHN, I. V., *Regionalism Reconsidered: the Economic Commission for Africa*, Westview Press, Boulder, Colorado, 1979.

GRUNDY, K., *Confrontation and Accommodation in Southern Africa*, University of California Press, Berkeley, 1973.

GUTKIND, P. C. W. and WALLERSTEIN, I. (eds), *The Political Economy of Contemporary Africa*, Sage Publications, London, 1977.

HAAS, E. B., *Beyond the Nation-State: Functionalism and International Organization*, Stanford University Press, Stanford, 1964.

HAAS, E. B., *The Uniting of Europe: Political, Social and Economic Forces; 1950–1957*, Stanford University Press, Stanford, 1958.

HAZLEWOOD, A. (ed.), *African Integration and Disintegration: Case Studies in Economic and Political Union*, Oxford University Press, London, 1967.

HAZLEWOOD, A., *Economic Integration: the East African Experience*, Heinemann, London, 1975.

INTERNATIONAL DIMENSIONS OF REGIONAL INTEGRATION IN THE THIRD WORLD, Proceedings of the 5th international conference of the Institute for International Cooperation, University of Ottawa, 10–13 April 1973, University of Ottawa Press, Ottawa, 1975.

JACOB, P. and TOSCANO, J. (eds), *The Integration of Political Communities*, Lippincott, Philadelphia, 1964.

JACOBSON, H. K., *Networks of Interdependence: International Organizations and the Global Political System*, A. A. Knopf/ Random House, Westminster, 1979.

JALLOH, A. A., *Political Integration in French-speaking Africa*, Institute of International Studies, University of California, Berkeley, 1973.

JOHNSON, H. G. and SWOBODA, A. K., *The Economics of Common Currencies*, Harvard University Press, Cambridge, Mass., 1973.

KAHNERT, F. et al., *Economic Integration among Developing Countries*, OECD, Paris, 1969.

KAMARCK, A. M., *The Economics of African Development*, Praeger, New York, 1971.

KOUASSI, E. K., *Les Rapports entre l'Organisation des N.U. et l'Organisation de l'Unité Africaine*, Bruyland, Bruxelles, 1978.

KRAUSS, M. B., *Economics of Integration: a Book of Readings*, George Allen and Unwin, London, 1973.

LALL, S., *Foreign Investments, Transnationals and Developing Countries*, Macmillan, London, 1979.

LEGUM, C., *Pan-Africanism: a Short Political Guide*, Praeger, New York, 1962.

LEGUM, C. et al. (eds), *Africa in the 1980s: a Continent in Crisis*, McGraw-Hill Book Co., New York, 1979.

LINDBERG, L. N. and SCHEINGOLD, S. A., *Regional Integration: Theory and Research*, Harvard University Press, Cambridge, Mass., 1971.

LIPSEY, R. G., *The Theory of Customs Unions: a General Equilibrium Analysis*, Weidenfeld and Nicolson, London, 1970.

LLEWELLYN, D. J., *International Financial Integration: the Limits of Sovereignty* (Problems of Economic Integration Ser.), Halsted Press, 1981.

LONG, F.(ed.), *The Political Economy of EEC Relations with African, Caribbean and Pacific States: Contributions to the Understanding of the Lomé Convention on North-South Relations*, Pergamon Press, Oxford, 1980.

LORTIE, P., *Economic Integration and the Law of GATT* (Special Studies), Praeger, New York, 1975.

MACHLUP, F., *A History of Thought on Economic Integration*, Columbia University Press, New York, 1977.

MAZRUI, A. A., *Africa's International Relations: the Diplomacy of Dependency and Change*, Westview Press, Boulder, 1978.

MAZRUI, A. A. and PATEL, H. H. (eds), *Africa: the Next Thirty Years*, Friedmann, London, 1974.

MAZZEO, D., *Foreign Assistance and the East African Common Services, 1960–70*, Weltforum Verlag, Munich, 1975.

MEHRETU, A., *Regional Integration for Economic Development of Greater East Africa: a Quantified Analysis of Possibilities*, Uganda Publication House, Kampala, 1973.

MITRANY, D. *A Working Peace System: an Argument for the Functional Development of International Organization*, The Royal Institute of International Affairs, London, 1943.

LES MULTINATIONALES AFRICAINES, Ediafric, 1978.

MUTHARIKA, B. W. T., *Toward Multinational Economic Cooperation in Africa*, Praeger, New York, 1972.

MYTELKA, L. K., *Regional Development in a Global Economy: the Multinational Corporation, Technology, and Andean Integration*, Yale University Press, New Haven, 1979.

NDEGWA, P., *The Common Market and Development in East Africa*, East African Publishing House, Nairobi, 2nd edn., 1968.

NGOUDI, N., *La Réussite de l'Intégration Économique en Afrique*, Presence Africaine, Paris, 1971.

NIXSON, F. I., *Economic Integration and Industrial Location: an East African Case Study*, Longman, London, 1973.

NSEKELA, A. J. (ed.), *Southern Africa: Toward Economic Liberation*, Rex Collings, London, 1981.

NYE, J. S. Jr, *International Regionalism*, Little Brown & Co., Boston, 1968.

NYE, J. S. Jr, *Pan-Africanism and East African Integration*, Harvard University Press, Cambridge, Mass., 1965.

NYE, J. S. Jr, *Peace in Parts; Integration and Conflict in Regional Organization*, Little Brown & Co., Boston, 1971.

OKIGBO, P. N. C., *Africa and the Common Market*, Longman, London, 1967.

O'LEARY, J. O., *Systems Theory and Regional Integration: the Market Model of International Politics*, University Press of America, Washington, 1978.

PENTLAND, C., *International Theory and European Integration*, Faber and Faber, London, 1973.

PLESSZ, N. G., *Problems and Prospects of Economic Integration in West Africa*, McGill University Press, Montreal, 1968.

POTHOLM, C. and FREDLAND, R., *Integration and Disintegration in East Africa*, University Press of America, Lanham, 1980.

RENNINGER, J. P., *Multinational Cooperation for Development in West Africa*, Pergamon Press, New York, 1979.

RIDEAU, A., *Legal Aspects of Economic Integration*, A. W. Sijthoff, Leiden, 1972.

RIVKIN, A., *Nation-building in Africa: Problems and Prospects*, Rutgers University Press, New Brunswick, N.J., 1969.

ROBAWA, A., *The Prospects for an Economic Community in North Africa: Managing Economic Integration in the Maghreb States*, Praeger, New York, 1973.

ROBINSON, R. S. (ed.), *Appropriate Technologies for Third World Development*, Macmillan, London, 1979.

ROBSON, P., *Economic Integration in Africa*, Allen & Unwin, London, 1968.

ROBSON, P. and LEYS, C. (eds), *Federation in East Africa, Opportunities and Problems*, Oxford University Press, Nairobi, 1965.

ROTHCHILD, D. (ed.), *Politics of Integration: an East African Documentary*, East African Publishing House, Nairobi, 1968.

RUSSETT, B. H., *International Regions and the International System; a Study in Political Ecology*, Rand McNally, Chicago, 1967.

SEERS, D. and VAITSOS, C. (eds), *Integration and Unequal Development: the Experience of the EEC*, Macmillan, London, 1980.

SHAW, T. and ONWUKA, R. (eds), *Africa and World Politics*, George Allen & Unwin, London, 1982.

SHAW, T. M. et al., *The Politics of Africa: Development and Dependence*, Longman, London, 1978.

SHOWP, C. P., *Fiscal Harmonization in Common Markets*, Columbia University Press, New York, 1967.

SIMAI, M. and GARAM, P., *Economic Integration: Concepts, Theories and Problems*, International Publications Ser., 1977.

SOHN, L. B. (ed.), *Basic Documents of African Regional Organizations*, Oceana Publications, Dobbs Ferry, 1972.

SWANN, D., *The Economics of the Common Market*, Penguin, Harmondsworth, 1975.

SYZ, J., *International Development Banks*, Oceana Publications, New York, 1974.

TANDON, Y. A., *Readings in African International Relations*, Vol. 1, East African Literature Bureau, Nairobi, Kampala, Dar-es-Salaam, 1972.

TANDON, Y. A. and CHANDARANA, D. (eds), *Horizons of African Diplomacy*, East African Literature Bureau, Nairobi, Dar-es-Salaam, Kampala, 1974.

TEITGEN, P. H., *Les Organisations Régionales Internationales*, Montchrestien, 1971.

TEVOEDJRE, A., *Pan-Africanism in Action: an Account of the Union Africaine et Malgache*, Harvard University Press, Cambridge, Mass., 1965.

THARP, P. A. Jr, *Regional International Organizations: Structures and Functions*, St. Martin's Press, New York, 1971.

THIAM, D., *The Foreign Policy of African States*, Praeger, New York, 1965.

THOMPSON, V., *West Africa's Council of the Entente*, Cornell University Press, Ithaca, New York, 1972.

THOMPSON, V., *Africa and Unity: the Evolution of Pan-Africanism*, Longman, London, 1969.

TIMBERGEN, J., *International Economic Integration*, Elsevier, New York, 2nd rev. edn., 1965.

TREMBLAY, R., *Afrique et Intégration Monétaire*, H R W, 1975.

VANEK, J., *General Equilibrium of International Discrimination: the Case of Customs Unions*, Harvard University Press, Cambridge, Mass., 1965.

VINER, J., *The Customs Union Issue*, Stevens and Sons, London, 1950.

WELCH, C. E. Jr, *Dream of Unity: Pan-Africanism and Political Unification in West Africa*, Cornell University Press, Ithaca, New York, 1966.

WIDSTRAND, C. C. (ed.), *African Boundary Problems*, Scandinavian Institute of African Studies, Uppsala, 1969.

WIDSTRAND, C. C. (ed.), *Multinational Firms in Africa*, African Institute for Economic Development and Planning, Dakar, 1975.

WILLETTS, P., *The Non-Aligned Movement: the Origins of a Third World Alliance*, Nichols Publ. Co., 1978.

WIONCZEK, M. (ed.), *Economic Cooperation in Latin America, Africa, and Asia*, MIT Press, 1969.

WOLFERS, M., *Politics in the Organization of African Unity*, Methuen, London, 1976.

YASSIN, El-Ayouty (ed.), *The OAU after Ten Years: Comparative Perspectives*, Praeger, New York, 1975.

YONDO, M., *Dimension Nationale et Dévelopment Economique*, R. Pichon et R. Durand-Auzias, Paris, 1970.

ZARTMAN, W. I., *International Relations in the New Africa*, Prentice-Hall, Englewood Cliffs, 1966.

ZARTMAN, W. I., *Contemporary Maghreb*, Blackwell's, London, 1973.

LA ZONE FRANC ET L'AFRIQUE, Ediafric, 2nd edn, 1979.

ARTICLES

ABDALLAH, R., 'L'unité africaine: de premiers congrés panafricains à la fin de la première décennie de l'OUA', *Revue juridique* (Tunis), i, (1974).

ADAMO LEBUM, L., 'Cooperation or Neocolonialism-Francophone Africa', *Africa Quarterly*, (New Delhi) xviii, 1 (1978).

ADEDEJI, A., 'Collective Self-reliance in Developing Africa: Scope, Prospects and Problems', Paper presented at the International Conference on ECOWAS, Lagos, (23–27 August 1976).

ADEDEJI, A., 'Prospects of Regional Economic Cooperation in West Africa', *Journal of Modern African Studies*, viii, 2 (1970).

ADERIGBE, A. B., 'West African Integration: an Historical Perspective', *Nigerian Journal of Economic and Social Studies*, (1963).

AFRICAN UNITY AND POLITICAL ALIGNMENTS, *Africa Research Bulletin*, (1982).

AGYEMAN, O., 'The Osagyafo, the Mwalimu and Pan-Africanism', *Journal of Modern African Studies*, xiii, 4 (1975).

AJOMO, M. A., 'Regional Economic Organizations, the African Experience', *International and Comparative Law Quarterly*, xxv (1976).

AKINDELE, R. A., 'The Organization of African Unity and the UN: a Study of the Problems of Universal-Regional Relationships in the Organization and Maintenance of International Peace and Security', *Canadian Yearbook of International Law*, ix (1971).

AKINSANYA, A., 'Afro-Arab Alliance: Dream or Reality?', *African Affairs*, lxxv, (1976).

ALUKO, O., 'The O.A.U. Liberation Committee after a Decade: an Appraisal', *Quarterly Journal of Administration*, viii, 1 (1973).

ALUKO, S. A., 'Nigeria's role of Inter-African Relations with Special Reference to the OAU', *African Affairs*, lxxii (1973).

ALUKO, S. A., 'Problems of Financial and Monetary Integration', *Nigerian Journal of Economic and Social Studies* (1963).

AMIN, S., 'Underdevelopment and Dependence in Black Africa: their Historical Origins and Contemporary Forms', *Journal of Modern African Studies*, x, 4 (1972).

ASANTE, S. K. B., 'Lomé II: Another Machinery for Updating Dependency', *Development and Cooperation*, iii (1981).

ASANTE, S. K. B., 'The Lomé Convention: towards Perpetuation of Dependence or Promotion of Interdependence?', *Third World Quarterly*, iii, 4 (1981).

AXLINE, W. A., 'Underdevelopment, Dependence and Integration: the Politics of Regionalism in the Third World', *International Organization*, xxxi, 1 (1977).

AYOOB, M., 'The Super-powers and Regional "Stability": Parallel Responses to the Gulf and the Horn', *The World Today* (1979).

AZARE, F. B., 'The Background to O.A.U.', *Africa and the World*, ii (1965).

BAKARY, L., 'Les chances d'une intégration monétaire et économique au sein de la sous-région ouest africaine', *Banque*, 374 (1978).

BALASSA, B., 'Avantages comparés et perspectives de l'intégration économique en Afrique de l'Ouest', *Cahiers économiques et sociaux*, xvi (1978).

BALASSA, B. and STOUTJESDIJK, A., 'Economic Integration among Developing Countries', *Journal of Common Market Studies*, xiv, 1 (1975).

BANAISA, G. L., 'Organization of African Unity and Decolonization: Present and Future Trends', *American Academy of Political and Social Science Annals*, 432 (1977).

BAZA, G., 'Tentatives de coordination industrielle au sein de l'Union douanière et économique de l'Afrique du centre', *Cahiers congolais de la recherche et du développement*, Kinshasa-Kalima (1970).

BIARNES, P., 'Industrialisation et unité en Afrique de l'ouest', *Le mois en Afrique*, x (1966).

BISHOP, A. S. and MUNRO, R. D., 'The United Nations Regional Economic Commissions and Environmental Problems', *International Organization*, xxvi (1972).

BOCKEL, A., 'Intégration régionale Ouest-Africaine et relations verticales-Afrique de l'Ouest ou Eurafrique?', *Cahiers économiques et sociaux*, xvi (1978).

BORNSTEIN, R., 'The Organization of Senegal River States', *Journal of Modern African Studies*, x, 2 (1972).

BOTCHWAY, F. A., 'A Reconsideration of the Pan-Africanism Reality', *Pan-African Journal*, iii (1970).

BOUTROS-GHALI, B., 'Addis Ababa Charter with Text of Charter', *International Conciliation*, 546 (1964).

BOUTROS-GHALI, B., 'Les relations entre la ligue Arabe et l'OUA', *Annuaire Français de droit international*, xxiii (1977).

BRUYAS, J., 'La convention ACP-CEE de Lomé (28 février 1975)', *Annuaire du Tiers Monde*, i (1975).

CAMARA, S-S., 'La Guinée et la coopération économique en Afrique de l'Ouest', *Cultures et développement*, viii (1976).

CAPORASO, J. A., 'Dependency Theory: Continuities and Discontinuities in Development Studies', *International Organization*, xxxiv, 4 (1980).

CAPORASO, J. A., 'Theory and Method in the Study of International Integration', *International Organization*, xxv, 2 (1971).

ČERVENKA, Z., 'Africa as a Case of Inter-regional Contradictions', *International Social Science Journal*, xxviii, 4 (1976).

ČERVENKA, Z., 'The Emergence and Significance of African Arab Solidarity', *Institute for Research on Peace and Violence*, iv, 2 (1974).

CHARTRAND, P. E., 'The Organization of African Unity and African Refugees: a Progress Report', *World Affairs*, xiii, 4 (1975).
CHIDZERO, B. T. G., 'The Meaning of Economic Integration in Africa', *East African Journal*, ii, 8 (1965).
CHUKWURAH, A. O., 'The Organization of African Unity and African Territorial and Boundary Problems: 1963–1973', *Indian Journal of International Law*, xiii, 2 (1973).
CHURCH, R. J., 'Some Problems of Regional Economic Development in West Africa', *Economic Geography*, xlv, (1969).
COBBE, J. H., 'Integration among Unequals: the Southern African Customs Union and Development', *World Development*, viii, 4 (1980).
COMMUNAUTE ECONOMIQUE DE L'AFRIQUE DE L'OUEST, Ouagadougou, 'Annuaire économique juridique de la CEAO', Ouagadougou, CEAO (1978).
CONSTANTIN, F., 'La Communauté européene et l'Est African Community: Les leçons d'un accord Nord Sud oublié', *Annuaire des pays de l'Océan indien*, iii (1976).
CONSTANTIN, F., 'L'intégration régionale en Afrique noire', *Revue française de science politique*, xxii (1972).
CONSTANTIN, F., 'Un echec politique', *Revue française d'études politiques africaines*, xiii (1978).
COPSON, R. W., 'African International Politics: Underdevelopment and Conflict in the Seventies, *Orbis*, xxii, 1 (1978).
DALAN, M. B. and TOMLIN, B. W., 'First World-Third World Linkages: External Relations and Economic Development', *International Organization*, xxxiv, 1 (1980).
DALOZ, P. J., 'Union et intégration monétaire', *Cahiers économiques et sociaux*, xvi, 2 (1978).
DAVID, J., 'La Communauté économique de l'Afrique de l'ouest', *Marchés tropicaux et méditerranéens* (1973).
DIEJOMOAH, V. P., 'Ecowas' Way Ahead', *West Africa* (1980).
DIESHIT, R. D., 'O.A.U. Promises and Performances', *Africa Quarterly*, vi, 1 (1966).
DOLAN, M. B., et al., 'Foreign Policies of African States in Asymmetrical Dyads', *International Studies Quarterly*, xxiv, 3 (1980).
DUGARD, C. J. R., 'The Organization of African Unity and Colonialism', *International and Comparative Law Quarterly*, xvi, 1 (1967).
ECONOMIC COMMISSION FOR AFRICA AND THE O.A.U.: 'Some Comparison of their Goals and Operation', *Africa* (1971).
ECONOMIC INTEGRATION AND THIRD WORLD COLLECTIVE SELF-RELIANCE, *Third World Forum*, Occasional paper, iv (1979).
ECOWAS after Freetown, *West Africa* (1981).
ECOWAS critique, *West Africa* (1980).
ECOWAS on energy, *West Africa* (1981).
ECOWAS' seventh anniversary, *West Africa* (1982).
EEC-ACP consultative Assembly meeting, *West Africa* (1981).
EKUE, A. K., 'L'organisation Commune Africaine et Mauricienne', *Revue française d'études politiques africaines*, 130 (1976).

EL-AYOUTY, U., 'O.A.U. Mediation in the Arab-Israeli Conflict', *Genève Afrique*, xiv, 1 (1975).

ELIAS, T. O., 'The Charter of the Organization of African Unity', *American Journal of International Law*, lix, 2 (1965).

ELIAS, T. O., 'The Commission of Mediation, Conciliation, and Arbitration of the Organization of African Unity', *British Year-book of International Law* (1964).

ELIAS, T. O., 'The Economic Community of West Africa', *Year Book of World Affairs*, xxxii (1978).

ELKAN, P. G., 'Measuring the Impact of Economic Integration among Developing Countries', *Journal of Common Market Studies*, xiv, 1 (1975).

EWING, A. F., 'Prospects for Economic Integration in Africa', *Journal of Modern African Studies*, v, 1 (1967).

EZE, O. C., 'O.A.U. Faces Rhodesia', *African Review*, v, 1 (1975).

FESSARD DE FOUCAULT, B., 'Vers un réaménagement des relations entre les états riverains du fleuve Sénégal?', *Revue de défense nationale* (1972).

FOREIGN TRADE REGULATIONS OF THE WEST AFRICAN CUSTOMS UNION: 'Dahomey, Ivory Coast, Mali, Mauritania, Niger, Senegal, Upper Volta and Togo', *Overseas Business Reports*, Washington (1970).

FOUGUET, D., 'African Unity in Europe', *Africa Report*, xx, 4 (1975).

FRANCE AND WEST AFRICA, *West Africa*, (1981).

FREDLAND, R. A., 'The O.A.U. after Ten Years: can it Survive?', *African Affairs*, lxxii, 288 (1973).

GALTUNG, P., 'The Lomé Convention and Neo-capitalism', *Africa Review*, vi, 1 (1976).

GAM, P., 'Les causes de l'éclatement de la fédération du Mali', *Revue juridique et politique* (Paris, juillet-septembre 1966).

GAUDIO, A., 'L'industrialisation des états de l'Union douanière et économique de l'Afrique centrale', *BCEAEC Notes et études documentaires* (Paris, Oct. 1971).

GAUTRON, J-Cl., 'L'aménagement du bassin du fleuve Sénégal', *Annuaire français de droit international*, (Paris), xiii (1967).

GAUTRON, J-Cl., 'De Lomé I à Lomé II: la Convention ACP-EEC du 31 octobre 1979', *Cahiers de Droit européen*, xvi, 4 (1980).

GAUTRON, J-Cl., 'Les métamorphoses d'un groupement sous-régional: l'Organisation des états riverains du Sénégal', *Année africaine* (Bordeaux, 1970).

GAUTRON, J-Cl. and JARMACHE, E., 'Les organisations régionales africaines', *Année africaine 1976* (1978).

GEISS, I., 'Pan-Africanism', *Journal of Contemporary History*, iv, 1 (1969).

GHAI, D. P., 'State Trading and Regional Economic Integration: the East African Experience', *Journal of Common Market Studies*, xii, 3 (1974).

GHAI, Y. P., 'East African Industrial Licensing System: a Device for the Regional Allocation of Industry', *Journal of Common Market Studies*, xii, 3 (1974).

GREEN, R. H., 'The Lomé Convention: Updated Dependence or Departure toward Collective Self-reliance?', *African Review*, vi, 1 (1976).

GREEN, R. H., 'Southern African Development Coordination: toward a functioning Dynamic?', *IDS Bulletin*, xi, 4 (1980).

GRUHN, I. V., 'The Commission for Technical Co-operation in Africa, 1960–1965', *Journal of Modern African Studies*, ix, 3 (1971).

GRUHN, I. V., 'The Lomé Convention: including towards Interdependence', *International Organization*, xxx, 2 (1976).

HAAS, E. B., 'International Integration: the European and the Universal Process', *International Organization*, xv, 3 (1961).

HANNING, H., 'Lifebelt for Africa: the OAU in the 1980s', *The World Today* (1981).

HANSEN, R. D., 'Regional Integration: Reflections on a Decade of Theoretical Efforts', *World Politics* (1969).

HEDRICH, M. and Von DER ROPP, K., 'Perspectives d'intégration régionale en Afrique de l'Ouest', *Afrique contemporaine*, xvi, (1978).

HIPPOLITE, M., 'De Nouakchott à Niamey, l'itinéraire de l'OCAM', *Revue française d'études politiques africaines*, xxxiv (1968).

HOSKINS, C., 'Trends and Development in the Organization of African Unity', *Yearbook of World Affairs*, xxi (1967).

IMOBIGHE, T. A., 'An African High Command: the Search for Feasible Strategies of Continental Defense', *African Affairs*, lxxix 315 (1980).

IYANDA, O. and STREMLAU, J., 'The Dilemma of an African High Command', *Nigeria*, i (1971).

JALLOH, A. A., 'Regional Integration in Africa: Lessons from the Past and Prospects for the Future', *Africa Development*, i, 2 (1976).

JODICE, D. A., 'Sources of Change in Third World Regimes for Foreign Direct Investment, 1968–1976', *International Organization*, xxxiv, 2 (1980).

JOHNSON, W. R., 'Africans and Arabs: Collaboration without Cooperation, Change without Challenge', *International Journal*, xxxv, 4 (1980).

JOUVE, E., 'L'OUA et la libération de l'Afrique', *Annuaire du Tiers Monde*, i (1975).

KAMARA, L., 'Intégration fonctionnele et développement accéléré en Afrique', *Tiers monde*, xii (1971).

KAMARA, L., 'Intégration territoriale et conflicts institutionnels en Afrique', *Tiers monde*, xi, (1970).

KAMARA, L. and D'HAUTERIVE, B., 'Aspects juridiques de l'intégration économique en Afrique', *Tiers monde*, xii (1972).

KAPPELER, D., 'Causes et conséquences de la désintégration de la Communauté est-africaine', *Politique étrangère*, xliii, 3 (1978).

KAY, D. A., 'The impact of African States on the United Nations', *International Organization*, xxiii, 1 (1969).

KURTZ, D. M., 'Political Integration in Africa: The Mali Federation', *Journal of Modern African Studies*, viii, 3 (1970).

LAWLER, J. and LAULICHT, J., 'International Integration in Developing Regions', *Peace Research Review*, iii, 4 (1970).

LECHINI, G., 'Une perspective historique', *Revue française d'études politiques africaines*, xiii (1978).

LEGUM, C., 'The Organization of African Unity: a Success or Failure?', *International Affairs*, li (1975).

LEGUM, C., 'The Specialized Commissions of the OAU', *Journal of Modern African Studies*, ii, 4 (1964).

LUKASA, T., 'Echange Commerciaux dans la sous-région d'Afrique centrale', *Cahiers économiques et sociaux*, v, 4 (1967).

LUKASA, T., 'Intégration économique et données nationales. La création de l'UEAC', *Etudes congolaises*, xi, 2 (1968).

MAGEE, J. S., 'ECA and the Paradox of African Cooperation', *International Conciliation*, 580 (1970).

MANIGAT, M., 'Les organisations régionales des pays du Tiers Monde', *Annuaire du Tiers Monde*, i (1975).

MARKAKIS, J., 'The Organization of African Unity. A Progress Report', *Journal of Modern African Studies*, iv, 2 (1966).

MATHEWS, R. E., 'Interstate Conflict in Africa: a Review', *International Organization*, xxiv, 2 (1970).

MAYALL, J., 'African Unity and the O.A.U.: the Place of a Political Myth in African Diplomacy', *Yearbook of World Affairs* (1973).

MAZRUI, A., 'Rights of States or of People – where should the OAU focus?', *New African*, London (1977).

MBOGORO, D. A. K., 'Un échec économique', *Revue française d'études politiques africaines*, xiii, (1978).

MBOGORO, D. A. K., 'Les groupements régionaux et le développement économique: quelques leçons tirées du plan d'intégration de l'Afrique de l'Est', *Cahiers économiques et sociaux*, xvi, 2 (1978).

MEYERS, B. D., 'Interregional Conflict Management by the Organization of African Unity', *International Organization*, xxviii, 3 (1974).

MEYERS, B. D., 'O.A.U.'s Administrative Secretary-General', *International Organization*, xx (1976).

MINI, M., 'Class Struggle and African Unity, Ten Years of O.A.U.', *Mainstream*, xi (1973).

MODERNE, F., 'Les dirigeants kenyans et la fin de la Communauté est-africaine', *Revue française d'études politiques africaines*, xiii (1978).

MULEI, C. M., 'African Boundary Disputes the OAU and International Law', *East Africa Journal*, vii (1970).

MUSKHAT, M., 'L'Afrique, le Tiers Monde et le système collectif de sécurité économique et politique internationale', *Africa* (Roma) xxxiii, 1 (1978).

MUSKHAT, M., 'Problems of Political and Organizational Unity in Africa', *African Studies Review*, xiii, 2 (1970).

MYTELKA, L. K., 'Common Market with some Uncommon Problems: UDEAC chooses Cooperation despite Unequally Shared Poverty and Some Severe Clashes of Interest', *Africa Report*, xv (1970).

MYTELKA, L. K., 'A Genealogy of Francophone West and Equatorial African Regional Organizations', *Journal of Modern African Studies*, xii, 2 (1974).

MYTELKA, L. K., 'New Departures in Equatorial African Integration', *Africa Today*, xv, 5 (1968).

MYTELKA, L. K., 'The Lomé Convention and a New International Division of Labour', *Journal of European Integration*, i, 1 (1977).

MYTELKA, L. K., 'The Salience of Gains in Third World Integrative systems', *World Politics*, xxv, 2 (1973).

NAHUMI, M., 'Looking for Unity at Accra: African Unity is a goal which seems further away today than it did in the past', *New Outlook*, viii (1965).

NAMBIAR, K. R., 'The Charter of the Organization of African Unity', *Indian Journal of International Law*, iii (1963).

NWORAH, D., 'The Integration of the Commission for Technical Cooperation in Africa with the Organization for African Unity: the Process of the Merger and the Problems of Institutional Rivalry and Complementarity, *African Review*, vi, 1 (1976).

NYE, J. S., 'Comparative Regional Integration: Concept and Measurement', *International Organization*, xxi (1968).

OAU Force in Chad, *West Africa* (1981).

OCAM, 'De Tananarive à Niamey', *Jeune Afrique*, supplement 367 (1968).

OJO, O. J. B., 'Nigeria and the Formation of ECOWAS', *International Organization*, xxxiv, 4 (1980).

OKOLO, J. E. and LANGLEY, W. E., 'The O.A.U. and Apartheid in South Africa: Constraints on Resolution', *World Affairs*, 137 (1974).

ONITIRI, H. M. A., 'Towards a West African Economic Community', *Nigerian Journal of Economic and Social Studies* (1963); reprinted in Carl K. Eicher and Carl Leidholm (eds), *Growth and Development of the Nigerian Economy*, East Lansing, 1970.

OTEIZA, E., and SERCOVICH, F., 'Collective Self-reliance: Selected Issues', *International Social Science Journal*, xxviii, 4 (1976).

PADELFORD, N. J., 'The Organization of African Unity: Background and Events in its Establishment', *International Organization*, xviii, 3 (1964).

PEIL, M., 'The Expulsion of West African Aliens', *Journal of Modern African Studies*, ix, 2 (1971).

PEUREUX, G., 'La création de l'union africaine et malgache et les conférences des chefs d'états d'expression française', *Revue juridique et politique d'outre-mer* (1961).

PONCELET, M., '60 ans d'expériences fédérales en Afrique de l'ouest franco-phone', *Canadian Journal of African Studies*, i, 2 (1967).

PREVOST, P., 'L'Union douanière et économique de l'Afrique central', *Revue française d'études politiques africanes*, xxxiv (1968).

PROCTOR, J. H., 'The Gambia's Relations with Senegal: the Search for Partnership', *Journal of Commonwealth Political Studies*, ii, (1967).

RAMAMURTHI, T. G., 'The Dynamics of Regional Integration in West Africa', *India Quarterly* xxvi, 3 (1970).

RANA, A. P., 'Regionalism as an Approach to International Order: a Conceptual Overview', *International Studies* (VIKAS), xviii, 4 (1979).

REPORT on ECOWAS, *West Africa* (1982).

ROBSON, P., 'The Problem of Senegambia', *Journal of Modern African Studies*, iii, 3 (1965).

ROBSON, P., 'L'UDEAC et la Communauté de l'Afrique de l'est', *BCEAEC Etudes et statistiques*, 131 (1968).

RONDOS, A., 'Making peace in Chad: Libya-OAU clash over Chad', *West Africa* (1981).

ROSBERG, C. G. Jr. and SEGAL, A., 'An East African Federation', *International Conciliation*, 543 (1963).

ROSSI, G., 'OAU: A Decade on Balance', *Africa*, xxviii, 2 (1973).

SAENZ, P., 'The Organization of African Unity in the Subordinate African Regional System', *African Studies Review*, iii, 2 (1970).

SAID, M., 'Integration as a Mode of Ethnic Conflict Resolution in Africa', *International Interactions*, viii, 4 (1981).

SANGER, C., 'Towards Unity in Africa', *Foreign Affairs*, xlii, 2 (1964).

SEGAL, A., 'The Integration of Developing Countries: Some Thoughts on East Africa and Central America', *Journal of Common Market Studies*, v, 3 (1967).

SHAW, T. M., 'Oil, Israel and the OAU, an Introduction to the Political Economy of Energy in Southern Africa', *Africa Today*, xxiii (1976).

SHAW, T. M., 'Regional Cooperation and Conflict in Africa', *International Journal*, xxx, 4 (1975).

SIRCAR, P. K., 'Regional Development through Cooperation: two examples from West Africa', *Africa Quarterly*, xvii, 1 (1978).

SIRCAR, P. K., 'Toward a Greater East African Community', *Africa Quarterly*, xvi, 3 (1977).

SKURNIK, W. A., 'France and Fragmentation in West Africa, 1945–1960', *Journal of African History*, viii (1968).

SLOAN, J. W., 'The Strategy of Developmental Regionalism: Benefits, Distribution, Obstacles, and Capabilities', *Journal of Common Market Studies*, x, 2 (1971).

SYMPOSIUM ON WEST AFRICAN INTEGRATION, *Nigerian Journal of Economic and Social Studies* (1963).

TANDON, Y., 'The Organization of African Unity: A Forum for African International Relations', *Round Table*, 246 (1972).

THOMPSON, V. B., 'A Catalogue of Betrayal: UN and OAU in the African Crisis', *Africa and the World* (1966).

THOMPSON, W. and BISSELL, R. R., 'Development of the African Subsystem: Legitimacy and Authority in the OAU', *Policy*, v, 3 (1973).

TIEWUL, A., 'Relations between the United Nations and the OAU in the Settlement of Secessionist Conflicts', *Harvard International Law Journal*, xvi (1975).

TOUVAL, S., 'The Organization of African Unity and African Borders', *International Organization*, xxi, 1 (1967).

UNECA, 'Planification du Développement et Intégration Economique en Afrique', *Journal de la Planification du Développement* (Addis Ababa), i (1970).

L'UNION AFRO-MALGACHE, *Bulletin de l'Afrique noire*, (1962).

VINAY, B., 'Coopération intra-africaine et intégration – l'expérience de l'UDEAC', *Penant*, lxxxi (1971).

WATERS, A. R., 'A Behavioral Model of Pan-African Disintegration', *African Studies Review*, xiii, 3 (1970).

WEIGERT, K. M. and RIGGS, R. E., 'Africa and United Nations Elections: an Aggregate Data Analysis', *International Organization*, xxiii, 1 (1969).

WESTERN SAHARA: a special report, *Africa Research Bulletin* (1982).

WILD, P., 'The OAU and the Algerian-Moroccan Border Conflict: a Study of New Machinery for Peace-keeping and for the Peaceful Settlement of Disputes among African States', *International Organization*, xx, 1 (1966).

WIONCZEK, M. S., 'Economic integration and Regional Distribution of Industrial Activities: a Comparative Study', *East African Economic Review*, ii (new series), 1 (1966); and iii (new series), 1 (1967).

WOOD, R. S., 'Public Order and Political Integration in Contemporary International Theory', *Virginia Journal of International Law*, xiv, 3 (1974).
WORONOFF, J., 'The Case for an African Defense Organization', *Africa Report*, xvi (1971).
YANNOPOULOS, T. and MARTIN, D., 'Domination et composition en Afrique: le Conseil de l'Entente et la Communauté est-africaine face à eux-même et face aux "Grands", *Revue algerienne de sciences politiques, économiques et juridiques* (1972).
ZARTMAN, I. W., 'Decision-making among African Governments on Inter-African Affairs', *Journal of Development Studies*, ii, 2 (1966).
ZARTMAN, I. W., 'Europe and Africa: Decolonization or Dependency', *Foreign Affairs*, liv, 2 (1976).

REPORTS AND UNPUBLISHED MATERIAL
AJJOUKI, K., 'Les conférences au sommet des Etats arabes 1964–1974', 3e cycle. Droit de la coopération, Bordeaux I (1977).
AKIWUMI, A. M., 'Institutional Arrangements for Multinational Decision-making in the Central African Sub-region? (Addis Ababa)', U.N.E.C.A. (1969).
ASARE, W., 'La Communauté de l'Afrique de l'Est', 3e cycle. Administration Internationale, Paris I (1977).
BALASSA, B. and STOUTJESDIJK, A., 'Economic Integration among Developing Countries', World Bank reprint Series, 30 (1975).
BECK, A., 'The East African Community and Regional Research in Science and Medicine', paper presented at the African Studies Association, Philadelphia (1972).
BEKOLO-EBE, B., 'Intégration et relations économiques interafricaines: bilan et perspectives', 3e cycle Economie internationale, Paris I (1977).
BENDOSOUPOU BRENDA, R., 'Les principaux problèmes relatifs à l'existence de la Banque africaine de développement', Thèse de 3e cycle. Sociologie politique, EHESS (1977).
BOREL, P., 'Problems of Plan Implementation: Economic Cooperation and Integration in Central Africa', New York, United Nations (1968).
BORRIBOON, R., 'Les relations commerciaux entre la CEE et six pays asiatiques et quarante-six pays d'Afrique, des Caraïbes et du Pacifique', DU. Science politique, Toulouse I (1977).
BOUAZIZI, M. M., 'Essai sur l'intégration économique, cas de la Libye, la Tunisie, l'Algerie et le Maroc', DE. Sciences économiques, Paris I (1977).
CENTRE DE DEVELOPPEMENT DE L'OCDE, 'La coopération régionale dans la recherche et la formation pour le développement', Paris (1978).
DOLAN, M. B., 'The Lomé Convention and Europe's Relationship with the Third World: a Critical Analysis', paper presented to the International Studies Association, St. Louis (1977).
DUBOIS, V. D., 'The Search for Unity in French-speaking Africa', American University Staff, Reports VII: 3, 1965.

E Z E N W E, U., 'The theory of integration: a further reassessment with particular reference to L D C', Paper presented at the international conference on E C O W A S, Lagos (1976).

G H A I, Y. P., 'Reflections on law and economic integration in East Africa', Scandinavian Institute of African Studies, Uppsala (1976).

G I L L E T, J. F., 'Les organismes communs aux états de l'Afrique centrale, Secrétariat général de la conférence des chefs d'état de l'Afrique équatoriale', Brazzaville (1965).

G R U H N, I. V., 'Functionalism in Africa: scientific and technical integration', unpublished Ph.D. dissertation. University of California, Berkeley, 1967.

H A N N I N G, H., 'The Organization of Africa Unity: a role for the 1980s; a report of the International Peace Academy', New York, I P A, 1980.

I M F, 'West African nations mark monetary union', I M F Survey, 1, 9 (1972).

J A L L O H, A., 'The politics and economies of regional political integration in Central Africa', unpublished Ph.D. dissertation, University of California, 1969.

K A H N E R T, F. et al., 'Economic integration among developing countries', Paris, 1969.

K H E R A D, R., 'La révolte du Tiers Monde sur la scène internationale: les non-alignés et le groupe des 77', D E. Droit public, Nice, 1977.

K O F F I, T., 'L'Union monétaires ouest-africaines', Diplome E H E S S, 1977.

K W I S H W E, 'Coopération monétaire et financiere et politique de développement dans les Etats d'Afrique centrale Francophone', 3e cycle. Economie E H E S S, 1977.

M A S E L L, B. F., 'East African Economic Union: an evaluation and some implications for policy', Santa Monica, Cal., Rand Corp, 1963.

M A U M O N, M., 'La coordination industrielle dans les pays de l'U D E A C, Paris, Secrétariat d'état aux affairs étrangères chargé de la coopération', 1968.

M E B A L E T-M'E S S O N E, M., 'La problématique de l'harmonization Fiscale dans le processus de développement économique de l'U D E A C', 3e cycle. Fiscalité et économie Financière, Clermont-Ferrand I., 1977.

N O W Z A R D, B., 'Economic integration in Central and West Africa', I M F staff Papers, Washington, D.C., X1, 1, (1969); reprinted in Paul A. Tharp, Jr. (ed.), *Regional International Organizations: Structures and Functions*, New York, 1971.

O A U, 'Lagos Plan of Action for the Economic Development of Africa 1980–2000', Institute of International Labour Studies, Genève, 1981.

O A U, 'What Kind of Africa by the year 2000?', Institute of International Labour Studies, Genève, 1979.

R A P P O R T D U P R E S I D E N T S E N G H O R A U 8ème Congrés de l'UPS, 'Le Communauté économique comme cadre du développement', *Bulletin de l'Afrique noire*, 718 (1973).

S A D A, P. O., 'Multinational planning of African Waters: the Case of Lake Chad Basin', a paper presented at the Council meeting of the African Studies Association, Philadelphia, 1972.

S C H U B E R T, J. N., 'Regional trends in Intergovernmental Organizations', Paper presented at International Studies Association Meeting, Washington, 1978.

S H A M U Y A R I B A, N. M., 'Documents and speeches on OAU Strategy for Liberation of Southern Africa', Department of Political Science, University of Dar es Salaam, 1975 (mimeo).

UNCTAD V, 'Arusha Programme for Collective Self-reliance and Framework for Negotiations', TD/236, 1979.

UNCTAD V, 'Current Problems of Economic Integration: Agricultural and Industrial Cooperation among Developing Countries', New York, 1971.

UNCTAD V, 'The Distribution of Benefits and Costs in Integration among Developing Countries', UN, New York, 1973.

UNCTAD V, 'Fiscal Compensation and the Distribution of Benefits in Economic Groupings of Developing Countries', UN, New York, 1971.

UNECA, 'Avant-projet d'un traité pour la communauté économique de l'Afrique de l'Ouest?, Addis Ababa, 1967.

UNECA, 'Rapport de la conférence sous-régionale sur la coopération économique en Afrique de l'ouest', Addis Ababa, 1967.

UNECA, 'Report of an ECA Economic Cooperation Mission to West Africa', Addis Ababa, 1970.

UNECA, 'Report of the Seminar on Intra-subregional Economic Cooperation and Trade in Agriculture in West Africa; Bathurst, Gambia, 1971', Addis Ababa, 1973.

UNECA, 'L'Union douanière des états de l'Afrique de l'ouest', Addis Ababa, 1967.

UNECA, 'Development of Trade in the Central African Subregion', Addis Ababa, 1969.

UNECA, 'Report of the Subregional Meeting on Economic Cooperation in Central Africa', Addis Ababa, 1970.

UNECA, 'Directory of Intergovernmental Cooperation Organizations in Africa', Addis Ababa, 1972.

UNECA, 'Economic Cooperation and Integration in Africa, Three Case Studies: East Africa, West Africa, and Central Africa', New York, 1969.

UNECA, 'The impact of Western European Integration on African Trade and Development', ECA, 1960.

UNECA, 'Intra-African Economic Cooperation and Africa's Relations with the European Economic Community', A report prepared by a team led by Prof. Kjeld Philip, Addis Ababa, 1972.

UNECA, 'Planification du développement et intégration économique en Afrique', in *Journal de la planification du développement*, Addis Ababa, 1, 1970.

UNECA, 'Report of the Panel of experts in intra-African Economic Cooperation and Africa's Relations with the European Economic Community', Addis Ababa, 1973.

UNITED NATIONS, Dept. of Economic and Social Affairs, 'Economic Cooperation and Integration in Africa: Three Case Studies', UN, New York, 1969.

WEST AFRICA NATIONS MARK MONETARY UNION, *IMF Survey*, i, 9 (1972).

WOILLETT, J. Cl., 'Sahel et technologies alternatives', Paris: Ministère de la coopération CINAM, Paris, 1977.

WOILLET, M. J., 'Appropriate technology: scope for cooperation among the countries of the West Africa Economic Community', International Labour Office, Geneva, 1980.

Abbreviations

AAPC	All African People's Conference
ACP	African Caribbean and Pacific Countries
ADB	African Development Bank
ADF	African Development Fund
ALC	African Liberation Committee
ASEAN	Association of South-East Asian Nations
BDEAC	Banque de Dévelopment des Etats de l'Afrique Centrale
BLS	Botswana Lesotho Swaziland
CAR	Central African Republic
CEAO	Communauté Economique de l'Afrique de l'Ouest
CIAS	Conference of Independent African States
COMECON	Council for Mutual Economic Assistance/Aid
EAC	East African Community
EACSO	East African Common Services Organization
EADB	East African Development Bank
ECA	Economic Commission for Africa
ECLA	Economic Commission for Latin America
ECOWAS	Economic Community of West African States
EEC	European Economic Community
FAO	Food and Agriculture Organization (UN)
F CFA	Central African Franc
GDR	German Democratic Republic
GNP	Gross National Product
IBRD	International Bank for Reconstruction and Development
IDA	International Development Association
IDRC	International Development Research Centre (Canadian)
LAFTA	Latin American Free Trade Area
MULPOCs	Multinational Programming and Operational Centres
NIEO	New International Economic Order
OAMCE	Organisation Africaine et Malgache de Coopération Economique
OAS	Organization of American States
OAU	Organization of African Unity
OCAM	Organisation Commune Africaine et Malgache

PADIS	Pan-African Documentation and Information System
PANAFTEL	Pan-African Telecommunications Network
PTA	Preferential Trade Area (for eastern, central and southern Africa)
SADCC	Southern African Development Coordination Conference
SATCC	Southern African Transport and Communications Commission
SELA	Latin American Economic System
SWAPO	South West Africa People Organization
UA	Unity of Account
UAM	Union Africaine et Malgache
UAMCE	Union Africaine et Malgache de Coopération Economique
UAMD	Union Africaine et Malgache de Défense
UAMPT	Union Africaine et Malgache de Postes et Télécommunications
UAR	United Arab Republic
UDE	Union Douanière Equatoriale
UDEAC	Union Douanière et Economique de l'Afrique Centrale
UDEAO	Union Douanière des Etats de l'Afrique Centrale
UN	United Nations
UNCTAD	United Nations Conference on Trade and Development
UN-DIESA	United Nations – Department of International Economic and Social Affairs
UNDP	United Nations Development Programme
UNESCO	United Nations Educational Scientific and Cultural Organization
UNIDO	United Nations Industrial Development Organization

Index

For EU product safety concerns, contact us at Calle de José Abascal, 56–1°,
28003 Madrid, Spain or eugpsr@cambridge.org.